Endorse

In a culture where biblical standards are routinely being ignored or marginalized, God's voice needs to be heard loud and clear, however unwelcome it may be. Old Testament prophets provide a powerful paradigm of this, and while biblical prophets have no like-for-like successors today, Christian pastors have a similar responsibility to 'reprove, rebuke and exhort,' directly challenging what seems to be the relentless drive towards framing a totally secular society. Michael Milton's book is an urgent, relevant, and powerful wake-up call. Every pastor should read it—and encourage his church members to do so.

> **John Blanchard,** Internationally known Christian
> preacher, teacher, apologist, and author

Michael Milton has biblically displayed for the evangelical church in general and the pulpit in particular how the prophetic voice of the church can and should speak to the issues of the day. This treatise displays with clarity how the prophets, the apostles, and our Savior call us to find a voice that exposes the sin of the day with a clarion call to repentance saturated in the preaching of the Gospel.

> **Harry L. Reeder, III,** Senior Pastor,
> Briarwood Presbyterian Church

Jesus Christ taught us to pray, 'Thy will be done on earth as it is in Heaven.' We sing 'God Bless America,' but our society ignores or even challenges His will. Preachers like me have so often remained silent. Let us teach and apply the Holy Bible, the Word and Will of God, to our national concerns, and as we obey His will, God blesses a people.

> **James M. Baird, Jr.,** Retired Senior Pastor,
> First Presbyterian Church, Jackson, MS

Mike Milton has sounded forth in clarion voice about the most important issue in preaching today—the prophetic pulpit. Contemporary preachers have lost the power of 'Thus saith the Lord.' I encourage all men in the pulpit to read *Silent No More* by my dear friend and colleague Mike Milton. His insights, clear-headed thinking, pastoral heart, and prophetic courage will both enlighten and encourage men to preach the full counsel of God. Great book!

> **Michael F. Ross,** Senior Pastor,
> Christ Covenant Church, Matthews, NC
> 40th Moderator of the PCA

It's hard to imagine Mike Milton's bothering to put words on paper without being assured that those words are carefully researched, artfully written, and helpful to God's people.

Joel Belz, Founder, *World Magazine*

It is only when Christian leaders courageously speak to the vital issues of the day that the distinctive fruits of Christian civilization can begin to flower in a culture: justice, mercy, and humility; art, music, and ideas; freedom, opportunity, and progress; beauty, goodness, and truth. In this much-needed book, Dr. Milton brilliantly, powerfully, and prophetically sounds that Good News proclamation from the rooftops.

George Grant, Pastor,
Parish Presbyterian Church, Franklin, TN

Dr. Michael Milton's challenge to be *Silent No More* is a thoughtful call for Americans to pause and consider where their country is headed. Apathy, fear, and indifference often seem to rule the day. His analysis is uncomfortably accurate but leads to solutions which are full of hope and encouragement. America is at a crossroads, and this book will assist thinking people in knowing which way to turn.

Douglas E. Lee, Chaplain (Brig Gen) USAR (Ret)

When Michael Milton speaks, we do well to listen. He is articulate and passionate. His concern for the Christian voice to be heard in our country should be shared by all believers in this time of cultural warfare and the loss of conscience in our nation and world. Dr Milton's insights are profound and moving. His recent appointment as chancellor of Reformed Theological Seminary affords him a platform for being a key player in the efforts to call the church back to its prophetic role in our country and in our world. I believe God has brought him into the kingdom for such a time as this.

Rev. Gordon K. Reed,
Missions & Conference Speaker, Bible Teacher

One of the great problems in the modern evangelical church is self-censorship. While our society is imploding, while traditional morality is held up to ridicule, while religious freedom and the sacred right of conscience hangs in the balance, many pastors are amazingly silent. Yet the Word of God is just as relevant today as it ever was. For that reason, I'm pleased to recommend Dr. Mike Milton's *Silent No More*. May God use this book for His glory and others' good during this critical time in our history.

Dr. Jerry Newcombe, co-host, Truth That Transforms
and spokesman for Truth in Action Ministries

My father, the late Dr. D. James Kennedy, believed passionately that the Word of God applies to all of life—including some of today's controversial issues. Dr. Mike Milton, seminary president and pastor, is willing to speak out. *Silent No More* shows the way for the Church to speak the truth in love.

Jennifer Kennedy Cassidy,
Member of the Board of Directors, Truth in Action Ministries

SILENT
NO MORE

MICHAEL A. MILTON, PH.D.

Chancellor and Chief Executive Officer
The James M. Baird, Jr. Chair of Pastoral Theology
Reformed Theological Seminary

Silent No More
by Michael A. Milton, Ph.D.

ISBN-13: 978-0-9852897-1-3
Library of Congress Control Number: 2012955575

© 2013 by Michael A. Milton
Published by Tanglewood Publishing

Printed in the USA.

Tanglewood Publishing
Fortress Book Service
1607 Tanglewood Dr.
Clinton, MS 39056
601-924-5020
www.tanglewoodpublishing.org

SILENT
NO MORE

*A Biblical Call for the Church
to Speak to State and Culture*

MICHAEL A. MILTON, PH.D.

In Memory of the
Forgotten Christian Martyrs of Communism
in the Twentieth Century (1917–1989)
and to our son,
John Michael,
who now takes his place to
prepare for the intellectual and
spiritual conflict that will transcend my own days

They cried out with a loud voice, 'O Sovereign Lord, holy
and true, how long before you will judge and avenge our
blood on those who dwell on the earth?'
—Revelation 6:10 ESV

And always to Mae

INTRODUCTION

Michael Milton has accurately diagnosed the potentially fatal disease that is so painfully eating out the vitals of our Western culture. The outward manifestation of that dread disease is statism, and it is a malignant (and understandable response) to the moral relativism that has resulted from the West's rejection of the truth of God and the salvation it sets forth.

No normal being would enjoy being told by the doctor that tests indicate that he or she has cancer, *unless* the indications are that it has been discovered in time for appropriate medical treatment to cure it. That is precisely the twofold function of *Silent No More*: it looks beneath the surface of the skin to find out what is the nature of the underlying disease that is inexorably taking away the life of our political culture and normal society, and in so doing it provides us bright and realistic hope of a profound cure and restoration to health (painful and disturbing though it may be), insofar as we humble ourselves to seek the healing grace of God so freely offered to us in the Gospel of Christ. Dr. Milton cannot, and wisely does not, predict whether our increasingly secularist society will ever bow the knee to the only One who can forgive and restore it, but those of us who know him cannot doubt the direction in which he is praying!

Major revivals are always unlikely, yet in the good providence of God they do break out with beneficent and transforming effects when least expected. Sometimes a humble and massive turning back to God may be related to a truer vision of where the church and country are and precisely what has gone wrong for them to have fallen into the filthy pit. I pray that Mike Milton's book may serve such a function. It is written in clear English and in terms that ordinary people in today's society can make sense of. At times it is uncomfortable, like some of the diagnostic procedures of a good doctor. In it, Milton is not afraid to discuss controversial matters that will not be acceptable to the politically correct hand that weighs so heavily on our contemporary public discourse. Although parts of it will be annoying to some, it will make others cry out with insight, 'Now I see, and now I know what must be done!'

A great value of this book is that it helps us grasp the parts in light of the whole; that is, it sheds much light on the confusing attacks that seem to keep coming every day in politics, education, the arts, and the media, against the largely Christian way of life that many of us were raised in. There is a fullness and wholeness about this little volume so that it does not leave us mounting a constant, tiresome, knee-jerk reaction against horrendous trends that keep washing against us like the waves of the incoming tide of the sea. I think its diagnosis enables the interested reader to make sense of the whole thing that is really happening that otherwise could overwhelm us with a plethora of depressing details. 'Yes,' we may say, ' we have grasped what is really wrong; we can make enough sense of it to begin taking action that will—with the help of the sovereign and gracious God of Holy Scripture—lead to a multitude of healings and restorations that may surpass our fondest dreams of revival and renewal.'

Dr. Milton will show you that statism essentially replaces worship in and obedience to the Triune God, with trust in and submission to the national state (or international world order). In the mentality of statism, all problems are basically caused by the central state not having enough power ceded to it. The solution is always a larger, stronger state, which requires withdrawing liberty from the churches, the local regions, and the family. The USSR that finally collapsed between 1989 and 1991 showed in flesh and blood where statism leads mighty nations. Siberia and other camps of the Gulag Archipelago, so terrifyingly described by Solzhenitsyn, are the end results of faith in the omnicompetent state. Yet that fall, and the human grief and unspeakable loss that lay behind it, seem not to have been seriously noticed by the majority of our Western intelligentsia, who are crying out for the same kind of statist control twenty years after Russia collapsed from within.

Why would very intelligent people try to repeat such disastrous historical experiments that have woefully failed in the recent past? Here is the reason, and you will find it in the pages of Dr. Milton's volume: when we turn our hearts away from God, we inevitably turn to something else to replace him. (The Apostle Paul discusses this same reaction in Romans, Chapter 1.) The Triune God is, generally in European and American thought since the eighteenth-century Enlightenment, replaced by the central state, which the famous nineteenth-century German philosopher Hegel famously termed 'God walking on earth.'

A Europe (soon followed by America) that wanted to get rid of the Triune God with his 'repressive moral code' and his unwelcome Lordship over its life, had to reject his written Word, and to replace that Word with something else in order to do so. In most cases it started with lifting up various shapes of humanist philosophy above a discredited Holy Scripture, and this secularist philosophy then became the basis of legislative enactments quite contrary to the divinely revealed moral code. An illustration would be the 1973 *Roe v. Wade* decision of the U.S. Supreme Court, which 'legalizes' that which God strictly forbids humans to do: the taking of innocent life of the unborn. More recently we see legislative actions seeking to allow homosexual unions, in the face of the prohibition of such things by God's written Word and by the consensus of nearly every nation for millennia. Such are the results of the cancer of willful spiritual blindness (to what God says in his Word and in also our own conscience, as we see in Romans, Chapter 2) and its never-failing offspring: moral relativism. Spiritual blindness to the true structure of human life and society always results in more potent statism, which exacerbates the underlying disease. The fall of the Berlin Wall and of the Soviet Union show us what will happen in due season unless we go in a different direction.

Silent No More will show you that infinitely better way if, by the grace of God, you are interested. I pray that you will be! No matter how dark our day may be, in terms of II Chronicles 7:14, I consider it definitely not too late for revival and renewal. This book could help push us in that direction, and that is why Michael Milton wrote it.

Douglas F. Kelly
The Jordan Chair of Systematic Theology
Reformed Theological Seminary
Charlotte, North Carolina

No one, believer or not, will argue that the revolution brought about by Jesus Christ is the greatest and most beneficial that has ever been accomplished in the world... The Author of this revolution was more than a man, yet he employed simple men, the apostles, as his instruments. Under him, they became the agents of the most extensive and most fruitful movement that has ever stirred mankind. The spiritual seed they scattered from place to place in the bosom of our poor earth has changed its face. The freeing of slaves, the emancipation of women, the elevation of domestic life, the improvement of walls, the softening of matters, the diffusion of knowledge, the progress of benevolence, perhaps even the world reborn to a new life—such is the fruit that we gather each day from their labor.

Adolphe Monod,
Saint Paul: Changing Our World for Christ[1]
(Translated by Constance K. Walker)

---

1   Adolphe Monod, Constance K. Walker, Editor and Translator, *Saint Paul: Changing Our World for Christ* (Solid Ground Books, Vestavia Hills, AL, 2012), 24–25.

TABLE OF CONTENTS

SECTION FOUR

SPEAKING OUT THROUGH SERMON AND CRYING OUT IN PRAYER FOR A NATION....... 195

PREFACE

This book seeks to express a biblical and theological and moral ground for a public theology, a public homiletic. While written most often with pastors in mind, it is hoped that the chapters, such as "Praying in Jesus' Name," will find a place in the thinking of all Christians, clergy or not.

The opening chapters reflect this aspiration in essays on the biblical–theological–historical grounds. This is followed by chapters on matters of public theology and prophetic speaking to critical areas of common life. The remaining chapters are essays on specific issues facing the Church in the West after a decade of following the Lord and living in this world in the twenty-first century. The material for the book comes from an attempt to provide fresh thoughts on the matters before us, as well as papers, essays, and sermons that have attempted to faithfully apply biblical truth in the context of worship.

I have written extensively on the matter of a pastoral theology that is focused on those competencies necessary for the ministry of the Gospel, particularly in the parish setting. This book is not an abandonment of that concern, or a new direction in emphasis, but a continuation. The application of all ministry must be to herald the Gospel of Jesus Christ to all men everywhere and to call the world to see the Lordship of the Savior over all and to compassionately offer new life and eternal life in Him alone. To expose darkness and to seek to guard a flock against the wiles of the devil is not popular pastoral work, but it is necessary. This is one pastor's humble plea to those who, understandably, might have been reticent, due to abuses, to be silent no more.

OTHER WORKS BY
DR. MICHAEL A. MILTON

BOOKS

Sacred Assembly: 15 Biblical Steps to Renew Your Church. P&R Publishing. 2012.

What God Starts, God Completes: Help and Hope for Hurting People, Third Edition with updates and a new Introduction. Christian Focus Publications. 2012.

What Is the Doctrine of Adoption? P&R Publishing. 2012.

Hit by Friendly Fire: What to Do When Fellow Believers Hurt You. EP Books. 2011.

Songs in the Night: How God Transforms our Pain into Praise. P&R Publishing. 2011.

Small Things, Big Things: Inspiring Stories of God's Everyday Grace. P&R Publishing. 2009.

What is the Doctrine of the Perseverance of the Saints? P&R Publishing. 2009.

Hit by Friendly Fire: What to Do When You are Hurt by Other Believers. Wipf and Stock Publishers. 2008.

What God Starts, God Completes: Help and Hope for Hurting People. Christian Focus Publications. 2007.

Cooperation without Compromise: Faithful Gospel Witness in a Pluralistic Setting. Wipf and Stock Publishers. 2007.

Oh the Deep, Deep Love of Jesus: Expository Messages from John 17. Wipf and Stock Publishers. 2007.

Following Ben: Expository Preaching for Frail Followers of Pulpit Giants. Wipf and Stock Publishers. 2006.

Giving as an Act of Worship. Wipf and Stock Publishers. 2006.

Leaving a Career to Follow a Call: A Vocational Guide to the Ordained Ministry. Wipf and Stock Publishers. 1999.

Authentic Christianity and the Life of Freedom. Wipf and Stock Publishers. 2005.

The Demands of Discipleship: Expository Messages from Daniel. Wipf and Stock Publishers. 2005.

MUSICAL RECORDINGS

He Shall Restore (2005, Music for Missions)
Follow Your Call (2009, Music for Missions)
Through the Open Door (2011, Music for Missions/Bethesda)
When Heaven Came Down (2012, Music for Missions/Bethesda/RTS)

For more information, see MichaelMilton.org

SECTION ONE

THE GROUND FOR SPEAKING OUT IN PASTORAL AND PROPHETIC PREACHING

There is an imperative need for Christians to confront responsibly the controversial social issues of our society today.

John Stott, Involvement

CRY ALOUD AND SPARE NOT

*The Biblical–Theological–Historical Ground
for Pastoral–Prophetic Preaching*

I utterly reject Theonomy. Theonomy is the wrong-headed theological idea that is a perennial minority position that the church continues to be governed by the theocratic laws that were imposed by God Himself over the ancient nation of Israel. The theocratic government is, as we know from modern Islamic examples, one in which God rules directly, mediating through a prophet like He did with Moses. I believe that the redemptive time frame in which we live has moved far beyond a theocracy. There is continuity and discontinuity in the Old and New Testaments. To impose a theocratic rule in the New Testament church violates the discontinuity which Jesus Christ himself declared had occurred. That cessation of theocracy happened not with the coming of the New Covenant under Christ but under the loss of their relationship through sin and the condescension of God to their demands for a king like the other nations. While there is a discontinuity with the direct rule of God or any expectation of such a rule now over political entities in this world, there certainly is, without any controversy, a continuity in the application of the moral law to our times. No administrative "dispensation" in the Bible has ever abrogated the moral law of God. Out of grace, God calls us to obey His law. It is in our very bones, and one thinks of Calvin's *sensus divinitatis*,[1] the sense of the divine which is the law in our very being.

We do not live under a theocracy, and thus the prophetic voice of the pastor today is given in the context of a New Covenant rule of Jesus Christ. Indeed, we live in the kingdom of love and grace in which our Lord and Savior Jesus Christ reigns. Yet His rule is all pervasive. We are told that Christ is the Lord of all and that there is no area of life separate from the Lordship of Christ. This does not mean that the believer seeks to impose the rule of Christ but rather to speak the Gospel of Christ before the powers of the earth, whether political or cultural or familial, and to remind them of the reality of Christ's reign. The reason that Christ mandates such a comprehensive announcement and application of His Gospel is not that we believe salvation of a people can come through culture or politics. God forbid! Salvation comes through Christ alone when human beings are set free from the bondage of the devil and the flesh, dead souls are awakened by the Holy Spirit, and through repentance and faith, Christ's righteousness is imputed to the penitent while his sin is imputed to Christ on the timeless cross, God's way of human salvation. Yet there are powers, of both human and demonic origins, that conspire to resist the redemptive work of the Spirit and also to torment humans, further distorting the image of God in man. It is the role of the pastor, the role of the Church, the role of the believer, to expose such and to offer a way out through Christ Jesus and His Word. To do this may have the appearance of "getting too involved with politics" or "getting too focused on culture." Those dangers exist and "hobby horses" are always waiting to be mounted (another lie and diversion from the redemptive

---

1   Jonathan David, O'Brien. *Theology and Reformed Epistemology: The Sensus Divinitatis, the Noetic Effects of Sin, and Regeneration.* 2003.

work of Christ). Yet the possibility of extremism or abuse of the biblical call to "cry aloud and spare not" and to "take every thought captive," to show the compassion of Christ to humanity by uncovering the idols and naming them, and to call for repentance and faith in Christ does not negate the mandate.

It is important for me to begin this chapter declaring that I do not believe that the Bible supports a theonomic continuity of Old Testament laws fulfilled in Christ. I do not call for any return to the foundational laws that established a theocracy. There will always be charges levied against those would urge that the church speak into the state and into the culture. Rather the Gospel call is to repent and turn to Christ and to urge believers to be warned of the idols of this present evil age lest thay are caught in the snare of the devil. Despite that distinction, some in the Church (and, understandably, many in the world) cringe at the sound of the pastoral voice that speaks into the powers of state and culture. In some cases it may be on target. But the bad exception should not indict the good example. Otherwise, as we shall see, we will have to label preachers from John Knox to Martin Luther King, Jr., from Albert Mohler and Archbishop Henry Luke Orombi as such. And that is simply not the case.

It is also important for me to confirm that our primary work is as a minister of the Gospel. We are ministers of Word, Sacrament, and Prayer. We are shepherds. Yet the shepherd is a watchman on the wall and responsible for announcing the arrival of devils, legions of demons, and even madmen who would attack the souls of the saints and hurt the image of God in Man. As John Stott wrote in his wonderfully simple and powerful portrait of the pastor's work, we are not only stewards and fathers in the faith, we, who have been called to preach, are prophets—small "p" only—yet prophets all the same. When we preach nothing but Christ and Him crucified, we preach, with St. Paul, that Gospel truth to all creatures and all powers that would obscure or deny that message or who could be saved by the glorious event of God's atonement through His only begotten Son.

2

BEING A PASTOR AND SPEAKING OUT IN TODAY'S CULTURE

Dangerous but Necessary

A pastor I know recently told me that he was criticized for being "too political." He has heard such an indictment all his ministry, he said. Today he leads a major ministry in America and battles daily for the rights of pastors to speak so that believers can speak. His prophetic word upsets the establishment. His voice is prophetic. His heart is pastoral. Can the two co-exist?

I have heard the similar charges in my ministry through the years. I accept the critique. However, if the matter is important enough for me to address in preaching or writing, I believe I am just being pastoral to God's people. I cannot compartmentalize the Lordship of Christ to only one area of life. He is Lord of all.

So, is it right that pastors should remain silent about important matters in society that are being debated in the public square because someone is trying to establish in our culture that there is no place in politics for religious beliefs or moral convictions that have been born out of a faith commitment? *Because people squirm when sin is exposed in politics or culture, does that mean we should refrain from preaching?* No. It may mean just the opposite.

Is a pastor solely limited to sharing the Gospel to his flock on Sunday mornings? Or was the late Dr. John Stott right that one of our identities as Gospel preachers, in a faithful biblical portrait of a pastor, is a "herald"? The pastor is not a prophet, yet he most certainly does carry a prophetic voice and speaks with biblical authority to other Beastlike powers when there are souls at risk or the honor of Christ and His Church under I have an intuitive concern that the liberal professor who won't let the young believer raise her hand in a state university and speak from her conviction is now trying to govern public discourse. Well, I am not governed by political correctness that has been born out of a liberal educational system or by the pressure of a liberal press but by the one and only true God. The public square is not the university professor's classroom nor is it the TV news studio. *This is my Father's world.* Therefore, I speak, and I speak publicly, as the Lord gives an open door, through media, because I am compelled by compassion for souls that may be victims of systems that will ultimately enslave them.

I believe that pastors must speak to our declining culture, whatever their pulpit. I am pastorally concerned that there are dangerous idols masquerading under the banner of politics in this increasingly secularized culture. These heaven-rejected powers prefer that we keep quiet. But when the powers move beyond the Machiavellian machinations of politics to the advocacy of principles at odds with God's Word, we must call them out.

The prophets and church fathers of old spoke forth concerning the actions of governments, individuals yielding power, and the idols of culture. Our Lord Jesus did when he said of Herod, "Go tell that Fox" (Luke 13:32), St. Paul did, the church fathers did, and the Reformers did. In the twentieth century I thank God that J. Gresham

Machen (1881–1937) was not afraid to speak to the ungodliness in his culture (read Stephen Nichols's fine new biography). And what of Bonhoeffer? Solzhenitsyn? Martin Luther King, Jr.? Today pastors like Ugandan Archbishop Henry Luke Orombi preach against the powers of darkness, expose evil in government, and even in churches in our own nation as missionaries to America, warn people while compassionately inviting them to Christ. Why? Because pastors are like watchmen on the wall (Ezekiel 33), required by God to sometimes warn of coming danger, even if others cry, "Off limits!" To do otherwise is to be disobedient to our calling. God says if there is harm to his people because the watchmen were silent, they will have the blood of the people on their hands. This is a sobering warning to pastors and trumps any criticism of being "too political."

Yet the challenge of discernment is acknowledged. What must we do?

1   Pastors must represent no man but God and no party but His Kingdom. We, therefore, refuse to be used as pawns by any political party. We are made aware by Psalm 2 that the rulers of this world conspire against God and His Son. We study. We pray. We speak when we must, therefore, on behalf of the truths of God's Word, to help people.

2   Pastors must diagnose the presenting ill to discover the real issue beneath it. Only then do we speak. Diagnosis requires prayer, wisdom, courage, and the leading of the Lord. Speaking requires courage and counting the cost. If it is a real or potential spiritual harm coming from the presenting issues of culture or politics, then we must deliver the diagnosis and offer the cure in the Person of Jesus Christ and His Word. If I happen to yell, "Warning!" and the demon under the cloak of culture is a straw man, then I have expended my pastoral capitol, perhaps compromising my ability to preach into real or more critical situations. But if it is not a straw man, and instead an instrument of the "devil, the flesh or

the world" that would further mar the image of God in man or further distance us from God, then woe to me if I speak not.

So we must preach, even when the culture labels our message "off limits." We will live with that criticism because we are pastors, and we follow One, and His disciples who also were criticized (and crucified) for assuming an authority that challenged the religious and political power-holders of their day.

3   Pastors must pray for each situation that startles our shepherding instincts and weigh whether a given issue is an assault on our conscience worth exposing. It is understood that some matters are just politics or a reflection of a sick culture, and such a pathology would be more ably addressed by other men and women.

4   Pastors must ground their preaching in God's Word, the Bible. We have no authority apart from His Word. We must also always offer the way out through the Gospel of Jesus Christ. To do less is to be embroiled in the political debate. But preaching with a conclusion that leads to freedom in Christ is above the storm, where it should be.

My pulpit is not for sale to any political party. I care not a whit for using my position to promote any political agenda. *I do care for souls.* That is my job. *And I will preach.* That is my calling.

Jesus said that we need to be as wise as serpents and harmless as doves. (Matthew 10:16) Thomas Watson, one the most pastoral of seventeenth-century Puritans, said of this passage, "To understand worldly affairs is the wisdom of the serpent; yet to not neglect the soul is the innocence of the dove."

Dangers exist on all sides for the pastor. But who said the job would be easy? Yet to silence the pastor in any realm is to cause the Church to retreat into a secluded ghetto where we can no longer be salt and light in the world. And that cannot be. We are pastors. We are shepherds. We comfort the afflicted and on occasion may afflict the comfortable, as it is sometimes put. The ground of our ministry is love from a pure conscience. Let us not abandon our post as long as God gives us the strength to stand. Let us be silent no more.

3

MY CONFESSION

Iranian Pastor Freed By Another's Prayers—Not Mine

I was awakened today by the news that an Iranian pastor, The Reverend Youcef Nadarkhani, held in captivity for simply being a Christian pastor, and therefore destined for imprisonment if not execution, has now been released.[2] We do not know what reason compelled the mad dictator of Iran to free the pastor. Or do we?

There were voices of the American State Department, the British Foreign Office,[3] Christian Solidarity Worldwide (CSW), and the American Jewish Committee among others who did not keep silent over this atrocity.[4] I believe that this pastor was liberated by the prayers of the saints from all over the world who were moved by the Holy Spirit, acting in obedience, and being used of God to glorify Himself and build His Body. As I am writing a book on being *Silent No More,* this case, with such a happy ending (thus far as I write),[5] is a perfect example of how the voices of the people, in

---

2   "Iranian pastor Nadarkhani acquitted, freed." 9 Sep. 2012 http://www.bpnews.net/BPnews.asp?ID=38680

3   "Pastor Yousef Nadarkhani—Christian Solidarity Worldwide." 2011. 9 Sep. 2012 http://www.csw.org.uk/nadarkhani.htm

4   "Iranian Pastor Freed | US Daily Review." 2012. 9 Sep. 2012 http://us-dailyreview.com/iranian-pastor-freed

5   "New court date set for jailed Iranian pastor Youcef Nadarkhani ..." 2012. 9 Sep. 2012 http://article.wn.com/view/2012/07/06/New_court_date_set_for_jailed_Iranian_pastor_Youcef_Nadarkha/

public as well as in private, as so many preached openly against this crime and even more prayed for righteousness and mercy, joined together in a chorus of prophetic witness. They were not silent. As a result destiny was changed. A river of blood was transformed into a stream of hope. But I was not there. I was not present, as it were, at the revolution. I did not write about the plight of this pastor. I did not preach, specifically, to call our people to speak. I cannot recall spending extended periods of time praying, though I joined in as a pastor led in prayer for the man from the pulpit. So I am a living example of what it means to sit on the sideline as others fight the fight. I am an example of what it means to be silent. And his freedom brings rejoicing to my soul but fear to my heart. "Let not many of you become teachers for you shall receive the stricter judgment,"[6] wrote James. And I feel the brunt of that hard saying in my own soul as I write. I was also drawn this morning to a passage that is before me like never before:

> When the Son of Man comes in his glory, and all the angels with him, then he will sit on his glorious throne. Before him will be gathered all the nations, and he will separate people one from another as a shepherd separates the sheep from the goats. And he will place the sheep on his right, but the goats on the left. Then the King will say to those on his right, 'Come, you who are blessed by my Father, inherit the kingdom prepared for you from the foundation of the world. For I was hungry and you gave me food, I was thirsty and you gave me drink, I was a stranger and you welcomed me, I was naked and you clothed me, I was sick and you visited me, I was in prison and you came to me.' Then the righteous will answer him, saying, 'Lord, when did we see you hungry and feed you, or thirsty and give you drink? And when did we see you a stranger and welcome you, or naked and clothe you? And when

---

6   "James 3:1 ESVBible.org." 2011. 9 Sep. 2012. http://www.esvbible.org/ James+3.1/

did we see you sick or in prison and visit you?' And the King will answer them, 'Truly, I say to you, as you did it to one of the least of these my brothers, you did it to me.'

Then he will say to those on his left, 'Depart from me, you cursed, into the eternal fire prepared for the devil and his angels. For I was hungry and you gave me no food, I was thirsty and you gave me no drink, I was a stranger and you did not welcome me, naked and you did not clothe me, sick and in prison and you did not visit me.' Then they also will answer, saying, 'Lord, when did we see you hungry or thirsty or a stranger or naked or sick or in prison, and did not minister to you?' Then he will answer them, saying, 'Truly, I say to you, as you did not do it to one of the least of these, you did not do it to me.' And these will go away into eternal punishment, but the righteous into eternal life. (Matthew 25:31–46 ESV)

The context of this teaching of Jesus is not about feeding the homeless, though there is application that can be made for that in comparing Scripture to Scripture. The context is the witness of faithful men and women of God who gave their all to speak up for the Gospel of Jesus Christ and who suffered as a result. The focus of this indictment is on those who did not stand with them publicly and privately. The judgment that Jesus warns is coming is for those who do not recognize that in their courageous voices is the voice of Jesus Himself. Thus, for those who were too busy with others things than to provide sustenance, comfort, and a ministry of presence, their true self is revealed and will be uncovered on the Day of Judgment. They will have shown themselves to be those who rejected Jesus Himself. John Stott's commentary is the guide for those who confuse devotion to Christ with public, prophetic preaching: "Our good works must be public so that our light shines; our religious devotions must be secret lest we boast about them."[7]

---

7   Stott, John R. W. *Sermon on the Mount.* Intervarsity Press, 2000, 69.

It is time to be silent no more, and I say that to myself first.

To ignore the plight of those who are suffering today because of their witness for Jesus Christ is to incur the wrath of God. To hear of those who suffer for preaching the Gospel and not even pause to pray, not even care to mention the crisis in a sermon, is not only to become isolated from those who need us most, it is to isolate one's self from Jesus. He is present in the preaching and in the ministry of those who will not be quiet. He is present with the Iranian pastor who refuses to bend the knee to the corrupt State of the Islamic Republic of Iran. Jesus shines upon the very soul of this pastor and those believers who are following Jesus in such harsh circumstances. As I sip on my Starbucks and write, others long for a drop of water on their parched tongue and sing praise in prison. They have given their last ounce of strength in witnessing to the cause of Christ in the presence of the Hell-born idols of this age as I have given little.

Joel C. Rosenberg wrote the following of the Iranian tyranny and its war on Christians:

> The rise of Mahmoud Ahmadinejad led to a dramatic acceleration of government-directed persecution of Iranian Christians—particularly pastors, many of whom have been arrested, interrogated, beaten, and even worse. "An Iranian convert to Christianity was kidnapped last week from his home in northeastern Iran and stabbed to death, his bleeding body thrown in front of his home a few hours later."[8]

---

8   Rosenberg, Joel C. *Inside the Revolution: How the Followers of Jihad, Jefferson, and Jesus are Battling to Dominate the Middle East and Transform the World.* Tyndale House Pub, 2011, 386.

Rosenberg wrote that this reign of terror against believers is the outcome of the evil policy of the dictator who declared, "I will stop Christianity in this country."[9]

I am ashamed. I am ashamed *of myself.* I ask God to forgive me. I pray He will cause me to be lifted above the damning indifference of my soul. I ask that the warning from Matthew 25:31–46 would bore a hole into my very soul and inject a new conviction of standing with those who cannot stand on their own, those who need me to welcome them, clothe them, visit them, pray for them. I do not want to be silent any longer. I am guilty of silence. I pray for a voice born out of love for Thee, O Christ, and Thy people, my brothers and sisters. *Lord have mercy. Christ have mercy.* I join in this good, old prayer for those who suffer, and I would make it mine today as an act of reaffirmation:

> Let us pray for all who suffer and are afflicted in body or in mind;
> For the hungry and the homeless, the destitute and the oppressed
> For the sick, the wounded, and the crippled
> For those in loneliness, fear, and anguish
> For those who face temptation, doubt, and despair
> For the sorrowful and bereaved
> For prisoners and captives, and those in mortal danger
> That God in His mercy will comfort and relieve them, and grant them the knowledge of His love, and stir up in us the will and patience to minister to their needs.[10]

Lord, hear my prayer. Open thou my lips.

---

9   Rosenberg, Joel C. *Inside the Revolution: How the Followers of Jihad, Jefferson, and Jesus Are Battling to Dominate the Middle East and Transform the World.* Tyndale House Pub, 2011.

10   *Book of Common Prayer.* 1979. Church Publishing, Incorporated, 279.

SECTION TWO

SPEAKING OUT
THROUGH SCHOLARLY ESSAYS

1

COOPERATION
WITHOUT COMPROMISE

Faithful Gospel Witness in a Pluralistic Setting

This chapter seeks to provide a framework for faithful Gospel witness in a pluralistic setting by considering the long-standing military praxis known as "cooperation without compromise." As a chaplain in the United States Army Reserve, a member of the adjunct faculty of two seminaries and a pastor of a local church seeking to equip my flock for works of ministry, I have a great interest in finding a working model. So that which I have received, as it were, I desire to share with you in this chapter.

I read recently a story about an ecumenical conference where it was being discussed how respective denominations would respond to demon possession. It was suggested that "Methodists would sing them out; Pentecostals would shout them out; Catholics and Greek Orthodox would incense them out; Baptists would drown them out; and Presbyterians would freeze them out!"[11]

---

11   See Biblical Reflections on Theological and Religious Pluralism by A. Vanlier Hunter, Th.D. at http://www.icjs.org/clergy/vanhunter.html.

As a Presbyterian I get a little tired of the "frozen chosen" jokes, but I get the point. And the point of that illustration is to get us to thinking about doing pastoral ministry—true to the Scriptures, to the Great Commission, and even to our distinctive and unique contributions to the Body of Christ—in a pluralistic setting. But I want to go beyond this hypothetical, tongue-in-cheek gathering into the very real world we live in today. The setting is not just Catholics and Baptists and Pentecostals and Presbyterians. The setting is more like what I saw when I stepped foot onto the soil of India last year, to teach in Chennai and in Dehradun: Hindus, Buddhists, Islamic sects, cults who operate in the name of Jesus, as well as atheists and agnostics, secularists and materialists. Now add to that Judaism of every brand, and the old standbys, Christian groups of every kind. What I wondered when I returned to my own nation was this: "Did I just see a snapshot of America and Great Britain fifty years from now?"

That is, as you all know, increasingly our world today, not only in American metropolitan areas, but also in almost every community in America.[12] Even rural areas, where plurality once meant (and still does in some communities) a Baptist Church, a Methodist Church, and an Independent break away congregation from both of those other two, are becoming more religiously pluralistic. Of course there were always those contemptible few who dared not claim any of those, as in where I grew up in the rural south (they are now

---

12   The religious makeup of America is 77% Christian, 3.7% Other Religions, 14.1% No religion, according to the American Religious Identification Survey-ARIS. See their excellent site for further study: Professor Barry A. Kosmin and Professor Egon Mayer; Study Director: Dr. Arela Keysar, American Religious Identification Survey [Internet] (The Graduate Center of the City University of New York, 2001 [cited November 14 2006]); available from http://www.gc.cuny.edu/faculty/research_briefs/aris/key_findings.htm.

the fastest growing group identified in the "American Religious Identification Survey" of 2001[13]). Those same places today are home, in an increasing way, to Muslims, various Eastern cults, and Mormons, and of course there seems to be more secularists and atheists. These are the teachers, the coaches, the students, and the next-door neighbors. Our nation, once ostensibly "monochrome," to use the word the late English missionary and Bishop of South India, Lesslie Newbigin (1909–1998) used to describe old Christendom,[14] is now pluralistic[15]. The decisive spiritual warfare that Reinhold Niebuhr foresaw in "The Christian Church in a Secular Age"[16] has broadened onto new fronts in these dawning years of the twenty-first century. His "five types" in *Christianity and Culture*[17] are ripe for reinterpreting as the cultural challenge itself has metastasized. John Howard Yoder in his critique in 1958,[18] and later, Hauerwas and Willimon in *Resident Aliens,* seek to do just that.[19] Old models of "coping" with plurality are no longer helpful

---

13   "The greatest increase in absolute as well as in percentage terms has been among those adults who do not subscribe to any religious identification; their number has more than doubled from 14.3 million in 1990 to 29.4 million in 2001; their proportion has grown from just eight percent of the total in 1990 to over fourteen percent in 2001." See Ibid.

14   As he did in Lesslie Newbigin, *The Gospel in a Pluralist Society* (Grand Rapids, MI; Geneva [SZ]: W.B. Eerdmans; WCC Publications, 1989).

15   See Ibid.

16   See H. Richard Niebuhr, *Christ and Culture*, 1st ed. ([San Francisco]: HarperSanFrancisco, 2001), Reinhold Niebuhr and Robert McAfee Brown, *The Essential Reinhold Niebuhr: Selected Essays and Addresses* (New Haven: Yale University Press, 1986).

17   Christ against culture, Christ of culture, Christ above culture, Christ and culture in paradox, and Christ the transformer of culture.

18   His unpublished critique was later published; see Glen Harold Stassen et al., *Authentic Transformation: A New Vision of Christ and Culture* (Nashville: Abingdon Press, 1996).

19   See Stanley Hauerwas and William H. Willimon, *Resident Aliens: Life in the Christian Colony* (Nashville: Abingdon Press, 1989).

as Glenn Lucke writes on his blog, *Common Grounds Online:* "The 1950s 'tripartite settlement' described in Will Herberg's *Protestant–Catholic–Jew*[20] no longer pertains as Muslims, Hindus, and Buddhists have swelled in numbers in recent decades."[21]

And writers like Robert Wuthnow and his *America and the Challenge of Religious Diversity,*[22] who welcomes the challenge, and Peter Wood in his *Diversity: The Invention of a Concept,*[23] who distrusts the claims, seem to be talking about our new identity but are less sure about how to live it out. And maybe none of us really are yet. We are just in the middle of it. We are just seeing it, to paraphrase Hans Urs von Balthasar, not really seeing through it.[24] But to be sure, things have changed. It is not just, "Toto, I've a feeling we're not in Kansas anymore"—it is more accurately, "Toto, Kansas isn't Kansas anymore."

But the question remains: How do we conduct faithful Gospel ministry in this environment?

Before I answer that question in this chapter, it might be helpful to differentiate between, at least, what I mean when I refer to pluralistic and pluralism. One is a matter of numbers and the other is a matter of ideology. Pluralistic, of course, refers to a undeniable plurality of beliefs and ideas and even customs and cultures that

---

20   See Will Herberg, *Protestant, Catholic, Jew: An Essay in American Religious Sociology* (Chicago: University of Chicago Press, 1983).

21   Glenn Lucke, Review of Robert Wuthnow, America and the Challenges of Religious Diversity [Blog] (Common Grounds Online, 2006 [cited November 13 2006]); available from http://commongroundsonline.typepad.com/common_grounds_online/2005/11/glenn_lucke_rev.html.

22   See Robert Wuthnow, *America and the Challenges of Religious Diversity* (Princeton, N.J.: Princeton University Press, 2005).

23   Peter Wood, *Diversity: The Invention of a Concept* (San Francisco: Encounter Books, 2003).

24   See Hans Urs von Balthasar, *Credo: Meditations on the Apostles' Creed* (New York: Crossroad, 1990).

are derived from those ideas. Even here, Lesslie Newbigin sees inconsistency:

> We are pluralist in respect to what we call beliefs but we are not pluralistic in respect of what we call fact. The former are a matter of personal decision; the latter are a matter of public knowledge.[25]

Nevertheless, pluralists we are, and pluralists we are becoming. Arguments not withstanding, for instance, even among conservatives like Pat Buchanan and Dinesh D'Souza on how immigrants truly become American ("American by creed" [Constitution] according to D'Souza and through "bonds of history and memory, tradition and custom, language and literature, birth and faith, blood and soil" according to Buchanan),[26] we are becoming more pluralistic each and every day. And within this global soup, chockfull of every religious morsel imaginable, there is the presence of the ideology of pluralism. It may be that, as I have seen suggested somewhere, pluralism is a faith that exists as a people are on their way from one orthodoxy to another. We are moving from a Christian West to something else, and pluralism serves as the necessary faith bridge, if you will, to get us there. We have mentioned Lesslie Newbigin before, but he is key in this study. In his *The Gospel in a Pluralistic Age*,[27] *The Open Secret*,[28] and *Foolishness to the Greeks*[29] among other increasingly important reflections on these matters, the late, great Bishop–missionary–church planter reminds us that we

---

25   Newbigin, *The Gospel in a Pluralist Society*.

26   See the excellent reflections on Dinesh D'Souza's What's Great About America and Pat Buchanan's State of Emergency: the Third World Invasion and Conquest of America on Chris Seck, Buchanan on Nationhood [Blog] (Buchanan.org, 2006 [cited October 7 2006]); available from http://buchanan.org/blog/?p=125.

27   Newbigin, *The Gospel in a Pluralist Society*.

28   Lesslie Newbigin, *The Open Secret: An Introduction to the Theology of Mission*, Rev. ed. (Grand Rapids, Mich.: W. B. Eerdmans, 1995).

29   Lesslie Newbigin, *Foolishness to the Greeks: The Gospel and Western Culture* (Grand Rapids, Mich.: W. B. Eerdmans Pub. Co., 1986).

may be cooperative with one, but without compromise with the other. In *The Gospel in a Pluralistic Age,* Newbigin wrote the following:

> I...believe that a Christian must welcome some measure of plurality but reject pluralism. We can and must welcome a plural society because it provides us with a winder range of experience and a wider diversity of human responses to experience, and therefore, richer opportunities for testing the sufficiency of our faith than are available in a monochrome society. As we confess Jesus as Lord in a plural society, and as the Church grows through the coming of people from many different cultic and religious traditions to faith in Christ, we are enabled to learn more of the length and breadth and height and depth of the love of God (Eph. 3:14–19) than we can in a monochrome society. But we must reject the ideology of pluralism.[30]

John Stott said, "Pluralism is an affirmation of the validity of every religion, and the refusal to choose between them, and the rejection of world evangelism...."[31] And of course this is the rub for Christians. Susan Laemmle, Rabbi and Dean of Religious Life at USC described the tenets of the ideology of religious pluralism as well as anyone when she said, "All spiritual paths are finally leading to the same sacred ground."[32]

---

30   Newbigin, *The Gospel in a Pluralist Society.*

31   John Stott, Orange County Register Interview with John Stott [Internet] (Religious Tolerance.org, 1998 [cited November 9 2006]); available from http://www.religioustolerance.org/rel_plur1.htm.

32   Susan Laemmle, Education as Transformation: A National Project on Religious Pluralism, Spirituality and Higher Education [Internet] (Education and Spirituality Network, on the Wellesley College website, 1998 [cited November 9 2006]); available from http://www.wellesley.edu/RelLife/transformation/edu-ngoverview.html.

Another scholar, an Episcopalean—Professor M. Basye Holland-Shuey of Belmont University[33]—said,

> Pluralism...holds to one's own faith, and at the same time, engages other faiths in learning about their path and how they want to be understood.... Pluralism and dialogue are the means for building bridges and relationships that create harmony and peace on our planet home.[34]

According to this idea of Pluralism, any denial of its validity would be paramount to blowing up bridges of common understanding and relationships among human beings. It is, according to Holland-Shuey and many others, to stand against world peace. The idea of religious pluralism as "the ideal cultural dynamic for our country" is developed and defended by Diana L. Eck, Ph.D., professor of comparative religion and Indian studies at Harvard University in works like her *A New Religious America: How a 'Christian Country' Has Become the World's Most Religiously Diverse Nation.*[35]

---

33 "M. Basye Holland teaches courses on World Religions and Biblical Studies at Belmont University in Nashville and is the Religion and Training Consultant for the Huntsville/Madison County Interfaith Mission Service, board member for the Alabama Faith Council, and presents programs on Inter-religious Dialogue for churches and universities." Taken from http://www.episcopalarchives.org/e-archives/bluebook/6.html.

34 M. Basye Holland-Shuey, Religious Pluralism and Interfaith Dialogue [Internet] (ReligiousTolerance.org, 2002 [cited November 9 2006]); available from http://www.religioustolerance.org/rel_plur1.htm.

35 See Diana L. Eck, *A New Religious America: How a "Christian Country" Has Now Become the World's Most Religiously Diverse Nation*, 1st ed. ([San Francisco]: HarperSanFrancisco, 2001). "Dr. Eck received the National Humanities Medal from President Clinton in a White House ceremony for her work in the area of religious pluralism" (http://www.renewnetwork.org/A%20New%20Religious%20America.pdf). Dr. Eck, a United Methodist, and her lesbian partner serve as the first homosexual house "parents" at the famous Lowell House dormitory at Harvard. They have been active in not only advocating religious pluralism but also promoting homosexuality as normative in the Christian faith.

But T. S. Eliot wrote in *Christianity and Culture,*

> Only a Christian culture could have produced a Voltaire or a Nietzsche. I do not believe that the culture of Europe could survive the complete disappearance of the Christian faith. And I am convinced of that, not merely because I am a Christian myself, but as a student of social biology. If Christianity goes, the whole of our culture goes.[36]

For Eliot pluralistic societies can only come through Christian societies, with its essential understanding of and necessary consequences of the idea of human freedom and Christian liberty. But Eliot is silenced beneath the cacophony of politically correct voices which equate pluralism with peace and exclusive truth claims with repression.

"Why do the nations rage and the peoples plot in vain?" asked the Psalmist. (Psalms 2:1 ESV) Yet in the postmodern city, the divergent voices find unity in opposition of the One who said I am the Way, the Truth, and the Life, even as the early Church in Acts prayed,"Indeed Herod and Pontius Pilate met together with the Gentiles and the people of Israel in this city to conspire against your holy servant Jesus, whom you anointed." (Acts 4:27 NIV)

And this is where we find ourselves in the modern public square where pluralism is the common denominator of the plurality. But we have been here before. Whether Noah standing against the unbelieving masses of the earth who had rejected God's truth in sexuality and marriage for their own truths, or whether Moses standing against the gods of Egypt, or Joshua preaching against the pluralism of Canaan, or Elijah challenging pluralism on Mount Carmel seeking to win back the hearts of Israel so enchanted by the religion

---

36   T. S. Eliot, *Christianity and Culture: The Idea of a Christian Society and Notes Towards the Definition of Culture* (New York: Harcourt, 1976).

of Baal worship, or Paul standing before the idolatry of Athens or
even preaching to the rabbinical Judaism of Jerusalem, the faith of
the One True God of Abraham, Isaac, and Jacob, of our Lord Jesus
Christ, has always been taught in the middle of a pluralistic setting.
The One True God, who has revealed Himself through General Revelation and through Special Revelation, becoming closest to us in
the Person of our Lord and Savior Jesus Christ, is a missionary God
whose revelation is centrifugal and expansive and victorious. God
has always made Himself known in this pluralistic setting and has
gathered in His children to the One among the Many. This God cannot be held in check by the ideology of pluralism and, therefore, can
never be presented by His ministers except as the One who stands
in judgment over the other pseudo gods, false religions, and harmful
thoughts of this present evil age and who calls for human beings to
escape the coming judgment on those religions and find the abundant life and eternal life that comes from trusting in Jesus Christ.

In short, then, pluralistic setting? Of course. Pluralism? Never.

Now the question is how do we do ministry in this environment? My answer is not a final answer, just an answer I am familiar with and want to share. It is the answer I use each time I do
ministry as an Army chaplain. It is a model commonly called "cooperation without compromise."

First, what is the model itself?

"Cooperation without compromise" is the Military, specifically
the U.S. Army chaplain way, for doing ministry, even fulfilling the
Great Commission, in a pluralistic setting. Cooperation without
compromise is a phrase that describes how military chaplains must
conduct their ministry, not only to troops of many faiths, but in a
chaplaincy with many different Christians denominations, as well
as chaplains from various branches of Judaism and Mormonism
and groups which we in the Evangelical Theological Society would

consider heterodox groups that call themselves "Christians" (I am thinking, for example, of Oneness Pentecostal groups) and now even different religions (with the advent of Islamic chaplains and even a Buddhist chaplain). This value emerged early on in the American military:

> As early as the French and Indian War (1754–1760) the Virginia Council, at the request of Colonel George Washington, had appointed a chaplain for his regiment. Washington was...Anglican, [and of course] that was the established church in Virginia. But at the same time, in 1758, provision had also been made for dissenting clergymen (Baptist) to serve with the troops when requested.[37]

So from the very beginning of military chaplaincy, "cooperation without compromise" has been a working model for the chaplaincy. The phrase and its modern implications were worked out more completely after World War II. The value is being put to the test with the advent of other surprising and perhaps unintended participants at the pluralistic table, including Wiccans.

Cooperation without compromise, as it is usually expressed in military chaplaincy settings, has a set of values that includes

- Respect for others
- Support of others
- No proselytizing
- Follow the existing laws
- No need to compromise one's own religious values and practices[38]

Our ears are immediately pricked by that sticky stated value of "no proselytizing." But it is important to think about that value in

---

37   United States Coast Guard Chaplains' Office, *United States Coast Guard Lay Reader Training Manual* (United States Coast Guard, 1995).
38   Ibid.

the context of military ministry. We must remember that among the recent cases making the headlines, no government authority, despite the tireless work of antagonists, has restricted, say, Gospel preaching, where a Pentecostal chaplain is preaching, or from restricting a Jewish rabbi from chanting a Hebrew prayer in Jewish chapel. Nor has there been a single outcome in which the government restricted the pastoral counsel of chaplains that would include the sharing of one's faith with a military member who sought that chaplain for ministry. As Chaplain (BG) David Zalis has written,

> United States Code Title X empowers and directs us to provide for the free exercise of religion to military members. Chaplains exist to provide religious services for all their soldiers and not just to fulfill the spiritual needs of those whose religious affiliation is like theirs. This in no way means that we are not representatives of our respective faith groups.[39]

The "no proselytizing" value of "cooperation without compromise" simply means that, in our case, the Gospel may be presented when there is an invitation for us to speak: in chapels or as soldiers come to us for counsel. It means also that we present the Gospel without knocking over the altars of other religions, so to speak. This may mean, for instance, that, say, an evangelical Methodist chaplain must cooperate by providing access to Catholic literature for his Roman Catholic soldiers. However, if once that soldier reads the Catholic material and then has questions about it and asks to see the Chaplain, at that moment, the Methodist chaplain, having cooperated within the pluralistic setting, may then share with the soldier how he believes that justification is by faith alone through

---

39   Chaplain (BG) David Zalis, The Army Transformation and Objective Force Unit Ministry Team [Internet] (The Army Chaplaincy, 2002 [cited November 9 2006]); available from http://www.usachcs.army.mil/TA-Carchive/ACwinspr02/Zalis.htm.

grace alone to God's glory alone, not through sacerdotalism. Perhaps he prays with the soldier. And let us say that the soldier then attends the Protestant chapel to hear more of the Methodist chaplain. Then the soldier decides that he has never really known Christ. The chaplain prays with the soldier to receive Jesus Christ as Lord. Then the chaplain, in seeking to make a disciple, gives him a book on Wesleyan theology, and the soldier decides that Methodism is an expression of Christianity most agreeable to him. The soldier joins the United Methodist Church where he begins a life of discipleship as a Methodist. In this scenario, the chaplain has cooperated within a pluralistic setting, shown respect for the rights of the Catholic soldier, even cooperating up to the point of providing avenues for that soldier to express his Catholic faith, yet never compromising his own commitments. Indeed, as the soldier then was drawn to him, perhaps even through his cooperative spirit, and the chaplain's firm faith, the soldier was converted to an evangelical understanding of the Christian faith, and even more distinctively, he became a Methodist.

That is cooperation without compromise. It gets tricky of course. Let us say that there is a chaplain who is a PCA chaplain or another denomination like the PCA that does not believe in or allow her ministers to ordain females into the ministry. That chaplain is a second lieutenant. He reports to his new assignment in Heidelberg, Germany, at U.S. Army Europe Headquarters. He walks in to meet his new section commander. The chaplain is an American Baptist female. And the woman is a colonel! Full Bird! Well, what about it? That is a pluralistic setting from the professional, vocational side of the house as well as from the ecclesiastical side (I am speaking about the issue of male–female working relationships in the military, which, in my own experience, is not fully and satisfactorily settled). In this hypothetical case, though, let us ask, "What about the faith commitment of the PCA chaplain? And the American Baptist female chaplain–colonel?" Well, the lower ranking chaplain is going to have to cooperate with the female American Baptist chaplain colonel in everything: military discipline, protocol, and daily assignments. *But* the PCA chaplain will not have to, say, co-officiate the Sacrament of the Lord's Supper in the same service with her since that would be a violation of his own commitments and understanding of his faith. Now, he may have to serve with her in a non-religious, involuntary military ceremony, such as a change of command or patriotic ceremony. But he will not be required to compromise the teachings of his own denomination, which are, presumably, his very own convictions.

So, while admitting that the military chaplaincy has unique ministry challenges distinct from civilian ministry in the public square and that the military culture is unique, I would nevertheless posit that the military chaplaincy is a good model for ministry in a pluralistic setting. Moreover, I would say, out of my own experience as Army Reserve chaplain, endorsed from my denomination, the Presbyterian Church in America, that such a model is successful, despite the growing tensions we have all read about.[40] The PCA, as has been mentioned, doesn't ordain females to the ministry, and thus, we are an even more restrictive denomination in terms of having to live out the "cooperation without compromise" military model. What I am saying is, to put it quite simply, "If we can do it, anyone can do it!"

And here is where this chapter is going: I believe that the military chaplaincy approach to ministry, "cooperation without

40   For some of the tensions, and from a liberal viewpoint, read Laurie Goodstein, The *New York Times*: Evangelicals Are a Growing Force in the Military Chaplain Corps [Internet] (Refuseandresisit.org, 2005 [cited November 9 2006]); available from http://www.refuseandresist.org/repro/art.php?aid=2123.

compromise," is a model to be considered for civilian ministry in pluralistic North America today. We have seen what it is; now is it biblical, and is it practical? I will go to one well-known Scripture and then to one well-publicized commentary for the answer to those questions.

Let's now ask whether "cooperation without compromise" is biblical.

I want to turn to one particular passage that is useful in the whole debate, and that is Paul at Mars Hill. Paul was on his way from Thessalonica to Corinth. He did not intend, necessarily, to go to do what he did in Athens. The surprising turn of events that led him into the "very religious" environment of Athens was in fact a providential open door to preach the Gospel. Can we make out a model of "cooperation without compromise" there? I want to first look at Athens' condition, then Paul's response, and lastly, Athens's reaction.

First, the condition of that city was both pluralistic and obviously committed to pluralism. That it was pluralistic can be affirmed by Luke's citing of the religious groups: the city was full of "idols," presumably spanning the gamut of possible deities of that period and that place; Jews who practiced and Jews who didn't; Stoics and Epicurean philosophers (and there is no reason that they should be dismissed from the orbit of other religious bodies), and those people who worshipped, among their other gods, the One known as "the unknown god" inscribed on an altar in one of the pagan temples. This is surely a pluralistic city. But we can also see pluralism in their midst. Though the ideology is certainly not stated as such, there is a peaceful co-existence of gods, of ideas, and a commitment of their time and, thus, their lives to "saying or hearing something novel."[41] Indeed, it is Paul and his teaching on the resurrection of Jesus Christ that is so "new" that they lay their hands upon him and lead him up to the Areopagus that they may discover the meaning of his message. So the pluralistic community and the ideology of pluralism, if you will allow me to call it that, provide a brief moment of opportunity for the Gospel.

Look at Paul's response. First, it is important to see what Paul did not do. Paul did not turn over the altars. In fact, he studied them. He did not take the opportunity to denounce their culture. In fact, he quoted from their poets. He did not resist the philosophers to retreat to the safety of the believing Jews, but went along with the game, so to speak. In short, at every turn, Paul cooperated with the pluralistic culture. But let us affirm that Paul never compromised. While cooperating, in the sense of that word as we have used it, we, the readers, know that Paul's spirit was "exasperated"—to use the translation of Richmond Lattimore—over the idolatry of Athens.[42] But Paul's exasperation is an energy put to good work as he preaches. At the Areopagus, Paul did not rail as an angry prophet against their idolatry (though he had been provoked in his spirit by it), nor did he protest their paganism (like an ancient Fred Phelps and his Westboro Baptist Church–Topeka followers, with "God Hates Athens" lifted high)[43], but approached the Athenian religious plurality with the care that God did when He sent Jonah to Nineveh. There is a graciousness in Paul's words. He is speaking into the

---

41   According to the translation of Richmond Alexander Lattimore, *Acts and Letters of the Apostles* (New York: Farrar, Straus, Giroux, 1982).

42   Ibid.

43   For more on this illustration of one way—an unbiblical, unprofitable and even inhumane way—to respond to plurality and pluralism, you need only to type in "Fred Phelps" to get 59,400 entries at Google [on November 15, 2006). I read from the site http://www.apologeticsindex. org/111-westboro-baptist-church.

pagan audience as a man unto men. (Acts 17:26)[44] His own humanity is wrapped up in theirs as he says, "Being then God's offspring,
we..." in Acts 17:29. Note these features of his message and their
powerful implication for our pluralistic, pluralism-committed generation: It is, first, a message that seeks for signs of God in the culture of the pagans, a recognition with Calvin[45] of the *divinitatis sen-
sum*, the innate awareness of God[46]. And this is evident from his
powerful introduction in which he points out the inscription to the
unknown god. (Acts 17:23)[47]

It is a message that seeks to disclose true faith in Christ by con-
necting what Reformed theology calls General Revelation with the
God of Special Revelation: "For as I passed along and observed the
objects of your worship, I found also an altar with this inscription,
'To the unknown god.' What therefore you worship as unknown,
this I proclaim to you. The God who made the world and everything in it, being Lord of heaven and earth, does not live in temples
made by man." (Acts 17:23–24)

---

44   "And he made from one man every nation of mankind to live on all the
face of the earth, having determined allotted periods and the boundaries of their dwelling place." (Acts 17:26)

45   Jean Calvin, Institutes of the Christian Religion, *The Library of Christian
Classics*, V. 20–21 (Philadelphia: Westminster Press, 1960).

46   "There is within the human mind, and indeed by natural instinct, an
awareness of divinity...God himself has implanted in all men a certain
understanding of his divine majesty" (Institutes, 1. 3. 1.).

47   "For as I passed along and observed the objects of your worship, I found
also an altar with this inscription, 'To the unknown god.' What therefore
you worship as unknown, this I proclaim to you." (Acts 17:23)

Paul shows that behind the seen and unseen forces of life (Acts 17:25–28)[48] there is the one true God. Paul declares that the world is moving towards a day in which this God will judge the world. He will judge the world through a man whom he has appointed to do this, after giving sure proof to all by resurrecting him from the dead. (Acts 17:31)[49]

It is a message of grace. (Acts 17:30)[50] This God has overlooked previous sins. (Acts 17:30) In his commentary on Acts, John Calvin warns about speculative theology at this point.[51] It means what it says, and we must live in the tension of the mystery of why God allowed darkness to reign in their world until that moment (or why God chose that time, in His goodness, to reveal Jesus Christ to them). This surely cannot mean that the Athenians' forefathers were

---

48   ...nor is he served by human hands, as though he needed anything, since he himself gives to all mankind life and breath and everything. And he made from one man every nation of mankind to live on all the face of the earth, having determined allotted periods and the boundaries of their dwelling place, that they should seek God, in the hope that they might feel their way toward him and find him. Yet he is actually not far from each one of us, for 'In him we live and move and have our being'; as even some of your own poets have said, 'For we are indeed his offspring'" (Acts 17:25–28).

49   "because he has fixed a day on which he will judge the world in righteousness by a man whom he has appointed; and of this he has given assurance to all by raising him from the dead" (Acts 17:31).

50   "The times of ignorance God overlooked, but now he commands all people everywhere to repent" (Acts 17:30).

51   On Acts 17:30, Calvin writes: "And assuredly we be not able to comprehend the reason why God did at a sudden set up the light of his doctrine, when he suffered men to walk in darkness four thousand years; at least seeing the Scripture doth conceal it, let us here make more account of sobriety than of preposterous wisdom." See Jean Calvin, Henry Beveridge, and Christopher Fetherston, *Commentary Upon the Acts of the Apostles*. Edited from the Original English Translation of Christopher Fetherstone by Henry Beveridge, Esq. (Grand Rapids, W.B. Eerdmans Pub. Co., 1949: 1949).

not responsible for their sins, but that rather than visiting the Athenians with wrath at this point in history, a good God had sent His apostle to them to announce the Good News of Jesus Christ. While Luke does not give Jesus' name in the sermon proper (whether this is the complete sermon or Luke's redacted account, we do not know), Luke tells us that Paul was in fact "preaching the good news about Jesus and the resurrection" in verse 18.[52]

It is, finally, a message that calls for repentance: "The times of ignorance God overlooked, but now he commands all people everywhere to repent." (Acts 17:30)

And what happened? Some scoffed, some wanted to hear more, and some believed, among them a man and his wife. (Acts 17:32–34)[53] A family in Athens was now Christian. Presumably, the God of Abraham, Isaac and Jacob had now engrafted a former Athenian pagan, from among the plurality of religions, out of the resistance of pluralism, to become members of the "Israel of God" (Galatians 6:16). In this case, according to Greek Orthodox endorsed history, St. Dionysius became the Bishop of Athens, and inspired by Paul, took the Gospel to Gaul and was martyred for Christ on what is still known as Montmartre. His name went into the French as St. Denis (he was confused with a saint of the same name from the third century)[54] and then into English as Sidney, and thus we have the

---

52   "...he was preaching Jesus and the resurrection" (Acts 17:18b).

53   "Now when they heard of the resurrection of the dead, some mocked. But others said, 'We will hear you again about this.' So Paul went out from their midst. But some men joined him and believed, among whom also were Dionysius the Areopagite and a woman named Damaris and others with them" (Acts 17:32–34).

54   Read more on him and the legend, as well as the pseudo Dionysius and his letters, at http://www.bartleby.com/65/di/DionysiuA.html.

name for the beautiful city in Australia![55] Out of the many came one who affected so many others with the Gospel. We are left to marvel and ask with confidence concerning the answer: "Can anything stop the Kingdom of God?"

It is clear that the "cooperation without compromise" motif is one that Paul used. When considered alongside other passages, far too many to deal with in the limits of this chapter, we could even say he used it self-consciously.[56]

Is "cooperation without compromise" practical for civilian ministry?

Conducting a faithful ministry in the public square of our culture, whether as preachers or educators or Christians in any employment, is not only the call of Christ for the Christian but also the plan of God for the world. The gospel goes forward in this way. And if you agree with me that Newbigin is exactly biblical when he says that the "only answer, the only hermeneutic of the gospel, is a congregation of men and women who believe it and live by it,"[57] then Christ will use the Church in a pluralistic society committed as

---

55   See the fine sermon by Fr Andrew Phillips, St Dionysius the Areopagite [Internet] (Orthodox England.org, 2006 [cited November 15 2006]); available from http://www.orthodoxengland.btinternet.co.uk/serm-dion.htm.

56   I am thinking now of Paul's appearance before Festus after having been charged by the Jews with crimes against the state. Paul said, "If then I am a wrongdoer and have committed anything for which I deserve to die, I do not seek to escape death. But if there is nothing to their charges against me, no one can give me up to them. I appeal to Caesar" (Acts 25:11 ESV). Paul would cooperate in many ways with the existing governments, even though they were pagan, anti-Christian, and even hostile to the faith. So, too, would Peter charge believers to do this: "Honor everyone. Love the brotherhood. Fear God. Honor the emperor" [1 Peter 2:17 ESV]. Much more has been and could be said about this matter. But for my purposes, it is clear that Paul—as well as Peter and their Christian auditors—could and must "cooperate" but without "compromise."

57   Newbigin, The Gospel in a Pluralist Society.

they may be to an ideology of pluralism to draw some, even a number no man can count, to Himself through our salt and light encounter with the religious people of our pluralistic world. And a framework of "cooperation without compromise" is a God-honoring, biblically sound, time-tested, and proven way of accomplishing that worthy end. Moreover, it does so by honoring human beings, even when an inconsistent pluralism doesn't honor Christ or His claims.

One final way that I want to apply this is to the case from a few years ago when a controversy arose in The Lutheran Church–Missouri Synod over the involvement of one of its clergy in a multi-faith service, held in Yankee Stadium in New York, after the tragedy of 9/11/01. The Rev. Dr. David Benke, President of the Atlantic District of the Lutheran Church–Missouri Synod, stood on the same stage, on September 23, 2001, with members of not only other Christian denominations, but other religions. Before 20,000 people on that Sunday, for a multi-faith service that expressed the grief of the largest city in the United States, Dr. Benke made his way to the microphone. He said that the "field of dreams"—referring to Yankee Stadium—had "turned into a house of prayer." He then prayed. And I quote from his prayer, made to God, whom he repeatedly called a "Tower":

> O Heavenly Father, un-bind, un-fear, un-scorch, un-sear our souls; renew us in Your free Spirit. We're leaning on You, our Tower of Strength. We find our refuge in the shadow of Your shelter. Lead

us from this place—strong—to bring forth the power of Your love, wherever we are.

In the precious name of Jesus. Amen.[58]

Now, without injecting this Presbyterian into Lutheran ecclesiology or, for goodness' sake,re adjudicating the case for them (if some of you are Missouri Synod Lutherans, please update me on any further developments!), and admitting that many believe that such multi-faith gatherings fail to aid in public crisis or celebration as much as monochromatic services, I would say that this case—a case which was brought about by one minister's response, along with the other religious leaders in his community, to the greatest public crisis since Pearl Harbor—is a classic example of what we will face as we seek to minister the Gospel in a pluralistic age, in a nation committed to pluralism as a public value. A faithful Gospel minister was asked to join with other religions to offer prayer. Yet, in this case, at least as I have found it, the minister did nothing less than Paul did at Athens. He cooperated with the many religions. He didn't use this as an opportunity to protest their religion, but to bring Christ to the culture and to the minds of the 20,000 people present plus millions of others around the world that read his words. He prayed to the God who is a tower to those who seek Him. And he prayed in the name of a "precious" Savior, Jesus Christ.

---

58   I quote from documents (located at http://72.14.209.104/ search?q=cache:tVlTipen-TIJ:www.cat41.org/News/Archives/2001/ BenkeDocs.doc+benke+in+the+precious+name+of+jesus+yankee+stadi um&hl=en&gl=us&ct=clnk&cd=1&client=safari) outlining the charges against The Reverend Dr. David Benke concerning his participation in the multi-faith prayer service at Yankee Stadium. The prayer is a direct quote from an October 13, 2001 letter from The Reverend Charles Hendrickson to officials of the Lutheran Church-Missouri Synod.

Ultimately his denomination ruled in favor of Dr. Benke, and his usage of "cooperation without compromise" was vindicated.[59]

Such scenes as Dr. Benke faced are being presented to Christian clergy and people alike all over pluralistic America. How do we respond? Scripture, as well as praxis, vindicates the military chaplaincy model of "cooperation without compromise," and this chapter commends that framework as a faithful response to the challenges of fulfilling the Great Commission in our pluralistic age.

We must be clear. The Gospel tells us, in essence, that "it is not over 'til it's over," to borrow the words of the very quotable Yogi Berra. Jesus is on the throne. His Kingdom is here and will grow through the fulfillment of the Great Commission given to the Church. He will come again and bring a New Heaven and a New Earth. Nothing can stop the forward movement of the Kingdom of Jesus Christ. Even India, mentioned earlier, that jewel of pluralistic visions and example of where pluralism can lead, is now witness to a phenomenal growth of Christian conversions.[60] Pluralistic societies and pluralism itself cannot stop the Gospel. They could not in the first century, they cannot in India, and they will not prevail, ultimately, in the West. We need not be intimidated.

I close with the words, once more, of Lesslie Newbigin:

> The church needs to be very humble in acknowledging that it is itself only a learner, and it needs to pay heed to all the variety of

---

59   The final verdict in the ecclesiastical case was given in the words of the panel investigating the event: "Rev. Benke's participation [in "A Prayer for America"] was neither a rejection of nor a challenge to the Synod's fellowship position and practice, but a discretionary response to a quite extraordinary set of circumstances in a quite unordinary event—a terrorist attack on the United States of America, specifically in New York City and the parochial area of St. Peter's Lutheran Church, New York, New York, and the Atlantic District of the LCMS." See Hillary Wicai, "Suspension Lifted for Missouri Synod Leader," *Christian Century*, May 31 2003.

60   See J. T. Sunderland, "Will India Become Christian?" *The New World: A Quarterly Review of Religion, Ethics and Theology* 7 (1898).

human experience in order to learn in practice what it means that Jesus is the King and Head of the human race. But the church also needs to be very bold in bearing witness to him as the one who alone is that King and Head. For the demonstration, the proof, we have to wait for the end. Until then, we have to be bold and steadfast in our witness and patient in our hope. For 'we are partakers of Christ if we hold our first confidence firm to the end.' (Heb. 3:14)[61]

---

61   Newbigin, *Foolishness to the Greeks: The Gospel and Western Culture*, 148–149.

2

GREEN OR EVERGREEN

The Secular Environmental
Movement and Biblical Care for Creation

The current cultural climate is a veritable greenhouse for grow-ing ever-mutating myths about Christians, particularly evan-gelicals, and their concern for the earth.[62] The charge that there is a "huge burden of guilt"[63] to be born by evangelical Christians con-cerning environmental abuses goes back several decades to the genesis of a popular concern for the environment as the cultural-political issue that we recognize today. The growth of environ-mentalism[64] as a political movement[65]—rather than a principled

62 Johnson, James JS. "Misreading Earth's Groanings: Why Evolutionists and Intelligent Design Proponents Fail Ecology 101." *Acts & Facts* 39.8 (2010): 8-9.

63 Lynn White is quoted on page 365 in Kearns, Laurel. "Noah's ark goes to Washington: A profile of evangelical environmentalism." *Social Compass* 44 (1997): 349-366.

64 Grove, Richard H. "Origins of Western Environmentalism." Scientific American 267.1 (1992): 42-47. Also see the more global historiographi-cal theories of environmentalism in Guha, Ramachandra, and Juan Mar-tinez-Alier. *Varieties of environmentalism: essays North and South.* Earth-scan Publications Ltd, 1997

65 Dryzek, John S., et al. *Green States and Social Movements: Environmental-ism in the United States, United Kingdom, Germany, and Norway: Environ-mentalism in the United States, United Kingdom, Germany, and Norway.* OUP Oxford, 2003.

scientific inquiry,[66] embraced by left wing political groups in Western Europe,[67] Britain,[68] and North America[69]—crafted a public narrative based on Lynn White's (1907–1987) 1967 article in *Science*.[70] This article is often used as a primer to set up Christianity as an enemy to any genuine concern for the planet. Lauren Kearns, in his essay, "Noah's Ark Goes to Washington: A Profile of Evangelical Environmentalism" (*Social Compass* 44 [1997]: 349–366), framed the debate by linking evangelical suspicion of an environmentalism divorced from a biblical fidelity and a leftist suspension of a Christian association with Republican and conservative movements that distrusted environmentalism as a major component of a larger Socialist agenda. Considering the growth of the debate, the clash of worldviews, and the resulting lack of any significant voice to speak to the movement, White concluded, "Thus it became common belief that Christians did not care about the environment."[71]

White went on to say that Christianity is unable to understand the "sacred grove"[72] of the Redwoods, arguing that Ronald Reagan, as governor of California was a prime example of a Christian who

---

66   Jamison, Andrew. *The making of green knowledge: Environmental politics and cultural transformation.* Cambridge University Press, 2001.

67   Rüdig, Wolfgang. "Peace and ecology movements in Western Europe." *West European Politics* 11.1 (1988): 26-39.

68   Carter, Neil. "Party politicization of the environment in Britain." *Party Politics* 12.6 (2006): 747-767.

69   Devall, Bill. "Deep ecology and radical environmentalism." *American Environmentalism* (1992): 51-76.

70   White Lynn, T. "The historical roots of our ecologic crisis." *Science* 155.3767 (1967): 1203-1207.

71   Kearns, Laurel. "Noah's ark goes to Washington: A profile of evangelical environmentalism." *Social Compass* 44 (1997): 350.

72   This article, appearing in *Science* (1967) was also published as White, Lynn, "The Historical Roots of our Ecological Crisis," in Santos, Miguel A. *Readings in Biology and Man.* Irvington Pub, 1974, 273.

was incapable of such ecological vision,[73] and that "For nearly 2 millennia Christian missionaries have been chopping down sacred groves..." [74] He sees historic, orthodox, and particularly evangelical Protestant Christianity, as lacking (what he appears to mean) a meaningful, ecological hermeneutic to join the environmental crusade.[75] The classical passages that inform a cogent, coherent framework for teaching a Christian care for the Creation is insufficient or at least insufficiently taught, according to White and others. Those passages often include

> And God blessed them, and God said unto them, Be fruitful, and multiply, and replenish the earth, and subdue it: and have dominion over the fish of the sea, and over the fowl of the air, and over every living thing that moveth upon the earth. (Genesis 1:28)

> And the LORD God took the man, and put him into the garden of Eden to dress it and to keep it. (Genesis 2:15)

> The land shall not be sold in perpetuity, for the land is mine. For you are strangers and sojourners with me. (Leviticus 25:23)

> The earth is the LORD's and the fullness thereof, the world and those who dwell therein. (Psalm 24:1)

> For the creation waits with eager longing for the revealing of the sons of God. (Romans 8:19)

White rejected common interpretations of Creation as unfitting for the deeper appreciation of the ecological crisis and how to find solutions. They were simply too focused on the earth as being

---

73   Ibid.

74   Ibid. 273.

75   White believed that the Creation mandate in Genesis 2:15 (15 The Lord God took the man and put him in the garden of Eden to work it and keep it.) needed an alternative worldview than the anthropocentric view that historic Christianity offered. See his "Historical Roots."

made for Man. He believed and argued for modeling any future "democratic" Christian understanding on the life of St. Francis of Assisi.[76] White did not address the fact that so much of St. Francis' life and works is inconclusive because of the apocryphal material about him. He would thus take enormous leaps from sound scholarship to launch into a vision of his alternative Christian ecology platform:

> Francis tried to depose man from his monarchy over creation and set up a democracy of all God's creatures. With him the ant is no longer simply a homily for the lazy, flames a sign of the thrust of the soul toward union with God; now they are Brother Ant and Sister Fire, praising the Creator in their own ways as Brother Man does in his.[77]

Robert Booth Fowler, in his *The Greening of Protestant Thought,*[78] admits the growing embrace of mainline American Protestant denominations to the environmental movement, the interest that is creating eco-theologies, process theologies, and eco-feminist theologies that are contributing to the debate. Fowler also seeks to establish theological reasons why "Fundamentalists" continue to be hostile to ecological concerns.[79] Fowler defines 'fundamentalists" as "the minority of evangelicals who normally defend

---

76   This article, appearing in *Science* (1967) was also published as White, Lynn, "The Historical Roots of our Ecological Crisis," in Santos, Miguel A. *Readings in Biology and Man.* Irvington Pub, 1974, 273, 274.

77   White, Lynn. "Natural science and naturalistic art in the Middle Ages." *The American Historical Review* 52.3 (1947): 433.

78   Fowler, Robert Booth. *The greening of Protestant thought.* University of North Carolina Press, 1995.

79   A deeper understanding of evangelical Christians who embrace the Bible as inerrant and infallible would be enough to understand that the very advocacy of ecofeminism is plenty enough to cause hesitancy or outright refusal to become engaged in meaningful discourse about what we would prefer to call "Caring for Creation."

the Bible as inerrant..."[80] Thus, the Evangelical Theological Society would be seen by Fowler and others as 'fundamentalists" and, thus, outside of the progression of ecological progressivism. This is due, in large part, according to Fowler and others, because those who hold to inerrancy actually embrace ecological decline as a welcome sign that the End is near. Such misunderstandings are not only absolutely baffling asserted by those who claim the high ground of objective scholarship, but they belie an ideological commitment that transcends scholarship. One would have thought that such stereotypes would have long been jettisoned by the significant contributions of Christians in the teaching of stewardship of Creation. Yet, therein, is the continuing rub: there are major disconnects, at the deepest philosophical, theological and existential level, that appear to obstruct any meaningful discourse.

Despite the growing concern among Christians committed to biblical authority and supernaturalism in Creation, whether Catholic or evangelical, to address the reality of "stewardship of Creation" (or "Caring for Creation," as the 63rd Annual Meeting of The Evangelical Theological Society theme puts it) and to differentiate between competing worldview "starting points"[81] which led to distortions of language, meaning, and goals in naming the crisis and engaging it, the resounding response of secularist points of view is to continue to believe that an evangelical and/or biblical response

---

80   Ibid., 45.
81   Kearns, Laurel. "Noah's ark goes to Washington: A profile of evangelical environmentalism." *Social Compass* 44 (1997): 352.

is simply not genuine.[82] This is the case in the Drew University dissertation by James Ball, re-worked as an essay in *Perspectives on Science and Christian Faith* as "Evangelical Protestants and the Ecological Crisis."[83]

> Ball divides evangelical eco-theology into four sub-strata—wise use, anthropocentric stewardship, caring management, and servanthood stewardship—of which three are genuinely pro-ecology, and one, the wise-use movement, masquerades as environmentalism but is more appropriately seen as private property rights advocacy.[84,85]

Although evangelical and Catholic responses to the movement range from earlier works by Francis Schaeffer, such as *Pollution and the Death of Man*,[86] to declarations by Pope John Paul II that the "ecological crisis is a moral issue,"[87] to editorial decisions at *Christianity*

---

82   Angela Smith, in her outstanding Brown University Masters of Arts in Environmental Studies dissertation on "Faith-based environmental groups," points to a lack of a common language as a problem in finding greater influence." Of course, every social movement has its weaknesses, and this is true for the faith-based environmental movement as well. The inability to agree on a common language is one area of difficulty for religious–environmental groups." See Smith, Angela M. "Faith-based environmental groups in the United States and their strategies for change." May. 200: 261.

83   Ball, Jim. "The Use of Ecology in the Evangelical Protestant Response to the Ecological Crisis." *Perspectives on Science and Christian Faith* 50 (1998): 32-40.

84   Kearns, Laurel. "Noah's ark goes to Washington: A profile of evangelical environmentalism." *Social Compass* 44 (1997): 362.

85   Pope John Paul II. "And God Saw That It Was Good," (1990): 200-206.

86   Schaeffer, Francis A, and Udo W Middelmann. *Pollution and the Death of Man*. Crossway Books, 1992.

87   Pope John Paul II. "The ecological crisis: A common responsibility." *This sacred earth: Religion, nature, environment.* New York: Routledge (1990): 202-209.

Today that "It's Not Easy Being Green,"[88] the evangelical voices that seek to enter into conversation with the environmental movements have not won any praise from the intelligentsia of the non-Christian movements. Secular worldviews distrust Bible believing Christians as "Fundamentalists." Creationists who simply are mired in a primordial supernaturalism that leaves them, necessarily, out of the more important evolutionary discoveries and dialogue in the larger world, including global warming, and other eco-sensitivities, or, sullied, politicized parties to a more Machiavellian approach to become more eco-sensitive in order to appeal to the populism within their pews or would be members. This cynical response to a recognition of biblical stewardship of God's creation is the exact response that Frazier-Crawford Boerl and Christopher Wayne advance in their research work at St. Antony's College,[89] Oxford.[90] Joseph Bulbulia summed up the attitudes of many, no doubt, when he wrote,

> In Darwin's classic statement religion serves no adaptive function. But if Darwin wasn't tempted to Darwinize religion, why should we? Starting in the 1990s cognitive psychologists began to seriously explore specific features of religious cognition. Following

---

88   "It's Not Easy Being Green." *Christianity Today.* 18 May 1992: 14.

89   "St Antony's College is the most cosmopolitan of the seven graduate colleges of the University of Oxford, specializing in international relations, economics, politics and history of particular parts of the world" ("St Antony's College - University of Oxford." 19 Oct. 2012 <http://www.sant.ox.ac.uk/>).

The issue of theology, environmental science as a political movement, and international relations seems to be a broad subject with to arrive at such strong theological conclusions. One might suggest that the work might have benefited from more collaboration with researchers from Wycliffe Hall (http://www.wycliffehall.org.uk/content.asp?id=14).

90   Frazier-Crawford Boerl, Christopher Wayne. "American Evangelicals and the Politics of Climate Change." *St Antony's International Review* 5.2 (2010): 147-163.

in Darwin's footsteps, they argued that the aspects of religious cognition are most fruitfully understood not as parts to a globally adaptive system but as spandrels of other systems. Once we understand how these other integrated, modular, information processors work, we'll understand how they wind up accidentally generating supernatural thought as noise.[91]

Evangelical Christianity's voice in the environmental movement is just "noise" to the pseudo-illuminati of the self-proclaimed, genuine, earth care groups. The "noise" is grating on the ears of the more self-proclaimed enlightened environmentalists and thus attempts by Christian environmentalists, like the Christian Society of the Green Cross, the Evangelical Environmental Network, and the Christian Environmentalist Association—as worthy as these ministries are of our support—are, many times, not taken seriously. Likewise, excellent Christian books such as *Redeeming Creation*,[92] *Saving God's Green Earth*,[93] *An Earth-Careful Way of Life: Christian Stewardship and the Environmental Crisis*,[94] *Cherishing the Earth*,[95] appear simply as more of the "noise" from evangelical Christians. This attitude of larger academic community, demonstrated here, not only distorts the voices of well meaning Christian ecologists but often causes an effect not unlike the child putting his hands over his ears so that he cannot hear the opposing views of the kid

91   Bulbulia, Joseph. "The cognitive and evolutionary psychology of religion." *Biology and Philosophy* 19.5 (2004): 655-686.

92   Van Dyke, Fred H et al. *Redeeming creation: the biblical basis for environmental stewardship.* IVP Academic, 1996.

93   Robinson, Tri, and Jason Chatraw. *Saving God's Green Earth: Rediscovering the Church's Responsibility to Environmental Stewardship.* Ampelon Pub LLC, 2006.

94   Basney, Lionel. *An Earth-Careful Way of Life: Christian Stewardship and the Environmental Crisis.* Regent College Pub, 2000.

95   Hodson, Martin J, and Margot R Hodson. *Cherishing the Earth: How to Care for God's Creation.* Monarch Books, 2008.

next door. Simply put, the environmental movement's ground of being is incompatible with biblical Christianity. Lynn White's understanding that when Christians see the ecology through the lens of the creation mandate, the view is not only untenable for meaningful dialogue and collaboration but also unworthy of it. This might remind the believer of the incompatibility that John Gresham Machen referred to in his title *Christianity and Liberalism*.[96] From the environmental movement perspective, it appears clear that Christians who see the earth as made for man and fallen due to sin and crying out for redemption, as St. Paul taught, in Romans 8:19–22,[97] is simply a theological conception that can never sync with the globalism[98], socialism,[99] feminism,[100] redistribution,[101] and even (loosely) confederated groups, including religious ones, like

---

96   Machen, J Gresham. *Christianity and liberalism*. Eerdmans Publishing Company, 2009.

97   "For the creation waits with eager longing for the revealing of the sons of God. For the creation was subjected to futility, not willingly, but because of him who subjected it, in hope that the creation itself will be set free from its bondage to corruption and obtain the freedom of the glory of the children of God. For we know that the whole creation has been groaning together in the pains of childbirth until now" Romans 8:19-22 (New King James Version) - Bible Gateway." 2009. 20 Oct. 2012 <http://www.biblegateway.com/passage/?search=Romans+8%3A19-22&version=NKJV>.

98   Rootes, Christopher. *Environmental Movements: local, national and global*. London: Frank Cass, 1999.

99   McCormick, John. *Reclaiming paradise: the global environmental movement*. Indiana University Press, 1991.

100 Plevin, Arlene. "The World Is Our Home": Environmental Justice, Feminisms, and Student Ideology." *Feminist Teacher* 16.2 (2006): 110-123.

101 Schlosberg, David. "The justice of environmental justice: reconciling equity, recognition, and participation in a political movement." *Moral and political reasoning in environmental practice* (2003): 77-106.

pagans[102] and Wiccans,[103] that oppose biblical revelation in explaining the problem and any solutions for the environment, or more preferably put, Creation. Governmental policies, international, multi-national agreements, as well as private and nonprofit efforts at addressing and solving true ecological problems are forever bogged down in the incompatibility of worldviews, or, as some see it, an inescapable narrative that "...religion [is] the primary cause of ecological crisis."[104] It is no wonder that some Christians, like H. Paul Santmire, in his *The Travail of Nature* speak about "ambiguity" of a distinctive Christian theology of ecology. Thus, the publishers described his work:

> *The Travail of Nature* shows that the theological tradition in the West is neither ecologically bankrupt, as some of its popular and scholarly critics have maintained, nor replete with immediately accessible, albeit long-forgotten, ecological riches hidden everywhere in its deeper vaults, as some contemporary Christians, who are profoundly troubled by the environmental crisis and other related concerns, might wistfully hope to find. This is why it is appropriate to speak of the ambiguous ecological promises of Christian theology.[105]

102 Harvey, Graham. "The roots of pagan ecology." *Journal of Contemporary Religion* 9.3 (1994): 38-41.

103 Wood, Gail. "Review of Wiccan Roots: Gerald Gardner and the Modern Pagan Revival by Philip Heselton." *Pomegranate: The International Journal of Pagan Studies* 6.1 (2007): 144-146.

104 Oelschlaeger, Max. *Caring for creation: An ecumenical approach to the environmental crisis.* Yale University Press, 1996: 1-2.

105 Santmire, H Paul. The travail of nature: The ambiguous ecological promise of Christian theology. Fortress Press, 1985. The quote is taken from the Publisher's description of the book. See http://store.augsburgfortress.org/store/product/1690/9780800618063-The-Travail-of-Nature-The-Ambiguous-Ecological-Promise-of-Christian-Theology-?notFound=true.

This chapter does not propose to solve the ambiguity of a Christian theology of ecology. We do not seek to solve the intractable positions of those who see Christian concerns for the stewardship of Creation as mere Machiavellian moves to appease a popular environmentalism at work in the pew. We do seek to demonstrate that a Christian relationship to our world has long drawn from the clear streams of biblical revelation to describe a theology of Creation. We will seek to establish a high regard for "Caring for Creation" from the a biblical worldview of the stewardship of Creation.

A BIBLICAL WORLDVIEW

To begin to understand the wide chasm between secular environmentalism and biblical Christianity's understanding of stewardship of the earth, one must begin with a clear Weltanschauung.[106,107] Indeed, it has been written[108] that it was the German philosopher Immanuel Kant who first introduced the word in 1906 to describe what is called a "worldview,"[109] or what Albert Walters calls "the comprehensive framework of one's basic beliefs about things."[110] Historic, biblical Christianity must always begin with the special revelation of God through the Scriptures. If Jesus Christ is really who he says he is (and over 500 people testified that he lived after

---

106 Scheler, Max, et al. *Philosophische Weltanschauung.* F. Cohen, 1929.

107 Mannheim, Karl. "On the interpretation of Weltanschauung." *Essays on the Sociology of Knowledge* (1952): 33-83.

108 Naugle, David K. *Worldview: The history of a concept.* Wm. B. Eerdmans Publishing, 2002: 58.

109 Sire, James W. *The universe next door: A basic worldview catalog.* IVP Academic, 2009.

110 Wolters, Albert M. *Creation regained: Biblical basics for a Reformational worldview.* Wm. B. Eerdmans Publishing, 2005: 2.

he was crucified and entombed[111]) and God incarnate was crucified and then rose on the third day, and Christ testified to the vera-
city of the Bible,[112] then the Bible is in fact the inerrant and infallible Word of God. This Almighty God revealed over time, as
Benjamin Breckinridge Warfield put it,[113] that he exists in perfect,
eternal, communal tri-unity—three persons within the Godhead
and yet one God. A biblical worldview begins with the special revelation[114] and understands that there is a threefold progress to the
great metanarrative.

There was a supernatural creation by this Almighty God. The
pinnacle of that creation was not the earth but was in fact mankind—male and female. The first two chapters of Genesis are
clearly not poetic material or mythology. Moses was a great sacred
writer composing among other things Psalm 90.[115] However, any
honest reading of the first two chapters of Genesis cannot escape
the fact that Moses was recording history from a supernatural
perspective—that is, he was not interested in conveying scientific
data to the people; he was interested in describing the supernatural activity of Almighty God in creating. This gives us an anchor.

We are not purposeless. The children of God were made for
the garden. They were made for *ha eretz*—the land.[116,117] Further-

---

111   1 Corinthians 15:6.

112   Luke 24:27.

113   Warfield, Benjamin B. "The Biblical Doctrine of the Trinity." *The Works
of Benjamin B Warfield* Volume II (1929): 133-172.

114   Berkouwer, Gerrit C. "General and Special Divine Revelation." *Revelation
and the Bible* (1959): 13-24.

115   Fraser, James H. *The Authenticity of the Psalm Titles.* Diss. Grace Theological Seminary, 1984.

116   Sailhamer, John H., Walter C. Kaiser Jr, and Richard Hess. Genesis—Leviticus. Eds. Tremper Longman III, and David E. Garland. Vol. 1. *Zonder-
van*, 2008.

117   Elohim, Bara. "Word Studies from Genesis." *Ancient World: Reader*: 147.

more, the zenith of God's creation, mankind, was placed in a special relationship with Almighty God in *ha eretz* as is recorded by Moses. While calling it a covenant in theological terms, we are merely describing what we read in the Scriptures from beginning to end—what is being called a scarlet thread that runs through all of the metanarrative of the Bible.[118] God made a covenant with man and in that covenant he required that man being obedient. The reward for the obedience was life. The reward for such obedience was in Eden without end. There is great emphasis in Genesis placed upon *ha eretz*—the land. It is to be tended. It is to be cared for. Man's highest achievement is to cultivate the land. And all of this is recorded prior to the fall. After the fall there is also emphasis upon the land. The land becomes a nemesis of mankind. It is no longer a completely hospitable habitat. Thorns and pain now form a ruling motif within this habitat.[119] So a biblical worldview begins with a special revelation that describes to us a threefold meta-narrative. We have advanced two of those: special creation and the fall of mankind. But the third component in this biblical worldview, which is so necessary for us to understand the differences between environmentalism and a biblical caring for creation, is redemption.[120,121] The redemption that Almighty God promised and has brought about and will bring about in an even greater way—in what George Eldon Ladd called the "cataclysmic in breaking" of the

---

118 Robertson, O. Palmer. "Genesis 15:6: New Covenant Expositions of an Old Covenant Text." *Westminster (The) Theological Journal Philadelphia, Pa* 42.2 (1980): 259-289.

119 Moo, Douglas J. "Nature in the New Creation: New Testament Eschatology and the Environment." *Journal-Evangelical Theological Society* 49.3 (2006): 449.

120 See Mohler, R. Albert. "The Christian Worldview as Master Narrative: The End that is a Beginning." (2011).

121 McGrath, Alister E. "The Christian Church's Response to Pluralism."" *JETS* 35.4 (1992): 487.

kingdom of God[122]—was that God would provide—"What God Requires, God Provides."[123] Thus in Genesis 3:15 we have a promise of one who will come to crush the head of the evil one, the serpent who led mankind astray through his temptations of woman and man succumbing to that as well. Though the heel of that one will be bruised, we are told yet the head of the serpent will be crushed. This begins to work its way out as what theologians call a covenant of grace.[124] The covenant of works remains in effect. The issue is simply this: either mankind will find redemption in itself, bring redemption to the fallen world, and rectify the expulsion from Eden, and create a new Eden without the help of anyone—that is, clearly, without the help of Almighty God—or, there is a redemption promised by God and fulfilled in the person of Jesus Christ—Jesus, who said come on to me and you will have life.

This is the one who also said if you believe in me, you are passed from death unto life. This is also the one who said that if you know me, you will know the truth, and the truth will set you free. This is also the one who said that no one will come on unto me demand less the father draws him. This is also the one who was stapled to a cross, never denying that he was God Almighty, the supposed blasphemy which placed him upon that cross, but looking

---

122 Ladd, George Eldon. *The Presence of the Future: The Eschatology of Biblical Realism*. William B. Eerdmans Publishing Company, 1996. See also Lunde, Jonathan M. "A Summons to Covenantal Discipleship." "The C. S. Lewis Institute," in *Knowing and Doing*. Summer, 2011: 5.

123 See the sermon by John Piper, "What God Requires, Christ Provides," January 1, 2004: http://www.desiringgod.org/resource-library/articles/what-god-requires-christ-provides.

124 See, e.g., Murray, John. *The Covenant of Grace*. Presbyterian and Reformed Publishing Company, 1988.

down from the cross upon the very creatures he had created and saying, "Father, forgive them, they know not what they do."

Jesus of Nazareth, the adopted son of a carpenter and the son of the Virgin Mary, anointed for priesthood by John. The Scriptures testify to us from beginning to end, and so we have eyewitness testimony of the resurrection of Jesus Christ. In fact, the apostle Paul says more than 500 people saw him alive after he had been entombed. He also said that many of those who saw him were living as if to say, "if you doubt my words go, check it out with those many who saw it and who can corroborate this true story of resurrection."

It is important to understand then that the centering point of the meta-narrative of Scripture is the resurrection of Jesus Christ, his rising from the dead on the third day after he was entombed, and, this is often overlooked in a biblical worldview, the ascension of Jesus Christ to the very dwelling place of Almighty God. From thence he shall come again to judge the quick and the dead says the Apostle's Creed.

This has an enormous impact and import not only for the believer but also for the world. Jesus Christ lived the life that we could never live, and he died the death which should've been ours, and this essential purpose of the coming of Jesus Christ, according to Paul in Romans 8, verses 1 through 11, forms an important link from a biblical worldview to caring for creation.

In a biblical worldview, while mankind is the apex of God's creation and the earth is created for him, as a home for him, the earth fell into sin as a consequence of man's own sin. We surely know what it means for the earth to become infected with the corruption and evil of mankind. We understand what it means, whatever our political views or our understanding of scientific data, that man can pollute the very planet on which he dwells. Thus, it is not that far reached at all, though it is supernatural and must not be explained away in naturalistic terms, that the earth was wounded by the very sinfulness of mankind. In a similar way as the earth was corrupted in all of its parts, expressed by some as the role seen in both storms and floods and earthquakes as well as cancer and tragedies of all kind, including wars and rumors of wars. Man and his environment are one in the fall. Yet man and his environment, the earth, *ha eretz,* are also one in their hope for redemption.

Indeed, the apostle Paul lays forth a clear presentation of the state of things in terms of the environment or, the more biblical phrase, creation. The apostle Paul tells us that creation is groaning underneath the weight of sin brought by mankind.[125] Yet creation is eagerly groaning for redemption. That redemption, which was brought forward through Jesus Christ, is not only to redeem man but also to redeem his habitat, the creation of God, which is the land. Thus, John Milton will not compose *Paradise Lost* (1667) but will record *Paradise Regained* (1671).[126] There is a yearning inside of creation itself, and this does not mean there is a pantheistic understanding of creation.[127] But it does mean that there is a systematic, deep, perhaps inexplicable, drawing forth of the flower toward the sun as it were, in anticipation of a new heaven and a new earth. Thus, redemption is not only personal but redemption, in a biblical worldview, is cosmic. There is going to be an Eden restored. This is what the believer looks forward to and, in some way, creation itself strains toward.

---

125   "For we know that the whole creation has been groaning together in the pains of childbirth until now" (Romans 8:221 ESV).

126   Find it at: http://www.sacred-texts.com/chr/milton/index.htm.

127   Lamm, Julia A. "Romanticism and Pantheism." The Blackwell Companion to Nineteenth-Century Theology 44 (2010): 165.

CARING FOR CREATION

Thus, a biblical understanding of the world confesses a supernatural creation, a comprehensive fall that impacted not only mankind but also the earth, but that in Jesus Christ there is redemption—there is a new heaven and a new earth on its way. Whether this is a radical destruction of this earth and remaking of it, or as Albert Wolters[128] and Michael Williams[129] and others suggest, that the New Heaven and the New Earth is a fiery reordering of the present earth yet with some continuity (as was before in Noah's flood) with Eden, and the world we presently know is another matter within the larger narrative and worldview to consider. Yet, the Christian worldview clearly establishes that the earth will be redeemed. While we live in that theological tension of "the already in the not yet"[130]—which is the theological tension filled not only by mankind but, again, according to St. Paul in Romans 8, at work within creation—we live with the teleological perspective that brings us hope and brings us a renewed Christian activism within creation. "Creation is teleological."[131] We are not ready to return to Eden just yet, and Eden is not fully restored, but it is on its way. That is enough to pick up the cultivating tools once again and to enter the earth with the vision of caring for God's creation. Therefore, this essay posits that a biblical worldview calls for the believer to respond to the redemptive acts of God by caring for creation.

---

128   Wolters, Albert M. Creation regained: Biblical Basics for a Reformational Worldview. Wm. B. Eerdmans Publishing, 2005.

129   Williams, Michael D. Far as the curse is found: the covenant story of redemption. Presbyterian & Reformed Pub Co, 2005.

130   An interesting relationship of this theological phrase and worship and creation is found in: Harbert, Bruce. "Paradise and the Liturgy." New Blackfriars 83.971 (2002): 30-41.

131   Jones, W. Paul (1963) "Evil And Creativity: Theodicy Re-Examined." *Religion in Life* 32:521–533.

The theological vision of the redeemed earth is now inaugurated. Though our "gardening without weeds,"[132] as C. S. Lewis described the New Earth work, is not yet here, it is under way. We are therefore very busy weeding until that time is here.

This writer has witnessed how local government and private enterprise can collaborate to bring about a care for Creation. Chattanooga, Tennessee was once known as one of the dirtiest places in America.[133] The causes of the polluted river and the dirty downtown could be attributed to many things, yet the observant believer and adherent to a biblical worldview, could point to a lack of care for creation. Yet, the same worldview fueled the efforts of local government and local businesses, of philanthropist and educators, and, indeed, in some sense, the whole community to roll up their sleeves and go to work and cultivate the land. Today Chattanooga has been cited as a model of what a downtown River city revitalization should look like.[134,135,136] This is also an example of the response of a believer, grounded in a biblical worldview of creation–fall–redemption, who looks upon creation, whether it is forest or river or wildlife or, indeed, unstoppable reproduction of mutated cells in the human body, or the human condition, whether physiologically,

---

132   Martindale, W., and W. Hooper. *Beyond the Shadowlands: C. S. Lewis on Heaven and Hell. Crossway*, 2005:27.

133   Rogge, Mary E., et al. "Leveraging Environmental, Social, and Economic Justice at Chattanooga Creek." *Journal of Community Practice* 13.3 (2006): 33-53.

134   Rogge, Mary E. "Toxic risk, community resilience, and social justice in Chattanooga, Tennessee." *Sustainable Community Development: Studies in Economic, Environmental, and Cultural Revitalization*, edited by Marie D. Hoff. Boston: Lewis Publishers (1998): 105-121.

135   Jacobson, L. "Tennessee Triumph. Chattanooga Attacks Its Biggest Problems With Gusto." *Planning* 63.5 (1997).

136   Portney, Kent E. "Local business and environmental policies in cities." *Business and environmental policy: corporate interests in the American political system* (2007): 299-326.

psychologically, spiritually, or sociologically, and recognizes the woundedness of the fall in that condition. Responding to the re-demptive work of Jesus Christ in his own life, the believer then be-comes an activist, not out of the pantheistic environmentalist movement, but out of gratitude to the creator God, to apply, in some measure, in some way, the redemption he has received to the brokenness before him.

One will note that the writer has not sought to engage issues such as population controversies, deforestation controversies, cli-mate change, destruction or possible destruction of the Earth's ozone, the relative impossible destructive powers of certain fuels, nuclear energy, or a host of other issues that or before Aldus. There are those who are experts in the field and those who have much more data to discern whether these are populist movements or observable, scientific issues which demand a biblical worldview responds. My concern has only been—and this is a big *only*, if I may say so myself—that biblical Christianity is *not* an enemy to the earth. Biblical Christianity is, in fact, a friend of the earth. A new heaven and a new earth are not here, but the program of re-demption has been inaugurated. And we who are not fully restored to Eden have also experienced the inaugural saving work of Jesus Christ in our own lives. In this, therefore, rather than in any pagan concept of unity of mankind and earth, we all are, in fact, united with creation.

A biblical Christian worldview is, therefore, most concerned about caring for God's creation because of one's faith and convic-tion, not in spite of it. This same faith and conviction compels a be-liever to care for the earth—and in a better way than pantheistic green activists do. The charge that Christians do not care for the earth is offensive on its face and categorically, historically, and theologically wrong at its core.

Populist movements within congregations or shrewd attempts to mollify activists who are demanding that clergy and church become more involved in green movements pose a danger on many levels. First and foremost, Christians must rely on God's instruction and not the instruction of movements or politicians. Second, there must be proper understanding (this takes reading and studying) of these movements, their leaders, and their real motives (which is almost always about more money and more taxes) and the wisdom to be able to adequately counter these movements (which, by the way, is always about money, but not taxes).

The proper teaching of the church about caring for the earth should be about a compelling conviction arising out of a personal encounter with the Redeemer, Jesus Christ. And just as the Apostle Paul reasoned with the leaders of his day with great wisdom and knowledge, so must we in this and in other concerns of our day, and with the same amount of enthusiasm. This is not a green movement. This is better. However, it is good to acknowledge that there are many concerns that would be common to both sides.

3

"IN JESUS' NAME I PRAY"

Exclusivity in Public Prayer and the Restrictive Contours of Civic Pluralism in the Early Twenty-First Century

ABSTRACT

This chapter seeks to examine the increasingly challenging goal of faithful, authentic Christian public prayer in the antagonistic arena of a civic culture committed to the cult of pluralism. While attempting to answer practical questions about the changing nature of civic expectations for public prayer in the West, this chapter will also present biblical models and principles for faithful witness in prayer. Finally, this chapter will also analyze current Christian responses to this critical challenge and provide possible alternatives for naming the name of Jesus Christ in public prayer.

There can be no denial of the culture wars in the early twenty-first century.[137] Scholars, authors, social observers, pundits, and entire institutes have all recognized the challenge and insult to give various opinions for the root of the problem, the description

---

137 An excellent resource for commentary on the continuing challenge of faith and culture is Executive Director Dr. Paul Kengor, The Center for Vision and Values | Grove City College. http://www.visionandvalues. org/. The Center won the 2010 Templeton Freedom Award and continues to produce excellent commentary and resources with great thoughtfulness, historic depth and biblical worldview. Their Center has been a resource for this chapter and I would like to thank Dr. Kengor and Fellows of the Center for the compendium of articles and scholarly work that helps shape my own thinking about the Church and Culture.

of the problem, and the possibilities for solution.[138] Some are more optimistic than others.[139] The red state/blue state division of our nation, so popularly put by political pundits on news shows, is only the beginning of the greater division that many believe we face. [140] Yet political and cultural wounds in the flesh of our society are not alone. H. Richard Niebuhr in his book, *The Social Sources of*

---

138 See, for example, these resources which all, from several points of view, helped to inform this chapter: L. E. Adams, *Going Public: Christian Responsibility in a Divided America* (Brazos Press, 2002); W. A. Donohue, *Secular Sabotage: How Liberals Are Destroying Religion and Culture in America* (FaithWords, 2009); M. McGough, *A Field Guide to the Culture Wars: The Battle over Values from the Campaign Trail to the Classroom* (Praeger, 2008); R. A. Mohler, *Culture Shift: Engaging Current Issues with Timeless Truth* (The Doubleday Religious Publishing Group, 2008). T. J. Demy and G. P. Stewart, *Politics and Public Policy: A Christian Response: Crucial Considerations for Governing Life* (Kregel Publications, 2000); ibid.; V. Havel and P. Wilson, *Summer Meditations* (Knopf Canada, 1993); P. B. Henry, *Politics for Evangelicals* (Judson Press, 1974).

139 I am particularly thankful, with so many others, for the outstanding contributions of Dr. Phillip Jenkins of Penn State University. His optimistic view of the future of immigration and its positive implications for biblical Christianity in America, for instance, is one of the most hopeful and refreshing perspectives today. See P. Jenkins, *The New Faces of Christianity: Believing the Bible in the Global South* (Oxford University Press, 2006). For a European take on the future of Christianity in a deeply secularized society, see P. Jenkins, *God's Continent: Christianity, Islam, and Europe's Religious Crisis* (Oxford University Press, 2007). In these books Jenkins proposes that the current fears of evangelicals, that immigration will dilute values, is turned upside down to show that Asian Presbyterians, Hispanic traditional Catholics—and the new Pentecostals of South America—African Anglicans and others groups whose theology is decidedly more conservative than contemporary American (and European) Christians, will, in fact, return the nation to the founding values of America.

140 Bishop Thomas Curry, Los Angeles, has argued that the nation is facing a deep crisis because of liberal attacks that are reinterpreting the First Amendment. See T. J. Curry, *Farewell to Christendom: The Future of Church and State in America* (Oxford University Press, 2001).

Denominationalism[141] (1929), makes the charge that "the gospel of the brotherhood of Jew and Greek, bond and free, white and black has sometimes the sound of irony, and sometimes falls upon the ear with unconscious hypocrisy..." and is still felt by many in our country. The riots in working class neighborhoods outside of London also point to a woundedness that is festering—the challenge of a twentieth-century social experiment which is no longer affordable.

Yet in the midst of all of these challenges of not being able to communicate with each other, there is an even greater challenge. It is the challenge of philosophical pluralism. I say "philosophical pluralism," for while plurality, or pluralistic, is simply a fact of the existence of diversity co-existing in one community, pluralism is an ideology.[142] For philosopher John Rawls, pluralism as ideology is a "fact" of Post World War II Western democracies:[143] "'Pluralism' goes further still, for its advocates reject exclusivism as 'presumptuous' and 'arrogant' and inclusive is seen as 'patronizing' or 'condescending.'"[144]

The charter of the European Union has a different way of putting it: "United Diversity."[145] It is also philosophical in the sense that it is a tenant, an ideal, and a commitment that has been largely embraced by the greater Western society.[146] The ideology of the

---

141 H. Richard Niebuhr, *The Social Sources of Denominationalism* (Hamden, Conn.: Shoe String Press, 1954).

142 See, for example, W. J. T. Mitchell, "Pluralism as Dogmatism," *Critical Inquiry* 12, no. 3 (Spring, 1986); John R. W. Stott, *The Contemporary Christian: An Urgent Plea for Double Listening* (Leicester: Inter-Varsity, 1992).

143 T. Hedrick, Rawls, and Habermas: *Reason, Pluralism, and the Claims of Political Philosophy* (Stanford University Press, 2010).

144 Stott.

145 Richard John Neuhaus, *The Naked Public Square: Religion and Democracy in America* (Grand Rapids, Mich.: W.B. Eerdmans Pub. Co., 1984).

146 In Hedrick.

philosophical pluralism is being buttressed by popular mass communication. The political correctness and increasing secularism has produced what Professor Stephen Carter has called "A Culture of Disbelief."[147] In the name of tolerance, the culture of the West is becoming increasingly and unbearably intolerant for Christians. Whereas John Rawls proposed in his *A Theory of Justice*,[148] that a liberal democracy is sustained by "restraint on the fundamentals," that is, by the citizen recognizing that there are, in such a free society, overlapping ideas and therefore a need for "fair social cooperation" between the views for the benefit of sustaining the democracy. Pluralism, as an ideology, knows no such restraint, it seems, for those who are want to contribute to the society out of their faith. There are many facets of this intolerance one could examine. For this annual meeting of the Evangelical Theological Society, I want to focus on only one of those: *praying in the name of Jesus Christ in the public domain.*

As Christians consider the topic of prayer in the name of Jesus Christ, we do so with a constellation of case studies moving in orbit: there is the decision by Mayor Michael Bloomberg of New York City not to invite clergy to the tenth anniversary services of the 9/11 attack.[149] There is the case of the atheist group led by Mickey Weinstein that successfully shut down the chaplain-taught

---

147 S. L. Carter, *The Culture of Disbelief: How American Law and Politics Trivialize Religious Devotion* (Anchor Books, 1994).

148 J. Rawls, *A Theory of Justice* (Belknap Press of Harvard University Press, 1999).

149 Thankfully the service included a reading of Psalm 42 by the President of the United States and references to God by former President Bush. See http://www.christianpost.com/news/obama-giuliani-read-bible-bush-mentions-god-at-9-11-service-55413/.

Christian Just War Theory at Vandenberg Air Force Base.[150] There are other cases of legislative prayer complaints,[151] prayer in school complaints,[152] prayers before football games,[153] and many other situations, that not only deserve attention by those following the cultural wars but give rise to a deeper discussion on how Christians can maintain a faithful Gospel witness in public prayer. One might add that for every issue that is raised publicly, there is very likely a multitude of other cases that we never hear about.

This writer was present in the very situation we are addressing—praying in Jesus' name in public prayer—at a local Rotary club. There, the Jewish rabbi insisted that there should be no more prayers in the name of Jesus Christ. Since he made this resolution in a medium-size, southern town, where the president and all the officers of Rotary are Christians, his resolution was bound for failure. His own constituency, members of his congregation, shrank as the young rabbi made the proposal. They knew it would go nowhere.

---

150 See my Commentary dealing with this matter: Michael A. Milton, "The Attack on Just War Is Not Just," *Christian News Wire*, August 11, 2011, (2011). This was published in numerous online journals including Michael A. Milton, "This Attack on Just War Is Not Just—Atheists Fiddling with Western Civilization While Nation Is at War," ArmyChaplaincy.com August 2011 (2011).

151 *Marsh v. Chambers*, in 463 U.S. 783, ed. ReligiousFreedom.lib.virginia. edu (1983). Concerning a complaint by a legislator named Chambers who sued that a chaplain's prayer using Jesus' name violated the establishment clause of the first amendment, "By a 6–3 vote the Supreme Court permitted the practice of beginning the legislative session with a prayer given by the publicly funded chaplain."

152 For example, see Susanne M. Schafer, "Complaints Prayer Rally Held at Sc Public School," Newsobserver.com (September 22, 2011). http://www.newsobserver.com/2011/09/22/1509547/complaints-prayer-rally-held-at.html (accessed October 3, 2011).

153 Santa Fe Independent School District v. 530 U.S. 290, 530 US Supreme Court 2000). See http://caselaw.lp.findlaw.com/scripts/getcase.pl?court=us&vol=530&invol=290.

That is not uncommon. For most of the United States, pluralism is now a way of life. And within that way of life there is an expectation of cooperation. There is, to use the phrase of the military on the title of the book that I wrote, "Cooperation without Compromise."[154] However, since that event happened, almost five years ago, the contour of tolerance in public pluralism has undergone a remarkable narrowing. Indeed, according to a former Rotary president and member of the congregation where I formerly pastored, that same club now *prohibits use of* the name of Jesus in the club's invocation. There is growing evidence that this is not an isolated incident, but represents an unsettling trend regarding Christianity and civic discourse.[155] It appears that all other religious prayers may be offered *except* for any prayer that is in the exclusive name of Jesus Christ of Nazareth. How shall we respond to this? Is there still space in the public square, or is it in fact now stripped bare of all references to Christ? There is much at stake in the answer. J. Howard Pew believed, "from Christian freedom

---

154 M. A. Milton, *Cooperation without Compromise: Faithful Gospel Witness in a Pluralistic Setting* (Wipf & Stock Publishers, 2007).

155 For example, see C. H. Lippy, *Faith in America: Changes, Challenges, New Directions* (Greenwood Publishing Group, Incorporated, 2006).

comes all of our other freedoms."[156, 157, 158] If he is right then any re-
strictions of the use of Jesus' name in public prayer should concern
all Americans. Others like David Tracy, the Andrew Thomas Greeley and Grace McNichols Greeley Distinguished Service Professor
of Catholic Studies at the Divinity School of the University of Chicago, representing another view of Christianity in the public
sphere, are pessimistic about any breakthrough as he wrote, "...
Until...Christian[s] develop a public set of criteria based upon the
communicative power of non-manipulative and emancipatory reason, the possibilities of an adequate public Christian theology of
praxis remain, I fear, remote."[159]

Greeley's analysis, if correct, is chilling.

Why can't Christians pray in Jesus' name in the public sphere
of our society? Do we really lack a "communicative power of

---

156 As quoted in L. J. V. Til, *Liberty of Conscience: The History of a Puritan Idea* (P&R Pub., 1992).

157 Our founding fathers felt so strongly about the freedom of religion in the public square that, as in the case of the 1776 Constitution of North Caro-lina, they prohibited office from anyone who objected to Christ in the public arena. Article XIX of North Carolina's 1776 Constitution reads, "All men have a natural and unalienable right to worship God according to the dictates of their own consciences." Article XXXII is specifically Christian in stating the following qualifications for public officers in the state: "No person who shall deny the being of God, or the truth of the Protestant religion, or the divine authority of the Old or New Testa-ments, or who shall hold religious principles incompatible with the free-dom and safety of the State, shall be capable of holding any office or place of trust or profit in the civil department within this State." See http://candst.tripod.com/cnst_nc.htm.

158 See also the arguments of J. Howard Pew in his work on the board of Grove City College to construct a curriculum which saw the essential connection between the doctrine of freedom in Christianity and the ex-pression of freedom in a democratic republic: L. Edwards, *Freedom's College: The History of Grove City College* (Regnery, 2000).

159 David Tracy, "Theology as Public Discourse," *The Christian Century*, March 19, 1975.

non-manipulative...reason?" Is a Christian minister praying in Christ's name at a national memorial no longer considered civil? Can't a businessman—Christian, Hebrew, or otherwise—still pray in public according to his own faith and conscience? The questions are meant to be rhetorical, but there are many who would shout out an answer, as I have found in my own research. This too is disturbing if our freedoms are indeed derived from the freedom of religious expression in the public square.

The difficulty has been given a name by J. H. H. Weiler[160] in chapter three of *The Naked Public Square Reconsidered.*[161] There, Weiler considers construction of the preamble to the Charter of the European Union, which disallowed the inclusion of an *invocation Dei,* as an example of what he calls *Christophobia,* an unreasonable fear of offending others by using the name of Jesus. Weller demonstrates that the name of Jesus is used in constitutional language for numerous member states, including Ireland, Denmark, Greece, Spain, Germany, as well as Britain's famous constitutional reference to the monarch as the Defender of the Protestant faith. Even the newer constitutions, like in Poland, recognize their religions heritage as being a source for their national values as well as those secularists who find those values originating from other sources (unnamed):

> ...We, the Polish nation—all citizens of the Republic, both those who believe in God as the source of truth, justice, good, and beauty, as well as those not sharing such date but respecting

---

160 Joseph Halevi Horowitz Weiler, Ph.D. (b. 1951), Joseph Straus Professor of Law; European Union Jean Monnet Chaired Professor; Director, Straus Institute for the Advanced Study of Law & Justice; Director, Tikvah Center for Law & Jewish Civilization; Director, Jean Monnet Center for International and Regional Economic Law and Justice; Director, J.S.D. Program, New York University School of Law, New York.

161 Neuhaus.

those universal values as arising from other sources, equal in
rights and obligations toward the common good...[162]

Despite the fact that Europe (I do not speak of Europe as sin-
gularity as Norman Davies[163] does, rather as, say, Paul Thibaud does,
when he states, "Europe remains an indeterminate political project
that has not managed to legitimate itself independently of states."[164])
is a continent of nations crafted on Christian and biblical principles
and an indisputable Christian heritage. Despite a still present
Christian majority, Brussels has sought to institute an economic–
political alliance—a "normative supranationalism"[165]—without
mentioning the philosophical–cultural–religious relevance of European nation–state's legacy, namely, Christianity. To accomplish
this is an extraordinary coup of disturbing intolerance for the faith
and history of the people the EU is presumed to serve.

How shall we think biblically, theologically, and humanly, about
this trial[166]—if I may call it such—that we face in our world today?
I believe the words of Miroslav Volf are prophetic and good for us,
when he writes,

---

162 C. Wolfe and R. J. Neuhaus, *The Naked Public Square Reconsidered: Religion and Politics in the Twenty-First Century* (ISI Books, 2009).

163 N. Davies, *Europe: A History* (Harper Perennial, 1998).

164 See L'Europe allemande... Définitivement ? *Esprit*, Mai 1996, pp. 53–65;
Jean-Marc Ferry and Paul Thibaud, Discussion Sur L'europe (Paris:
Calmann-Le\0301vy, 1992).

165 See the use of this phrase by Jean-Marc Ferry, La Question De L'etat
Europe\0301en ([Paris]: Gallimard, 2000); Riva Kastoryano, An Identity
for Europe: The Relevance of Multiculturalism in Eu Construction, 1st
ed., The Sciences Po Series in International Relations and Political Economy (New York: Palgrave Macmillan, 2009).

166 Persecution.Org calls it "persecution" in America, as in http://www.per-
secution.org/2011/06/03/banning-prayer-in-jesuss-name-in-america/
(accessed October 2, 11),

A genuinely Christian reflection on social issues must be rooted in the self giving love of the divine Trinity as manifested on the cross of Christ; all the central themes of such reflection what have to be fall through from the perspective of the self giving love of God.[167]

The cross of Christ therefore must be central in reflections on the use of the name in Jesus Christ in public prayer. Any thinking about opposition, any reflections on strategy, any opining about what to do or what not to do in this present state of affairs, must be radically grounded in the biblical identification of the apostle Paul's mission "to know nothing among you except Jesus Christ, and him crucified." (1 Corinthians 2:2) Such an approach to this problem or to any other assumes that the cross of Christ, the ruling motif of the selfless love towards sinners, which saved us, will save others. It also assumes that we naturally embrace the fundamental focus of the Scriptures—the supreme identity of Jesus as Lord and Savior. In doing so, we may be, in Christ, both uncompromising in our public faith and civil towards those with whom we disagree. We therefore agree with Demy and Stewart in their excellent work on faith and public discourse, *Politics and Public Policy: A Christian Response*:

> ... We believe that Christians operating in politics should be the exemplars of stability. Too much of politics is overheated rhetoric and ad hominem attack. Christians with a full understanding of the limits and possibilities of politics, and of the precarious state of their own souls should be the last to engage in such tactics despite the obvious temptations to do so.[168]

---

167 Miroslav Volf, *Exclusion and Embrace: A Theological Exploration of Identity, Otherness, and Reconciliation* (Nashville: Abingdon Press, 1996).

168 Demy and Stewart.

With our own Gospel requirement for a Christian charity acknowledged, we are still left with the colossal present-day challenge that Lesslie Newbigin described:

> ...to commend the truth of the gospel in a culture that has sought
> for absolute certainty as the ideal of true knowledge but now de-
> spairs of the possibility of knowing truth at all...[169]

Some theologians see the present secular resistance to Christians praying in Jesus' name as specifically related to the "powers"[170]
of this "present evil age."[171,172]

With our difficulty now stated, a motivation for discovering an
answer (namely, our faithfulness as Christ's servants as well as our
freedom as citizens in a Western democracy) recognized, and some
Gospel sensitivities affirmed as we move along, I would like to approach this chapter with a simple thesis that *Christians should pray*

---

169 Lesslie Newbigin, *Proper Confidence: Faith, Doubt, and Certainty in Christian Discipleship* (Grand Rapids: W. B. Eerdmans Pub. Co., 1995).

170 "For we do not wrestle against flesh and blood, but against the rulers,
against the authorities, against the cosmic powers over this present
darkness, against the spiritual forces of evil in the heavenly places."
(Ephesians 6:12 ESV)

171 "Grace to you and peace from God our Father and the Lord Jesus Christ,
Galatians 1.4 who gave himself for our sins to deliver us from the present evil age, according to the will of our God and Father," (Galatians
1:3–4 ESV)

172 See Ambrosiaster and G. L. Bray, *Commentaries on Galatians–Philemon*
(INTER VARSITY PR, 2009); C. E. Arnold, *Ephesians, Power and Magic:
The Concept of Power in Ephesians in Light of Its Historical Setting* (Cam-
bridge University Press, 1989); H. Berkhof, *Christ and the Powers* (Her-
ald Press, 1962); F. F. Bruce, *The Epistle to the Galatians: A Commentary
on the Greek Text* (Grand Rapids, Mich.: W.B. Eerdmans Pub. Co., 1981);
G. B. Caird, *Principalities and Powers: A Study in Pauline Theology: The
Chancellor's Lectures for 1954 at Queen's University, Kingston Ontario*
(Wipf & Stock Pub, 2003); W. Wink, *Unmasking the Powers: The Invisible
Forces That Determine Human Existence* (Fortress Press, 1986).

in the name of Jesus Christ in public prayer. I do not mean to imply such a recalcitrant view that those who offer public prayer and sincerely pray to God in Jesus' name yet omit a closing phrase should be held to theological libel! Many of us, I think, have prayed, perhaps through extemporaneous forms, and omitted the name of Jesus in our "prayer closet," yet praying in His name from the heart. I believe that this is a necessary qualification lest anyone suppose that I'm advocating praying in Jesus' name as a sort of incantation. That would, of course, amount to Jesus' warning about heathen prayer and their wrong-headed assumption that many words (and that could be applied to other religious prayer rituals) can bring about greater effectiveness in prayer.[173] Indeed, the pleasant familiarity of being in a Christian context reinforces the possibility of omitting the phrase, "in Jesus' name I pray," since we assume that our audience is "with us" in our faith. I would respectfully contend, however, that such a thought is a naïve assumption in these days (not only in public prayer in a broad civic context, but even in many churches that are called Christian and some identified as evangelical).

My thesis also has a sub-text: *that believers should not feel any civic guilt for witnessing to the authority of Jesus in their public prayers in this increasingly pluralistic age.* I will seek to acknowledge the difficulties with my proposition (and its subtext), which are held and defended by other fair-minded believers. In order not to set up a "straw man," I will seek to document Christian rebuttals to any necessity of praying in Jesus' name in public—not for the sake of picking a fight, for I agree with much of what others have said on the subject, but for an attempt at fair-mindedness and for the utmost appreciation of objectivity among Christians. There are

---

173 "And when you pray, do not heap up empty phrases as the Gentiles do, for they think that they will be heard for their many words." (Matthew 6:7 ESV)

indeed those who sincerely disagree with what I propose, and I want to give them their due, at least through several representative voices. I also want to move to my main concern by providing a response—I trust a biblical response—to those objections. In my rejoinder, I hope to demonstrate my argument by showing that a Christian prayer in the public realm rests on the three-legged stool of *authority, context, and witness.* Finally, I will seek to provide some practical responses to the growing sense of *Christophobia* in public prayer.

OBJECTIONS AND RESPONSES

The crisis, and I believe I'm justified in calling it that, over public prayer in the name of Jesus Christ evokes responses from within the church that are, not surprisingly, diverse. Some of the responses have included objections, or at least cautions, about public prayers in the name of Jesus Christ for theological, political, or even missional reasons. There have been objections to prayer in the name of Jesus in the public setting because, theologically, some have said (we will document these as we come to them in the chapter) that there is no example in the Bible where one prays in the name of Jesus. That much is admitted if praying in His name is using the phrase in question, "I pray in Jesus' name," or "in Christ's name I offer this prayer." Secondly, there are some believers who maintain that praying in the name of Jesus outside of the Church (or church) is to unnecessarily push the idea of separation of church and state, or more charitably, to dilute, or even adulterate, the spiritual mission of the Church in the world. Under the rubric of "don't mix faith and politics in the public domain," other sincere Christians believe that we simply should not participate in public prayer where there is the tendency to surrender doctrine for the sake of civility. Approaching these objections to public prayer using

Jesus' name, one thinks of Richard Niebuhr's classic work *Christ and Culture*[174] (as well as D. A. Carson's recent update[175]) and his analysis of five normative responses in the Christian faith.[176] Indeed, D. A. Carson is helpful in expressing the problems that we face in his first chapter on *Christ and Culture* revisited: D. A. Carson and his *Christ and Culture Revisited* introduced what he called "the contemporary challenge." Carson wrote,

> In the move from the Old Covenant to the New, the locus of the Covenant people passed from the covenant-nation to the international covenant-people. That inevitably raises questions about the relationships this people should have with the people around them who were not part of the new covenant. In political terms, Christians had to work through the relationship between the church and state, between the kingdom of God and the Roman Empire. Somewhat different answers were called up by different circumstances: contrast, for instance, Romans 13 and Revelation 19. But the issues the church faced by being an international community claiming ultimate allegiance to the kingdom not of this world were much more than governmental. They also had to do with whether Christians should participate in socially expected customs..."[177]

The Constantinian settlement eased the persecutions that resulted from these challenges to the early Church but did not

---

174 H. Richard Niebuhr, *Christ and Culture*, 1st ed. ([San Francisco]: Harper-SanFrancisco, 2001).

175 D. A. Carson, *Christ and Culture Revisited* (William B. Eerdmans Pub. Co., 2008).

176 In *Christ and Culture*, Helmet Richard Niebuhr proposes 5 responses to what he calls, "the enduring problem." These common responses within the church include "Christ against culture," "the Christ of culture," "Christ above culture," "the theology of the dualist," and Christ the transformer of culture."

177 Carson.

completely remove the tensions. Carson went on to say that it was
not his intention to treat the history of these debates, except to
note in passing that we must never fall into the trap of supposing
that we are the first generation of Christians to think about these
things [this is a point well remembered for many contemporary
challenges we face]:

> My focus is on how we should be thinking about the relations be-
> tween Christ and Culture now, at the beginning of the twenty-first
> century. We have the same biblical texts that earlier generations
> of Christians thought their way through, of course, but our reflec-
> tions are shaped by ... [new] factors.[178]

This chapter does not have the luxury of further interactions
with Niebuhr or Carson's diagnosis of the problems we have faced
and face now as citizens of Another Kingdom living in a kingdom of
this world, other than to agree that there remains the classic, dif-
fering answers from within the Church.[179] Some would meet the
tension of the two kingdoms by withdrawing from culture, thus
withdrawing, in our case, from the potential land mines of civic
discourse and faithful witness. There are also those who assert
that prayer is communication with God, and therefore, to be so
pre-meditatively intentional about inserting the name of Jesus in a
prayer before the Lion's Club or a high school football game is to
corrupt the essential nature of prayer—of communication between

---

178 Ibid.
179 For reflections on evangelicals in the public sphere in America in the
present, see M. Cromartie, *A Public Faith: Evangelicals and Civic Engagement* (Rowman & Littlefield, 2003); J. D. Hunter, *Culture Wars: The
Struggle to Define America* (BasicBooks, 1992). A reflection on the topic
from a global and multi religious perspective is found in the volume of
essays, G. Moyser, *Politics and Religion in the Modern World* (Routledge,
1991).

creature and Creator,[180] and, therefore, is to leave the sphere of prayer and to enter the sphere of evangelism. Some believe that entering into this fray in the public square amounts to an unnecessary squabble. Some have decided that praying in Jesus' name is just forcing the issue, and crossing the lines of civility. Let's get to some specific examples and some hopefully helpful responses that will guide us in prayer in the public square.

THE CHARGE OF CONTRIVED PRAYER BY PRAYING IN JESUS' NAME

We begin with the notion that to add "In Jesus' name I pray" is unnecessary, or some might say even contrived, in the Machiavellian sense of that word. The ground of this argument is that the authority of the Name by the Christian need not be understood by anyone other than the one praying.

The objection is supposedly given greater support because nowhere in the Bible is there an example of a prayer concluding with "in Jesus' name I pray." This view has been advanced, for instance, by Mark D. Roberts in his article, "Praying in the Name of Jesus: What Is It? How Should We Do It? Should We Do It When We Pray

---

180 C. S. Lewis in his *Letters to Malcolm: Chiefly on Prayer* writes about the essence of prayer being between creature in the Creator. This question related to the prayers of the reprobate, or an unbeliever, is particularly interesting to us. The issue could merit further study and discussion. One helpful thought for this chapter, at least for the writer of this chapter, came from C. S. Lewis when he wrote,

> Where there is prayer at all we may suppose that there is some effort, however feeble, towards the 2nd condition, the union of wills. What God labors to do or say through the man comes back to God with the distortion which at any rate is not total. See C. S. Lewis, *Letters to Malcolm: Chiefly on Prayer* (Houghton Mifflin Harcourt, 2002).

in Public, Civic Gatherings?"[181] Roberts's argument, representing others,[182] uses many of Scriptures that I would use to advance prayer in Jesus' name. However, Roberts raises the issue of authority *without* admitting the biblical testimony to witness and context in prayer. Roberts writes that he is praying in Jesus' name, in public forums, whether or not he uses a phrase such as "I pray in Jesus' name" when prayer is being made in a broad public square amidst the presence of competing gods. I will develop these ideas from Scripture shortly.

Roberts recalls the passages about praying in Jesus' name and agrees that this is the way he prays. No one else may know that he is praying like this, but he seems to be saying that is not the point. The point is *only* authority and he meets the authority issue because that is what he believes. He could not pray in another way but in the name of Jesus. Of course, again, I agree with him as far as that goes. All Christians would readily agree that the Scriptures teach us that authority is the real issue behind prayer being offered in Jesus' name. John records Jesus' own words about how we should offer prayer through His authority:

> Whatever you ask in my name, this I will do, that the Father may be glorified in the Son. (John 14:13)

> If you ask me anything in my name, I will do it. (John 14:14)

---

181   Mark D. Roberts, "Praying in the Name of Jesus: What Is It? How Should We Do It? Should We Do It When We Pray in Public, Civic Gatherings?," patheos.com (2011). http://www.patheos.com/community/markdroberts/series/praying-in-the-name-of-jesus/ (accessed September 25, 2011); ibid.

182   For a quick survey on this topic, including Mark Robert's opinions and others who agree with him, see the article, Ruth Moon, "In Jesus' Name: Must Christians Pray in Public Forums Using Jesus' Name?," (2010). http://www.christianitytoday.com/ct/2010/september/8.18.html.

You did not choose me, but I chose you and appointed you that you should go and bear fruit and that your fruit should abide, so that whatever you ask the Father in my name, he may give it to you. (John 15:16)

In that day you will ask nothing of me. Truly, truly, I say to you, whatever you ask of the Father in my name, he will give it to you. (John 16:24)

Until now you have asked nothing in my name. Ask, and you will receive, that your joy may be full. (John 16:24)

In that day you will ask in my name, and I do not say to you that I will ask the Father on your behalf. (John 16:26)

The Scriptures are clear enough about praying in Jesus' name as the Mediatorial authority we are given to access the throne of Almighty God. The dissenting point seems to be that authority does not need further testimony. But can it be self-evident to all that this is so? Is Jesus *really* the authority of my public prayer if I fail to mention His name or allude to his Deity in my prayer?

For John Calvin there could be no other meaning in these verses but that prayer should be offered in the name of Jesus Christ:

This is not a useless repetition. All see and feel that they are un-worthy to approach God; and yet the greater part of men burst forward, as if they were out of their senses, and rashly and haugh-tily address God; and afterwards, when that unworthiness, of which I have spoken, comes to their recollection, every man con-trives for himself various expedients. On the other hand, when God invites us to himself, he holds out to us one Mediator only, by whom he is willing to be appeased and reconciled.[183]

---

183 See Calvin's commentary on John 14:14 in John Calvin, *Calvin's Commentaries* (Complete), ed. Calvin Translation Society (Edinburgh: Accordance electronic ed., 9.0, 1847).

Matthew Henry wrote, "Asking in Christ's name is acknowledging our unworthiness to receive any favours from God and shows full dependence upon Christ as the Lord of our Righteousness."[184]

William Willimon, Bishop, North Alabama conference of the United Methodist Church, agrees that one does not have to mention a particular phrase, but we do need to establish that we are praying in the name of Jesus:

> In public praying, I think Christians attempt to be as hospitable as they can, knowing there are people from other faiths there. On the other hand, we pray in Jesus' name, whether we mention Jesus or not. So whether Jesus' name is mentioned, we do have to pray in Jesus' name. That would mean when I pray a public prayer, I want to sound like a Christian, and I'm not offended if somebody comes up and says, "Gee, that was a Christian prayer." I think, "Well, you know I'm a Christian."[185]

Stanley Hauerwas, Professor of Theological Ethics, Duke Divinity School, and former colleague of Bishop Willimon, added, "We pray to God, and the God we pray to is the Father, Son, and Holy Spirit, and we know God as the Father, Son, and Holy Spirit because Jesus is the Son of God. So prayer must be directed to the appropriate subject. That means we pray not to some vague God but to the Father of Jesus Christ. So prayer is appropriately Christocentric, since it's to God."[186]

Praying in Jesus' name does not require that I use a certain phrase that will get the e-mail there faster, as Walter Wangerin, Jr.,

---

184 See his commentary on John 14:14 in Mathew Henry, "Matthew Henry's Commentary" (Condensed) (Altamonte Springs: Accordance electronic ed., OakTree Software, 1996).

185 Moon.

186 Ibid.

responded,[187] but it does mean that we make clear that our prayer is distinctively Christian.[188]

It is good at this point to remember, however, that the name of Jesus is *the* most distinguishing qualifier in our public prayers. Whether one uses this precise phrase or not, the Name of Jesus Christ is central to the issue. Authority is joined to witness. The name of the Covenant God of Abraham, Isaac, and Jacob, whose fullest revelation came through Jesus Christ, is not only the authority we must assume in prayer, but also the confession we must claim in prayer.[189] The Name is not meaningful unless it is admitted in some way (speaking again, of public prayer). If we were to take a more in-depth look at this whole matter—the matter of the name of God could go deep into the Old Testament and New Testament theological understanding—we have to admit that authority and witness in prayer are joined. Either one approaches the Creator on his or her own merits, or on the merits of another. The Old Testament prayer was made for Almighty God based upon the invitation and the merits of God himself. This was so with the shepherd boy,

---

187 Ibid.

188 We will consider this more in the last section on practical suggestions.

189 G. W. Bromiley wrote that "To pray 'in Jesus' name' seems to mean to pray emboldened and inspired by the word that he has spoken (John 15:7), by the grace he has shown, and out of the difficulties and problems of the situation into which his service has led "(cf. Mark 11:22–24). See G. W. Bromiley, *International Standard Bible Encyclopedia*: E-J (Eerdmans Pub Co, 1982).

David, indignant over the Philistinian siege of Israel. The concern of David, which he reminds us of, is that heathen defied—desecrated—the one and only God by defying His covenant people:

> And David said to the men who stood by him, "What shall be done for the man who kills this Philistine and takes away the reproach from Israel? For who is this uncircumcised Philistine, that he should defy the armies of the living God?" (1 Samuel 17:26 ESV)

This was the case on Mount Carmel when Elijah, in 1 Kings 18, differentiates himself and his prayers from the names of the gods of the Baal priests by calling on the One True God:

> "Answer me, O LORD, answer me, that this people may know that you, O LORD, are God, and that you have turned their hearts back." Then the fire of the LORD fell and consumed the burnt offering and the wood and the stones and the dust, and licked up the water that was in the trench. And when all the people saw it, they fell on their faces and said, "The LORD, he is God; the LORD, he is God." (1 Kings 18:37–39 ESV)

Public prayer in the presence of other clergy demanded that the prophet be clear about his faith, His God and the object of his prayers. This continues in the New Testament with the fuller understanding that Jesus Christ is the mediator between God and man[190] and, therefore, the way, the truth, and the life[191] and the only way to pray. Peter and the early disciples preach, admittedly not pray, and declare their faith in the name of Jesus Christ. When they are told to be silent, they appeal to the higher authority of

---

190   "For there is one God, and there is one mediator between God and men, the man Christ Jesus," (1 Timothy 2:5 ESV)

191   "Jesus said to him, 'I am the way, and the truth, and the life. No one comes to the Father except through me.'" (John 14:6 ESV)

God.[192] Their right, if you will, to demonstrate both the authority of Jesus and to witness concerning Jesus does not come from human authority.[193] They must obey God rather than man. Similarly, prayer, as an expression of the Christian faith, should admit that we have

---

192 "And as they were speaking to the people, the priests and the captain of the temple and the Sadducees came upon them, greatly annoyed because they were teaching the people and proclaiming in Jesus the resurrection from the dead. And they arrested them and put them in custody until the next day, for it was already evening. But many of those who had heard the word believed, and the number of the men came to about five thousand.

On the next day their rulers and elders and scribes gathered together in Jerusalem, with Annas the high priest and Caiaphas and John and Alexander, and all who were of the high-priestly family. And when they had set them in the midst, they inquired, 'By what power or by what name did you do this?' Then Peter, filled with the Holy Spirit, said to them, 'Rulers of the people and elders, if we are being examined today concerning a good deed done to a crippled man, by what means this man has been healed, let it be known to all of you and to all the people of Israel that by the name of Jesus Christ of Nazareth, whom you crucified, whom God raised from the dead—by him this man is standing before you well. This Jesus is the stone that was rejected by you, the builders, which has become the cornerstone. And there is salvation in no one else, for there is no other name under heaven given among men by which we must be saved.'

Now when they saw the boldness of Peter and John, and perceived that they were uneducated, common men, they were astonished. And they recognized that they had been with Jesus. But seeing the man who was healed standing beside them, they had nothing to say in opposition. But when they had commanded them to leave the council, they conferred with one another, saying, 'What shall we do with these men? For that a notable sign has been performed through them is evident to all the inhabitants of Jerusalem, and we cannot deny it. But in order that it may spread no further among the people, let us warn them to speak no more to anyone in this name.' So they called them and charged them not to speak or teach at all in the name of Jesus. But Peter and John answered them, 'Whether it is right in the sight of God to listen to you rather than to God, you must judge, Acts 4:20 for we cannot but speak of what we have seen and heard.'" (Acts 4:1–20 ESV)

193 Acts 4:20.

only One Mediator, the Lord Jesus Christ, and also confess that He is Lord before others, lest we be seen as religious window dressing for public forums, praying to an unknown God, or a Civic God, whom we believe does not exist.[194]

No less than the great Princetonian, Doctor Samuel Miller, in his *Thoughts on Public Prayer* reminds us that the church father Origen spoke of the performance of public prayer and urged, "But when we pray, let us not *battologize* [i.e., use vain repetitions], but *theologize.*"[195]

THE MATTER OF
MIXING POLITICS AND RELIGION

Another objection made by some Christians to praying in Jesus' name in the public sphere goes like this:

---

194   Even if one is a heathen and discovers his or her own condition and cries out "Oh God save me," that prayer is actually made in the name of another. That prayer of desperation calms at the end of one's own self and perhaps there is not greater example of praying in the Mediatorship of God Himself than to cry out to Him, even if His name, the name of the Savior, is not fully known, as it was in the Old Testament. So to say that since there are no examples of the phrase "in Jesus' name I pray" and therefore we are simply being invasive in the public square by mentioning that name or demanding that we must pray in that name is unfounded. Ole Hallesby wrote "to pray is nothing more involved than to open the door, giving Jesus access to our needs and permitting him to exercise his power in dealing with them." See Ole Hallesby, *Prayer* (Minneapolis: Augsburg, 1994). Is there any more genuinely beautiful prayer that attributes the authority and witness of the Name than the Psalmist's cry, "Oh, magnify the LORD with me, and let us exalt his name together! I sought the LORD, and he answered me and delivered me from all my fears. Those who look to him are radiant, and their faces shall never be ashamed. This poor man cried, and the LORD heard him and saved him out of all his troubles." (Psalms 34:3–6 ESV)

195   S. Miller and Presbyterian Church in the U.S.A. Board of Publication, *Thoughts on Public Prayer* (Presbyterian Board of Publication, 1849).

In the controversies over legislative prayer, Christians should be especially mindful to pray in a way that does not tend to associate the government with a particular religious perspective. Current controversies over legislative prayer come out of using a government forum to push a particular type of prayer. That pushes the boundaries of constitutional law and threatens to send the message that the government is a proper forum for pursuing particular matters of faith.[196]

One does not have to be a theologian to respond that bringing faith into the political realm is not exactly radical when considering the history of the United States, not to even mention the nations of the world. Is the First Amendment really threatened by praying in Jesus' name?

Recently I was reading in the two-volume series, *Political Sermons of the American Founding Era,* 1730–1805, edited by Ellis Sandoz.[197] There is simply no doubt after reading the 1,733 pages of sermons and discourses from the Puritan Pulpit that the early public squares of America were gilded with the name of Jesus. Now one may say that the pulpit is not the public square and that no one is disputing the matter of preaching in the sovereign sphere of the Church, but the fact remains that the pulpit and meeting house were the equipping station for citizens to be sent into the public square. The force of this collection of American Puritan sermons is that Christians were being admonished to take their faith into the public square—indeed, to build the public square with the name of Jesus Christ. Detractors of the idea of such an American founding faith point to the uses of the word "providence," "Creator," and

---

196 Hollyn Hollman, general counsel, Baptist Joint Committee for Religious Liberty, quoted in Moon.

197 E. Sandoz, *Political Sermons of the American Founding Era, 1730–1805* (Liberty Fund, 1998).

other non-specific designations of the Deity (and even make a case that this is how we might pray today in our pluralistic age). But one could equally point to the use of the name of Jesus Christ by George Washington,[198] and an impressive post of other founders who used the name of Christ in official United States Government papers.[199] Dr. David L. Holmes, the Walter G. Mason Professor of Religious Studies at the College of William and Mary, in a book advertised to demythologize the Fundamentalist notion of a Christian nation, acknowledges that founders like Samuel Adams made clear, cogent claims of saving faith (as evangelicals would understand it) in Jesus Christ while also using Deistic names for God. Deistic names of God were used because they were a popular expression of the Deity, but their usage did not deny true faith in Christ or restrict the use of Jesus' name in public discourse by those same individuals.[200] Holmes wrote,

Until age prevented it, Samuel Adams walked to church on Sunday with his family, a sight that neighbors were accustomed to seeing. As early as 1765, John Adams wrote that his cousin possessed "real as well as professed piety." His religious language is also strikingly Orthodox. Like other Orthodox Christians of the time, he was able to describe God in terms shared with Deism. But most of his religious phrasing, even in state documents, is unabashedly Christian. He uses such terms as "the common Master,"

---

198 See, for example, G. Washington and W. H. Burk, *Washington's Prayers* (Published for the benefit of the Washington memorial chapel, 1907).

199 D. L. Holmes, *The Faiths of the Founding Fathers* (Oxford University Press, 2006). See also T. Pitkin, *A Political and Civil History of the United States of America: From the Year 1763 to the Close of the Administration of President Washington, in March, 1797: Including a Summary View of the Political and Civil State of the North American Colonies, Prior to That Period* (H. Howe and Durrie & Peck, 1828).

200 Holmes.

"our Divine Redeemer," "Him... who has given us his Son to purchase for us the reward of eternal," and "all those who love the
Lord Jesus Christ in sincerity." Even at the height of Deism, when
governor of Massachusetts, Adams issued a Thanksgiving proclamation "that holy and happy period, when the kingdom of our Lord
and Savior Jesus Christ may be everywhere established, and all...
willingly bow to the scepter of Him who is the Prince of Peace."[201]

My point is not to press that our founders were all standard-
bearers of evangelical faith, but as Steven Waldman has demonstrated, they were unanimous about religious freedom and the
right to express that freedom in the marketplace.[202] There simply is
no record in the founding of our nation of any hesitance of bringing the specific name of Jesus Christ to the public square. The reason? John Van Til of Grove City College in his *Liberty of Conscience:
The History of a Puritan Idea* shows how deeply engrained liberty
of conscience is in the American republic:

> While liberty and sovereignty of conscience failed in old England,
> it 1st in America from the earliest days the colonial. In addition to
> persistent individual defenses of liberty of conscience, as in the
> case of Roger Williams, liberty of conscience was provided for in
> most of the 17th century charters, Massachusetts Bay colony
> being the outstanding exception. By the end of the 17th century it
> became clear that liberty of conscience in its parallel idea of
> sphere sovereignty were emerging as important elements in the
> formation of an American political ideology. During the years after
> 1689, when John Locke published an important defense of liberty
> and sovereignty, colonial Americans increasingly drew upon his
> writings, and those of other defenders of the idea, such as the
> Westminster Divines, to defend the claim of individual liberty.

---

201 Ibid.
202 S. Waldman, *Founding Faith: Providence, Politics, and the Birth of Reli-
     gious Freedom in America* (Random House, 2008).

Liberty of conscience also was used in this period to argue for the separation of institutional spheres of jurisdiction... Liberty of conscience had its roots deep in the past, in the works of the Puritan, William Perkins. It's history to the era of the American Revolution, and beyond, is the history of a Puritan idea.[203]

Others have appealed to the living principles of Western Democracy to defend the right of one to pray according to conscience and, therefore, to pray in Jesus' name. Indeed, to express one's faith, even argue for the its logical and spiritual superiority over others, much less to simply pray according to one's own faith, forms the very bedrock of a self-governing society. Democratic civility demanded, then and now, that religious conviction be able to overlap with religious doubt or skepticism. Culture was stronger because of the expression of religion, not weaker. This is the point of Stephen Carter in his *Culture of Disbelief*.[204]

THE ISSUE OF
WITNESS IN PUBLIC PRAYER

The objection that to pray in Jesus' name, that is, to use the phrase "in Jesus' name I pray," is to engage in uninvited evangelism seems to me to be one of the most common objections. A surprising statement from a paper on public prayer published by the National

---

203 Til.

204 Carter. See also S. L. Carter, *God's Name in Vain* (Basic Books, 2001).

Association of Evangelicals on civic prayers[205] supported this
position (and an excellent rebuttal from Russell Moore of
Southern Baptist Theological Seminary was given in *Touchstone*

---

205 The 23-page Statement on Religious Freedom for Soldiers and Military
     Chaplains, which seems intended to uphold the constitutionality of
     chaplains praying in public at all, reviews the relevant law and the his-
     tory of ceremonial prayer in the United States, starting with George
     Washington. It concludes with recommendations for specific issues, in-
     cluding not only the work of chaplains but also soldiers' religious rights
     and the duties of commanders. An appendix offers some examples (pre-
     sumably NAE-approved) of ceremonial prayer. With most of the state-
     ment, no traditional Christian will have a problem. The problem comes
     with its solution to the most contentious question. "A military chaplain
     may preside, preach, or pray in sectarian language with a likeminded
     congregation that has voluntarily assembled," it states at the end of its
     section on general principles, but "the same chaplain ought to use the
     more inclusive language of civic faith when praying at memorials or
     convocations with religiously diverse audiences."
         The reason the NAE gives for this is that the purpose of the prayers
     offered at these events is neither to favor one religion over another nor
     to proselytize. It is to dignify and mark a public occasion by reflecting
     upon the deeper significance of that which has or is about to transpire.
     It is to honor the most basic human impulses of giving thanks and of in-
     voking God's protection, guidance, and blessing, and it is to reflect upon
     those religious values that unite the American people. Praying "in the
     name of Jesus" would both "exclude believers from other faith tradiz-
     tions" and "violate the Establishment Clause," the NAE argues. "[C]om-
     mon courtesy, pastoral judgment, and constitutional principle commend
     offering a religious message or prayer respectful of all present." Read
     more: http://www.touchstonemag.com/archives/article.php?id=19-06-
     003-e#ixzz1Z5plj2rI

Magazine).[206] The objection is easily addressed; we consider the following:

> We all understand, as believers, that there are different contexts for prayer. There is the prayer closet, that is, devotional prayer, or private prayer. How we pray to God in private is markedly unlike the way we pray to God in public. Authority is still a necessary component in the devotional prayer, obviously. However, our hearts soar, and often our language is freely, and most personally, expressed before the Lord in such prayer. Our understanding that we are approaching the throne of grace through the name of Jesus Christ is understood as we come to God. While I still might want to conclude my prayer within Jesus' name I pray, there is no necessity for a verbal acknowledgment in this scenario, for it is a heart acknowledgment. Witness is tethered to authority, but the witness is of one's own spirit in the secret prayer. And God knows my heart as I pray. There is no other name which I can approach God except in the name of Jesus. Whether or not I say that is inconsequential.[207] So private prayer, while demanding the same authority of the Mediator, namely, our Lord and Savior Jesus Christ,

This is fine for private pr.

---

206 "For many Christians, including especially most Evangelical Protestants, a prayer not offered through Jesus is not a prayer. These Christians are "Christian" precisely because they believe with the Apostle Paul that "there is one God and one mediator between God and men, the man Christ Jesus" (1 Tim. 2:5). They can appeal to God as Father only because they share the Spirit of Christ, through whom they cry "Abba" (Rom. 8:15). When Christians maintain this belief, they are not being bigoted against others, or even trying to proselytize. They are simply asserting what Christians throughout the ages have always defined as the way to pray to God. Christians have never, until recently, distinguished a way of public prayer from a way of private prayer." Read more: http://www.touchstonemag.com/archives/article.php?id=19-06-003-e#ixzz1Z5oNuxMN

207 The arguments that Mark Roberts makes are perfectly valid for private prayer.

the necessity of speaking that name, or qualifying and acknowledging that mediatorship, is not necessary. There is also prayer in small groups. And as I begin to think about the broadening of the audience for prayer (for we must remember the prayer is made in the context of others as well as privately), and I think about prayer in small groups, I begin to understand that the name of Jesus Christ as the authority for the approach to the throne of God in prayer is now needed. If I'm in the company of other believers, there is unity in our faith and an understanding that prayer can only be made to Almighty God in the name of Jesus Christ, the requirements for effective prayer may be made without mentioning a phrase such as "In Jesus' name I pray." The same could be said for the pulpit prayer or for pastoral prayer in a public worship service.[208] However, I would add a caveat: there are often "God fearers"[209] who are present in the morning and evening worship services of our churches who do not understand the concept of authority and the need to pray in the name of Jesus according to the New Testament. Therefore, as a pastor, I seek to pray in the name of Jesus Christ. Thomas Cranmer (2 July 1489–21 March 1556) modeled this so well as did the other contributors to the *Book of Common Prayer* by grounding all of public prayer Collects in the

---

208 For a study of pastoral prayers, see Hughes Oliphant Old, *Leading in Prayer: A Workbook for Ministers* (Grand Rapids, Mich.: W. B. Eerdmans, 1995).

209 "The term 'God-fearers' in Acts has traditionally been described as a technical term to designate Gentiles who attended the synagogue and were attracted by Jewish monotheism. They were not converts, however, because they did not submit to circumcision. Thus when Paul visited Jewish synagogues he found three groups of people: Jews, proselytes, and God-fearers. Paul was especially successful among God-fearers because the latter were reluctant to undergo the painful operation of circumcision, and they enthusiastically embraced Christianity because Paul contended that the rite was unnecessary." See G. W. Bromiley, *The International Standard Bible Encyclopedia* (William B. Eerdmans Publishing Company, 2007).

name of Jesus.[210] Even though prayers were going to be made in a
Christian worship service, the framers of the *Book of Common
Prayer* could not imagine making a prayer without using the name
of Jesus Christ in the prayer.[211] So it is interesting that as an audience is broadened, in that case, the classical Christian framers of
the public prayer felt the necessity to mention the name of Jesus
all the more. It is only when there is an absolute certainty that there
is unity of the faith that one would omit the name of Jesus in prayer.
Therefore, when one enters into the broader public square of different religions, and diverse expressions and understandings of
the Christian faith, one might all the more seek to pray in the name
of Jesus. It can no longer be presumed in our pluralistic society
that hearers understand the Mediator for prayer. Within this context, one might also consider that there is an element of prayer
that goes beyond speaking from creature to Creator; there is the
matter of witness in prayer to others who hear the prayer. It is
here, again, that so many objections are leveled. The objection
that prayer becomes an evangelistic exercise or the objection that
prayer becomes preaching or the objection that prayer becomes a
form of coercive opportunism in the presence of others. It may be
that a Christian unwisely forms a prayer in such a broad public
context, but it does not follow that we should omit the name of Jesus
Christ because of these objections. Injections are easily overruled
when we begin to see from the Scriptures that their prayers were
made with the intent of not only communicating with Almighty
God in the name of Jesus, but also advancing the mediatorship,
uniqueness and deity of Jesus Christ in front of others. I would
point, for example, to the very prayer and work of Jesus Christ in

---

210　See Church of England and J. H. Blunt, *The Annotated Book of Common
　　Prayer: Being an Historical, Ritual, and Theological Commentary on the
　　Devotional System of the Church of England* (Rivingtons, 1866); Church
　　of England and others, *The Collects of Thomas Cranmer* (W.B. Eerdmans
　　Pub., 1999).

211　Ibid.

John 11. In the story of Jesus raising Lazarus from the dead we see an example of witness and public prayer. There we read,

> Then Jesus, deeply moved again, came to the tomb. It was a cave, and a stone lay against it. Jesus said, "Take away the stone." Martha, the sister of the dead man, said to him, "Lord, by this time there will be an odor, for he has been dead four days." Jesus said to her, "Did I not tell you that if you believed you would see the glory of God?" So they took away the stone. And Jesus lifted up his eyes and said, "Father, I thank you that you have heard me. I knew that you always hear me, but I said this on account of the people standing around, that they may believe that you sent me." (John 11:38–42 ESV)

We hear the Lord's phrase, "I thank you that you have heard me. I know that you always hear me, but I said this on account of the people standing around, that they may believe that you sent me." Jesus Christ prayed in a very broad context. All there at Bethany were not believers in him as the mediator of the new covenant. He indicates, unequivocally, that he was praying the way he did in order to be a witness before them. This is a prime example—and if we had no other examples except this example it would be enough. Prayer does indeed possess an important element of witness to Jesus Christ in public prayers. Yet we could also point to the Old Testament. We can point to the case of David who was indignant that the Philistine army and Goliath should defy the people of God and defined the very name of God. David's diverse religious context had no problem whatsoever in announcing his intentions to do battle in the name of the Lord. Likewise, Elijah on Mount Carmel, before the pluralistic clergy of his day, made public prayer in the name of his God. Therefore, I reiterate my proposition that prayer in the pluralistic public square *should be* made in the name of Jesus Christ. The objections cannot overwhelm the demonstration of Jesus himself praying this way.

SOME PRACTICAL MODELS FOR PRAYING IN JESUS' NAME IN THE PUBLIC ARENA

It may be wise to seek to advance prayer in Jesus' name through an appeal to the pluralistic ethic itself (which is hypocritical when it does not allow for Christians to exercise public faith in prayer while it may allow others). In other words, I don't think it is enough, or as effective, to tell a group of unbelievers that we must pray in the name of Jesus Christ because "that is our faith." Rather, I believe the case has to be made using their own sense of fairness. To think more about this, I would turn to the philosophical–theological reflections of Nicholas Wolterstorff.[212]

Nicolas Wolterstorff writes that our religious actions in the public arena should be conducted

> as reasonable and rational, and knowing that they affirm a diver-
> sity of reasonable religious and philosophical doctrines, they
> should be ready to explain the basis of their actions to one an-
> other in terms each could reasonably expect that others might en-
> dorse as consistent with their freedom and equality.[213]

Another principle on being a faithful witness to one's own convictions—while collating that conviction with the other "overlapping" convictions in a fair, liberal democracy—is summed up in
Wolterstorff's Chapter 11 in *Practices of Belief, Volume Two: Selected Essays*, entitled, "On Being Entitled to Beliefs about God."
Wolterstorff rightly states that to have a religion is more than holding to abstract belief, but actually bringing faith propositions to the
life through "obedience, worship, prayer, self-discipline, meditation

---

212 See his biography at http://www.yale.edu/philos/people/wolterstorff_
nicholas.html.

213 Robert Audi, Nicholas Wolterstorff, *Religion in The Public Square: The
Place of Religious Convictions in Political Debate* (96).

and acts of justice and charity."[214] In a fair society, one may make
claims and follow those claims within the social order, yet concede
that others may hold an opposite view. Again, this is "cooperation
without compromise." For our purposes, and with this presenter's
convictions, a believer should be able to pray in the name of Jesus
in the public arena, and there must be ways to allow for the ability
to defend one's faith in that arena recognizing that others may not
(will not) agree.

Stephen Carter has written much about the decline of civility
in public discourse. If Carter is correct, and I believe that he is, then
even in the appeal to liberal democratic ideals being applied to the
matter of religion in public discourse and the "rights" of a Christian
to pray in the name of Jesus Christ will be met with disdain. In fact,
the Bible reveals that there is a diabolical agenda at work in the
world, and I'm thinking of the use of the term "this present evil
age" by the apostle Paul in Galatians, to remove the name of Jesus
Christ, the authority of Jesus Christ, and the influence of Jesus
Christ in this society. I would say even in this chapter that we must
be aware that there are powers at work within people unwitting as
they may be to create hostility toward the name of Jesus and toward
those who would use the name Jesus. Therefore, after all appeals
have been made for Democratic ideals to be applied, suitability to
be practiced, and a "cooperation without compromise" approach
to religious plurality, the end result may still be the same. In this
case the Christian is faced with the same scenario Peter faced when
he was told not to preach; we all remember that Peter asked
whether we, believers, should obey God or man. The Christian in
the broad public square must not allow the broad public square to

---

214 Wolterstorff, *Practices of Belief*, Volume Two, page 313.

remain naked, to borrow the phrase, but to clothe it with the authority of the name of Jesus in our prayers.

It is possible to do this without an intention of creating a stir, as it were. It is possible to do this with prudence. In fact, the whole matter of praying in the name of Jesus Christ in public requires a great deal of private prayer before addressing public prayer. It is interesting that the controversy of prayer itself in public is likely leading Christians to a deeper sense of prayer. In fact, the hostility of this present evil age, so steeped in the ideology of pluralism, may become the very instrument that God uses to bring the church to its knees in our generation.

I mentioned civic associations as being laboratories for praying in Jesus' name in public prayer, but nowhere is the issue more pointed than in the United States military. I've written earlier articles and a book on the matter of praying in the name of Jesus in public. Again, I want to say that even following this bit of wisdom one is not guaranteed insulation against the hostility of an unbelieving world. However, I have appealed to the First Amendment of the Constitution, and to the very ideals of pluralism, which would allow me, as a Christian chaplain, to pray in a way that is consistent with my faith, even as I would be expected, and would desire, to encourage someone of another religion to pray publicly according to his or her own beliefs. Therefore, whenever I pray, I pray like this:

> ...And thus, oh God, recognizing that there are many here of varying faiths and understandings about the relationship of man and God, I ask that your blessing would come down upon us, even as I make my prayer in the name of my Lord and Savior Jesus Christ, the only authority I recognize for coming to you this day. When you hear our prayer according to his name. Amen.

I'm certain that many of you are already employing this technique. Because I feel that it is important to pray in the name of Jesus Christ in public because of authority, because of witness and because of context. I'm also aware of stability and fairness and understanding of the overlapping of ideals and liberal democratic society. So I make my prayer in Jesus' name rather than saying or assuming that "we pray in the name of Jesus."

I have stated that it may be wiser to appeal to the very ethic that the pluralist proposes. I did not mean to be speaking in only a fleshly way but to be innocent as a dove and as wise as a serpent.[215] But in the end, the only sure path is faithfulness to bear witness to Christ's authority in our lives and in our prayers. This may meet with ruin in the world but will meet with favor in heaven.

SUMMARY

We have sought to present the problem of praying in Jesus' name in twentieth-century American experience, posited a thesis that we should seek to pray in the authority of Jesus Christ and with witness to His Deity. We have differentiated between classifications of prayer. We have sought to do this with a respectful presentation of objections to this thesis from other Christians. Our biblical mandates remain, however, and I would hold to my thesis based on Scripture. We pray in Jesus' name in public because of authority, witness and context. We ground our thesis in the Word of God, particularly, in the public prayer of Jesus in John 11 and in the ministry of the disciples in Acts 4. We also appeal to classical, Western democratic values of fairness and civility.

---

215 "Behold, I am sending you out as sheep in the midst of wolves, so be
     wise as serpents and innocent as doves." (Matthew 10:16 ESV)

In Stephen Carter's *God's Name in Vain*, the problem of faith in the public space—in this case—the broader issue of the state—is summarized with a simple and powerful last thought:

> The trouble is that the state and the religions are in competition to explain to their people the meaning of the world. And the meanings provided by the one differ from the meanings provided by the other, it is natural that the one the losing would do what it can to become a winner. In today's mass–produced world, characterized by the intrusion into every household of the materialistic interpretation of reality, religions often are just overwhelmed, which leads some of them to change and many of them to die. But more subtle tools are available in the assault on religious meaning. Indeed, all through history, the state has tried to domesticate religion, sometimes by force, simply eliminating dissenting faiths; sometimes through the device of creating an official, established church; sometimes—as in the twentieth-century American experience—through the device of reducing the power of religion by combining its freedom within a state-granted, state-defined, and state-controlled structure of constitutional rights.

Religion, however, is no idle bystander.[216]

That final observation is powerful because it was a key component in the demise of the Soviet Union and Eastern Block nations held in captivity. It is the ever present witness of Christ, with humility and genuine concern for the world that opposes it, that ultimately has demonstrated that it cannot be quieted; and is seen in

---

216 Carter, *God's Name in Vain*.

the ingenious way that Christians continue to bring Christ to the public square even in days like these.[217]

The following is a statement that was read over the PA system at the football game at Roane County High School, Kingston, Tennessee, by school Principal Jody McCloud, on September 1, 2000.[218]

I thought it was worth sharing with the world, and hope you will forward it to all your friends. It clearly shows just how far this country has gone in the wrong direction.

> It has always been the custom at Roane County High School football games to say a prayer and play the National Anthem to honor God and Country. Due to a recent ruling by the Supreme Court, I am told that saying a prayer is a violation of Federal Case Law.
>
> As I understand the law at this time, I can use this public facility to approve of sexual perversion and call it an alternate lifestyle, and if someone is offended, that's OK.
>
> I can use it to condone sexual promiscuity by dispensing condoms and calling it safe sex. If someone is offended, that's OK.
>
> I can even use this public facility to present the merits of killing an unborn baby as a viable means of birth control.
>
> If someone is offended, no problem.
>
> I can designate a school day as earth day and involve students in activities to religiously worship and praise the goddess, mother earth, and call it ecology.

---

217 For example, see also "Crowd Says Prayer at Bell County Football Game," Associated Press article in Kentucky.com, October 3, 2011. In this report, "A few weeks after Bell County Schools stopped its practice of having public prayer before high school football games, the crowd who came recited the Lord's Prayer." Read more: http://www.kentucky.com/2011/10/ 03/1906304/crowd-says-prayer-at-bell-county.html#ixzz1ZkIJJCaS

218 Michael Walker, "Christophobia: An Irrational Animosity Towards Christians" (http://www.associatedcontent.com/article/5890986/christophobia_an_irrational_animosity_pg3.html?cat=34), accessed September 22, 11.

I can use literature, videos and presentations in the classroom that depict people with strong, traditional, Christian convictions as simple minded and ignorant and call it enlightenment.

However, if anyone uses this facility to honor God and ask
Him to bless this event with safety and good sportsmanship, Federal Case Law is violated.

This appears to be at best, inconsistent and at worst, diabolical. Apparently, we are to be tolerant of everything and anyone
except God and His Commandments.

Nevertheless, as a school principal, I frequently ask staff and
students to abide by rules which they do not necessarily agree.
For me to do otherwise would be at best, inconsistent and at
worst, hypocritical. I suffer from that affliction enough uninten-
tionally. I certainly do not need to add an intentional transgression.

For this reason, I shall "Render unto Caesar that which is Caesar's," and refrain from praying at this time.

However, if you feel inspired to honor, praise and thank God,
and ask Him in the name of Jesus to bless this event, please feel
free to do so. As far as I know, that's not against the law—yet.[219]

The principal's complaint and ultimate concern to bring faith
into the public square, even if he had to do it through the back door,
was simply affirming the critical importance of not just having
ideas about faith but expressing those ideas. He would no doubt
agree with Professor Stephen Carter's assessment:

Only religion possesses the majesty, the power, and the sacred
language to teach all of us, the religious and the secular, the genuine appreciation for each other on which a successful civility must
rest. Without religion, civility, like any other moral principle, has
no firm rock on which to stand. Civility that rests on the shifting

---

219   This story is validated at http://www.truthorfiction.com/rumors/j/
jodymccloud.htm.

sands of secular morality might topple with the next stiff political wind.[220]

I maintain, from the Bible, from Western Civilization, the American founding and even contemporary legislation,[221] as well as from the practice of civility and tolerance inherited from both the Bible and Western democracy, that public prayer in the name of Jesus is a cornerstone for all true tolerance and civility, and from that free exercise of faith in prayer flows the right for others to pray, worship, and share their faith as well. Any claim of tolerance and true plurality that denies this practice is itself, intolerant, *Christophobic*, unfair, hypocritical, and self-defeating. Yet we remain hopeful as we seek to stand next to the jagged contour of public discourse in this age, because the truth of Christ is greater than deceits of the flesh, the devil, and the world; and untarnished freedom is better than prejudicial boundaries imposed on public prayer. We are encouraged by the words of Václav Havel: "My experience and observations confirm that politics in the practice of morality is possible."[222]

Yet we are even more emboldened by the words of our Savior, "I know your works. Behold, I have set before you an open door,

---

220 S. L. Carter, *Civility: Manners, Morals, and the Etiquette of Democracy* (Basic Books, 1998).

221 For example, see the Religious Freedom Restoration Act of 1993. The Religious Freedom Restoration Acts ("RFRA") of 1994 was a dramatic piece of legislation passed by Congress and signed by President Bill Clinton that sought protect religious express in American life. Professor William P. Marshall of the University of North Carolina wrote that "the only other legislation that even compare are with the protections provided to religion by RFRA are the provisions of the Civil Rights Act of 1964..." See William P. Marshall, "The Culture of Belief and the Politics of Religion," *Law and Contemporary Problems* 63(2000). http://heinonline.org/HOL/LandingPage?collection=journals&handle=hein.journals/lcp63&div=23&id=&page= (accessed October 2, 2011).

222 Havel and Wilson.

which no one is able to shut. I know that you have but little power, and yet you have kept my word and have not denied my name." (Revelation 3:8 ESV)

SECTION THREE

SPEAKING OUT
THROUGH COMMENTARIES

1

CIVILIZATION COMING UNGLUED?

The Most Important Question Facing Us in 2012 Is More than an Election

The most important fact of the coming year is not "who will be the next occupant of the White House?" The single most important matter before us all is a question of value. It is a question that may be stated, "Will the Western world embrace the very thing that holds it together. Or will it continue the denial of the obvious and seal its inevitable decline?" Let me explain.

In historiography—the study of history—professional historians are often torn between what is called "lower history" and "higher history." Higher history aims to chronicle the past through grand events such as kings and queens and wars and treaties. Lower history, on the other hand, traces the record of mankind through often unseen events, underlying popular philosophies, and frequently, obvious facts. Thinking about lower history, British historian, Dr. Niall Ferguson, has drawn our attention to a lower historical fact that he proposes in his latest and most exceptional (if not unsettling) work, *Civilization: The West and the Rest* (Penguin Press, 2011). Ignoring political-correctness in favor of the obvious, Ferguson appeals to his readers to see that the remarkable civilization called the West is just so because of what he refers to as "six killer apps" (using a computer metaphor). These apps are fundamental common commitments—a worldview, if you will—which has brought about the greatest advances in human history and the greatest opportunities for men to live free, happy lives. These "killer apps," according to Niall Ferguson, are "competition, science, property rights, medicine, the consumer society, and the work ethic" (p. 13)—specifically, the Protestant work ethic that came as a result of the reformation in the 16th century. Ferguson describes this sixth application of Western civilization as "the glue of the dynamic" (p. 13) that allows the other features to work. Yet Ferguson also observes that, "the Protestant ethic of thrift that once seemed so central to the Western project has all but vanished" (p. 17). I believe that Ferguson is absolutely spot on. He is spot on because Jesus Christ declared, "You shall know the truth and the truth shall set you free." We don't have to look any further than here, in John, chapter eight, to uncover the roots of the present Euro–Anglo–American debt quandary.

Before the Protestant Reformation and the counterreformation that influenced the Roman Catholic Church, freedom and that which we call Western Civilization was hardly free. The truths that Luther recovered and that Calvin taught were galvanized in the popular conscience of their time and afterwards gave rise to the other five "apps" that Ferguson cites and "activated" them. The "activation code" that unlocked Western Civilization was nothing less than the Gospel of Jesus Christ. That blessed One who said that He was "the way, the truth, and the life" opened up a new world of opportunity for mankind. This was the operating system, according to Ferguson, that nations embraced and thereby became "Western civilization" as we know it. The question is now, "Will the Western world disavow the very worldview—the glue, the Protestant work ethic, the Reformation truth–that activated the "software" that generated Western civilization, and that brought so much life, liberty, and happiness? Or will we foolishly ignore it in the name of a secular substitute that is powerless to re-boot the system?" No one will deny that (still using the computer metaphor) there is a giant "Error Message" on the screen of Western civilization. Something has malfunctioned and every other application is either no longer operational or running too sluggish to be productive. Ferguson helps us to see what is going on is not the absence of a "higher historical" figure to fix us, but a "lower historical" faith to free us: the faith of the Bible and of the Redeemer it presents: Jesus Christ. Ferguson ends his excellent treatise by declaring, "Today...the biggest threat to Western civilization is posed not by other civilizations, but by our own pusillanimity—and by the historical ignorance that feeds it" (p. 325).

The greatest challenge before us in 2012 is not merely to elect an individual in America who will become president and expose this ignorance and lead us back to the truth, but to recover what Churchill called for, "a large majority of mankind united together to defend" the truth that got us where we are today. We have every hope that since it has been done before, it can be done again. Let's pray so. Our civilization depends upon it.

GRACE IN THE TRENCHES

Chaplains on the Front Lines of
the Repeal of Don't Ask, Don't Tell

The senior chaplain came to me for counseling, struggling with how he would face the repeal of *Don't Ask, Don't Tell* (DADT). I put my hand on his shoulder and looked him square in the eyes, "Chaplain, this nation needs you to stand strong for your convictions *now more than ever.* It is not time to retreat, but to minister as the pastor to our military that God has called you to be."

While budget battles rage in D.C., radiation leaks in Japan, and the Middle East rumbles with uncertainty, the U.S. military has quietly but dutifully began following orders to train for the probable repeal of DADT, the policy which disallows military service to avowed homosexuals.

The repeal of DADT (which cannot be initiated until 60 days after the President, Defense Secretary, and Chairman of the Joint Chiefs certify that lifting the ban won't hurt the military's ability to fight) remains a decisive story. But the 24-hour news cycle on this one is up. Our soldiers, sailors, airmen, Marines and guardsmen are on their own. Yet this story is not over. At the center of the story are now chaplains.

Chaplains are the unheralded heroes of the military. They are, to use Army language, "force multipliers." Providing religious services is only one important task they do. Chaplains are there to counsel all military members, guide the commander about world religions, and ensure that all have the opportunity to follow their religion, even when it is different from their own.

Asking chaplains to minister biblical truth to what the Bible condemns is nothing new. Asking chaplains to keep quiet about what the Bible condemns is. *So far* no agency is trying to stop chaplains from preaching the doctrines their denominations ordained them to teach or obstructing them from counseling homosexuals (or adulterous heterosexuals, for that matter) according to their confessions. Yet will there be pressure applied tomorrow by militant homosexual activists to change that?

If challenged, evangelical chaplains I know will not capitulate. They will preach the truth in love. They will minister to homosexuals in the same way they minister to all, in the love and grace of Jesus Christ whose commands are life. However, they will call sin a sin and offer forgiveness and salvation. Let's pray that the chaplains' freedoms continue, for our freedoms rest on the moral foundations they seek to build.

Let's pray they stand strong. For if ever we needed our chaplains, it is now.

3

ANARCHY IN
SEARCH OF MEANING

G od hates rebellion.
    "For rebellion is as the sin of witchcraft, and stubbornness
is as iniquity and idolatry" (1 Samuel 15:23a) [*see also* Numbers
20:12–14; Isaiah 30:1; Isaiah 63:10; Psalm 68:6; Psalm 107:10–11;
Nehemiah 9:26. Rebellion is described throughout the Bible as a
certain path to judgment and destruction, unless there is repentance and an embracing of godly order].

Christianity has changed government and culture in many ways.
One way has been to inject the very concept of order. Order is a
communicable attribute of the Triune God. There is order in His
creation of the world and, through redemption in Jesus Christ,
order in our lives may be recovered—cosmically and personally
(though the fallen world, still suffering from that disorder, awaits
the consummation of the Kingdom of Christ, when all Edenic order
will be restored).

> For God is not a God of disorder but of peace.... (1 Corinthians
> 14:33 NIV)

Just go to a country where the residual faith of Judeo–Christianity is culturally, historically absent. You can almost say that it is
a universal, "If there is no Christian influence in the culture, you
don't want to drive there!" Chaos in traffic, a simple but real example
of "ideas have consequences," is just one consistent indicator of a

void of a Christian world and life view. The way a people treat women and children is another more profound and infinitely more important feature of such cultures.

So back to the point. God hates rebellion. He calls for order. He would tell Peter, who cut of Malchus's ear (a Roman soldier who kept his head but lost his ear to the impulsive Peter), that "those who live by the sword die by the sword." Yet many look upon the "Occupy Movement" in America as being a positive, nonviolent movement that is seeking justice for all people. But that is not the story that is unfolding before us. It is, to quote my son, "simply anarchy." Leftover-Abbie-Hoffman-wannabe" rebels called occupiers have found a "movement" to vent their inner angst. It reminds me of disproven but once radically fashionable Students for a Democratic Society who, in the 1960s, stormed administrative buildings of campuses, shutting down education in the name of democracy. It sounded more like lawlessness and mobocracy then and it does now. I hear the passage in my mind as I see the images of chaos and disorder in our streets:

> "In those days there was no king in Israel. Everyone did what was right in his own eyes." (Judges 21:25 ESV)

But there is hope.

This morning my son and I got up at "zero-dark-thirty" to vote. The polls opened at 0630 here in North Carolina. We wanted to be first up. My son just turned eighteen, and this was his first time to vote. He was excited to do so, and I was excited to watch him sign in and cast his vote after carefully examining the candidates and their stance on issues (with Safari and his iPhone). That is order, albeit order with technology! Order is the way to effect change. Yet even that process is a by-product of a biblical past which continues to leave a positive influence in this increasingly secularist culture.

We should all pray that we "occupy" ourselves more with the Bible, with the truth of Jesus Christ which sets men free, and that less time be occupied with scenes of anarchists who have no idea why or what they are protesting.

Let them get up at 5:00 A.M. and go vote.

4

ANNE RICE, AMERICAN CHRISTIANITY, WEEDS IN MY GARDEN, AND BARBARA BUSH

My wife and I enjoyed an early morning cup of steaming hot and freshly ground Pike Place coffee together on this late summer day. And then it happened. I walked through my garden and discovered, in spite of a valiant effort by my wife in recent days to control the infestation in our yard of every breed of weed, yet more weeds! I hate them! My visceral response to weeds can sometimes go embarrassingly public, like when the True Green fertilizer man comes around and leaves me a piece of paper that says, "Yard looks good, but you should take care of some of those weeds."

"What?" I cry to my wife who vicariously bears the brunt of my indignation. "I thought that was supposed to be what he took care of! I hate weeds!" She nods as I, Hank-like (as in Hank on King of the Hill) rage against the mere indecencies of suburban life. Well, what I hate mostly about weeds is not just that they grow randomly, but that they grow, the devils, right next to good, healthy plants.

I had planted a nice row of azaleas, the Southern beauties, six white ones, on the side of our drive way, under two dogwoods and two magnolias. As I surveyed my front lawn, my would-be-arboretum, my eyes fell upon the dastardly villains. Though I had just cleared the area, by hand, of several different varieties of weeds, there they were. I repeat: they do not grow indiscriminately, but intentionally next to that which is good. They seek to find that which is healthy and growing, that which is green and filled with life, with potential for greater glory, and with inherent beauty. And they live like a lousy leech off of them. I pull the weeds, but they come back.

Before I continue further, let me say that my son has recently caught me in my apparently delirious, perhaps even maniacal, state of mind, actually speaking curses (in a pastoral way, mind you) against these weeds as I bent over (with my bad back, mind you) and pulled the weeds away from my bushes.

"Dad, why are you talking to the weeds?" he asks, as if he is witnessing the final mental breakdown of his father.

"Because, Son, the weeds are a sign of the devil!" I seethe and spit as I speak, not even looking at him, still pulling a deep-rooted weed that won't come up.

He observes me for a few seconds before asking, "Dad, are you OK?"

"No!" I respond, throwing down the trowel and rising halfway up with my hand on my back. "No, I am not OK! I hate weeds! They are signs of the fall, attacking my roses and my azaleas and my dogwoods and my crepe myrtles and my vegetables!"

"Why can't they grow out in a field somewhere?" he asks!

I tell my son,

These things are like sin itself that grabs on to human beings at the prime of their lives and sucks away life and potential and beauty. I am a pastor, Son. I see these things every day when I see broken marriages due to selfish desires attached to an otherwise godly man, or a 'root of bitterness' for a husband attached to a woman who is also capable of extraordinary acts of kindness to strangers. I see it, Son, every day. I am, indeed, fearful of the weeds in my own life. I look at your life and I know that the weeds will attack you in the prime of your life! They will come upon you unaware, and unless you are vigilant in tending the garden of your soul, the weeds of hell, growing up from the world, the devil or your old sin nature, will begin to slowly but purposively wrap its ugly tentacles around your life. I have seen what weeds do to azaleas, and I have seen what sin does to good men and women who have such potential for greatness.

By this time, well into my sermonic response, I can actually stand up straight, the kinks and pain in my lower back finally surrendering to my movements. I look my son in the eye: "That, my boy, is why I hate weeds! And that is why I shall toil, for so said the Bard:

O, my lord, You said that idle weeds are fast in growth...[223]

The sixteen-year-old son looks at me. "Gotcha, Dad." He turns, pauses, looks away into the sky as if to ask God to help his poor, suffering father, and walks down the pathway to the front door. I watch him, praying that our family devotions, our times of prayer, and, hopefully, the sincerity of his mother and father in private and public worship will help keep the weeds away. My racing heart slows as I see him pause, look down, and then bend over to grab a weed. He looks back at me. I am still standing and watching him. I smile.

Yes, I hate weeds. I see them not only in my pastoral work, but I read of them in our culture today. For instance, this morning, I was confronted with a news item that has been on my mind in recent days. Anne Rice, the extraordinarily gifted authoress, resident of my native New Orleans, who publicly announced her fidelity to

---

223 York at III, I in William Shakespeare and John Jowett, *The Tragedy of King Richard III*, The Oxford Shakespeare. (Oxford [England] ; New York: Oxford University Press, 2000).

her childhood Catholic faith has now renounced it. The renouncing of faith is fodder for news, even more so than the acceptance of Christ. And sure enough the papers are running with it repeatedly. Yet the story does not shock those of us who have seen this happen in our own congregations and sadly, among our own friends and family. We know that there are complications of the human soul due to the weeds of sin, that can smother potential, strangle away good intentions, and kill human desire to do good. We also know the passage from 1 John: "They went out from us, but they were not of us; for if they had been of us, they would have continued with us. But they went out, that it might become plain that they all are not of us." (1 John 2:9 ESV)

If Anne Rice has left the faith then you can be sure that she was never in the faith. She may have been in a visible church, but her heart had never surrendered to the Prince of Peace. If this were the case, she was never a member of the invisible Church known to God. Her soul had never undergone a genuine, supernatural conversion. This sort of genuine, radical transformation of her very nature would have had nothing to do with her desires and everything to do with the sovereign grace of a gloriously untamable Spirit. He roams across the lives of our generation, calling out transgressors to confess their sin and look up to their Savior, Jesus Christ. These repentant ones looked to Jesus Christ, not as the leader of a great tradition, but they looked to Him as dying Israelites in the desert looked at the brazen serpent on the pole to be healed of the original sin that was killing them over and over again. Such people look to Jesus the righteous, Jesus the Atoning One, and Jesus the "friend of sinners."

On the cross, God pulled up the first deep-rooted weed of original sin and destroyed all weeds in His garden by crucifying His only begotten Son on our behalf. If Anne Rice had seen her own condition and looked upon Jesus as her only life, her only hope, her eternal security, you can be sure that while she might fall away for a season, she would never, could never, depart fully from this Savior. She could not renounce Jesus. It is impossible to do so and even continue to live. Thus, it may be that Anne Rice was not converted. Maybe she was, and this is but a momentary stumble in her longer journey of faith. But the weeds of hell found a most choice plant in this gifted woman with this announcement. I do pray, if she reads this, that she might realize that she, like all of us, is in desperate need of soul-healing through Jesus Christ. I pray that she recognizes, through the power of the Holy Spirit, that she is entangled in weeds that are sucking away the life and purpose for living that God would have for her, if only she would turn to Him in truth. She has departed either for a season, if she is a true believer, or she has departed because she was never an authentic, God-drawn, disciple of Jesus.

William Lobdell's article[224] in the paper this morning is revealing. This former religion writer for the *Los Angeles Times* has written a book that is gaining some attention, particularly with the Rice announcement. The title of his book is *Losing my Religion: How I Lost My Faith Reporting on Religion in America—and Found Unexpected Peace.* It all sounds rather nice and assuring to those who believe that we can live in a world without weeds. Lobdell asserts that, like Anne Rice, having shed the remnants of religion he has found a new peace. He demonstrates how America, too, is losing her faith. He says this almost with hopefulness. While he calls America a Christian nation, still, he quotes George Barna to prove what we all see: that many who talk the talk are not walking the walk. He

---

224 William Lobdell, *Losing My Religion: How I Lost My Faith Reporting on Religion in America–and Found Unexpected Peace*, 1st ed. (New York: Collins, 2009). *Charlotte Observer*, August 11, 2010, 13A.

writes, "American Christianity is not well and there is evidence that its condition is more critical than most realize or at least want to admit." Pollsters, most notably evangelical George Barna, have reported repeatedly that they can find little measurable difference between the moral behavior of church goers and the rest of American society."[225]

There is not one genuine believer in Jesus who would argue with his premise that America is sick, "sin-sick," we would say. But we would deny that the answer is that America should just walk away from Christ. Some may need to walk away from tradition, from religion that is apart from the radical, Spirit-born faith that is preached by the Prophets, by St. Paul, St. Peter, and all of the New Testament writers, and by Jesus Christ Himself. You may need to renounce that. But the way to "peace" will not be through denial of Jesus. For the weeds will come. They will creep unannounced into your life. They will, for Anne Rice and William Lobdell (for whom I dedicate this article with ardent prayer for their souls' true conversion to the Lord Jesus Christ) and for all of us, come and seek to strangle life and potential and hope. In sorrow, and finally in death, they and all of us will be like the death of a fine oak, that at length, and after great struggle for life, gives way to the weeds of this world.

Just the other day I shared the news of sin, but also the glory of grace through Jesus Christ, as my wife and I stood in a Starbucks and prayed for the salvation of a lawyer from Lincoln in Banff, the great Canadian National Park. He was on vacation like we were. But God led us together in a "divine appointment" that yielded to a time of conversation and possibly conversion. So while many turn from religion, many are turning to Christ. The backdrop of the

---

225 Ibid.

weedy condition in America is also providing a clear demarcation between those who follow Jesus Christ as Lord and those who have followed an idea about Him, but not truly left all to embrace the Lord of life.

I read the article, thought about my experiences with the weeds, but also about our recent experience of praying with a vacationing lawyer for new faith in Jesus Christ, and then strolled past my roses. They are in a stone-surrounded, raised bed right in front of our porch, where I can enjoy them in the early mornings and late evenings. Just a few weeks ago, deadly, sinister Japanese beetles (the arch enemy of every American rose) had buried themselves, diabolically, in every single bud. The beetles from Eden-lost seemed to be killing our lovely, deep red "Mr. Lincoln" roses and our cheerful scarlet "Let Freedom Ring" bushes and our fragrant "John Paul II" specimens. But this morning, after doing great battle through the summer to save them, the wretched beetles are gone. Our rose plants are now radiant and are putting on a great end-of-the-summer speculator show! My favorite rose is "Barbara Bush." This morning, "Mrs. Bush" is in full glory! She is displaying the most delightful pink petals set against the perfect backdrop of her deep green foliage. I beheld the glorious sight, and with hope rising like a new season, I told my wife, "Heaven is on its way."

Anne Rice renounces her faith. William Lobdell finds peace away from religion. And yet a lawyer from Lincoln prays to receive Christ in Banff, and "Mrs. Bush" blooms in all of her glory. There are weeds. There are pests aplenty. But there is a movement of the Holy Spirit that is calling out to men and women, boys and girls, lawyers and students and writers to come and follow, not religion or tradition, but the life-giving, weed-killing Christ of the Scriptures.

> "Truly, truly, I say to you, whoever hears My word and believes Him who sent Me has eternal life. He does not come into judgment, but has passed from death to life" (John 5:24 ESV).

5

DEFENSE DRAWDOWN TALK WHILE THE NATION IS AT WAR

Irresponsible and Immoral

The failure of the bipartisan super committee to take decisive action to reverse the 15 trillion-dollar debt crisis this country needs from becoming another Greece has, predictably, failed. Now the Washington blame game begins. However, the greatest losers are the American people and, specifically, those Americans who courageously and proudly wear the uniform of the armed services. As I write, the Ambassador to Libya has been killed along with three other foreign service workers. Embassies are being stormed. Our military and our civil servants are also losers, as are those who work for our companies doing business on the high seas or in foreign countries. The military exists for good reasons.

As threats of cuts are made to their very mission, our brave troops are on the ground, in the air, and on the seas fighting, defending, and protecting this nation from the continuing threats to our very existence as a people. The absurd decision to tie massive cuts to the U.S. military as an "incentive" to force action by the super committee was one of the biggest mistakes ever made by Washington DC, and they have made a few recently. Of all the things that the government does, providing a military to "defend the Constitution of the United States against all enemies, foreign and domestic" just happens to be one of the clearest.

Scripture teaches that God has ordained government for the good of man. Civil authority, according to St. Paul, has been granted the power of the sword to punish evil, thereby protecting the innocent: "For he is the minister of God to thee for good. But if thou do that which is evil, be afraid; for he beareth not the sword in vain: for he is the minister of God, a revenger to execute wrath upon him that doeth evil." (The Epistle to the Romans 13:4 KJV) The present talk of defense cuts flies in the face of our nation's duty and our proud heritage.

We have had drawdowns before—after WWII, after Vietnam, and after the Gulf War, but we have never had to think about draconian reductions while we were in the middle of a war! It is this very point that is deeply disturbing, and recklessly dangerous. The consequences of even the talk of such tinkering with our defenders, even if reasonable heads prevail to stop this absurdity, will have their consequences.

Have we not learned our lesson? Reagan's military buildup in the 1980s reversed the ill-advised drawdowns after Vietnam (just one front in a larger, trans-generational Cold War) and, according to scholars like Paul Kengor of Grove City College and the American Center for Vision and Values, "All of these ventures [the strengthening of defense] had the effect of demonstrating a stronger, resurgent America, not only economically but also militarily. Suddenly, the country that had left Vietnam no longer appeared to lack resolve" (The Crusader: Ronald Reagan and the Fall of Communism by Dr. Paul Kengor, HarperCollins, 2007, 82).

Kengor went on to demonstrate that President Reagan understood that America was still at war. According to this preeminent Reagan scholar, his action in strengthening the military greatly contributed to bringing down the Soviet Union. Why now, when our sacred military members are risking their lives to fight "over there" so we don't fight "over here," would the president and other congressional leaders think that it is any different? To reduce military strength or even to talk about it as an option is to demoralize our troops while they are literally in the midst of a battle for our way of life.

Some may call it treason. I would call it self-destructive. As a minister of the gospel I would also call it irresponsible and immoral, given that God has called our civil authorities to protect our people against evil. May God have mercy and bless the troops who bravely carry on their mission to defend this nation, even while others who have taken the same oath are allegedly using the military as pawns in a Washington election year. There are times when the Church should speak up. Because our life and liberty are at stake, I think that time is now.

6

GUTTER TALK
GOING MAINSTREAM

Timothy Jay is one of the leading authorities on, of all things, cursing. In an article by Melanie Glover that appeared in the *Charlotte Observer's* front page on 2/25/08, I read that cursing by teens is up "90 swear words" per day. In fact Jay, a psychology professor at MIT, says that curse words are used as "fillers." That is, when a teen can't think of anything else to say, or is pausing to think, instead of uttering, "uh" or "well" he utters an obscenity. Now what strikes me first about this article is the lengths that the scientist had to go to obtain his data. But after that I thought, "Is there any wonder?" This report comes fresh on the heels of Jane Fonda (didn't I read that she became a Christian?) using an obscenity on a morning talk show. There have been numerous other obscenity incidents in recent days. Indeed, through obscene talk in movies, television sit-coms and talks shows, and even public sporting events, gutter talk has gone mainstream. Our children, if they are led by their parents into theaters where filthy language is used, with tacit approval of the parents, come to believe that such talk is normal. And of course if parents pay good money for their little ones to be assaulted by gutter language they are, most often, using it themselves. But is there anything really wrong with it? Or is language and word usage just evolving? The Bible says that filthy talk, or "obscene talk" as the English Standard Version puts it, is a sign of a filthy heart. Such talk should be removed from the lips of God's children. And as God's people our lips should, through the literal cleansing of our souls, reflect words that build up, that heal, that reflect the ministry of the Holy Spirit within us. We are reminded that our bodies are God's temple. Filthy talk is to be shunned. Moreover, we ought not to let such talk come into our hearts where we can help it. Obscene language is the overflow of a stench of the soul and the presence of the world, the devil, and an unregenerate soul. What is the answer to the situation we are facing as a nation with filthy language becoming more acceptable by society? There are ways to combat it. My wife and I demanded that we did not want our family (ourselves!) hearing obscene language in our own home, through television and DVDs. So we purchased a "TV Guard" to filter language on our television. It has helped. But our child actually first heard foul language at a Christian school. The greatest way to impact our children and even the larger society is to model Christ Jesus in our own lives, to talk a new language. And that comes from a new heart. There is no other real way. But what if you are "addicted" to cursing? Perhaps you are a new believer, and it is a habit that it proving too hard to break?

First, read more and more of God's Word. God's Word is a cleansing power that will begin to heal you from the inside out.

Second, "pray without ceasing."

Third, begin to offer thanks to Christ frequently. I am not advocating the sort of "praise the Lord" language that some Christians have adopted to use as "fillers" in their discourse. Rather, I am suggesting that the speaking of thanks to Jesus Christ is, in itself, a cleansing exercise of the tongue and of the heart.

Fourth, pray for revival. Many have heard that when the Welsh revival came to that land in the early 1900s the coal-mining mules had to be retrained, because they only responded to curses. The men had been changed from the inside out by the work of the Holy Spirit. And unless God raises up a genuine movement of the Holy Spirit from heaven among us today, we will continue to hear of such reports.

7

IN THE LAND OF BOCHIM

At the broken places of disobedience, the ruined places of prophetic warning fulfilled, the severe grace places where we hear the voice of the Lord convict us of our sins and call us to himself, when we realize that the blessings gained have been forfeited: that is the place called Bochim—the land of weeping in the original Hebrew.

This is what happened to the people of Israel in Judges 2:1–5. They had settled into a life of comfort in which the surrounding culture penetrated their lives more than they influenced that culture. They were people who had been transformed, yet by then they were not transforming others with the Word of God. And if you're not moving forward in faith you are moving backward. As a result God warned of coming judgment.

The place where we stand as a people in our day is *Bochim*. We cannot watch an old clip of Ronald Reagan giving a message about a "city on the hill" without weeping. It is difficult to watch a movie prior to the 1960s, because there we see an innocence lost. We see how an industry self-regulated itself to protect the morals of the nation. To even say such a thing today sounds like censorship. Then it sounded like responsibility.

We are watching the earnings of generations of anonymous preachers all over this land, through the ages, come to chilling fulfillment.

Our forefathers, our spiritual ancestors, the pilgrims, made a covenant with God, and out of the covenant with God a nation was formed. No one is saying that the constitutional documents are absolutely biblical or that the Bible itself is part of our Constitution or that Thomas Jefferson was a devout, orthodox believer. We are saying that, undeniably, people of God claimed this land long before those men ever thought about a Constitution. Their forefathers had established not a constitution, but a covenant. They claimed this land and they consecrated themselves and covenanted with God to create that City on the Hill that would influence the other nations for the cause of Jesus Christ. And if you are not a Christian, there is no better place to be than in a nation whose God is the Lord. In such a culture, the essential nature of God—the freedom of God, the love of God—will be more fully expressed in the public square. All will be blessed.

If you want to know about that, read the sermons of John Robinson (1576–1625), the pastor to the pilgrims who did not come but sent his elders instead to lead the people. The pastor remained in England with the older folk and a majority who could not make the trip. In several of his sermons, John Robinson warns the sojourning saints that their cause was not only religious, but because it was religious, that is because it was a Christian mission, it would touch every area of life, including, and especially the public life. He believed that the sojourning saints of England were on a holy mission: "I Charge you before God and his blessed angels that you follow me no further than you have seen me follow Christ...for I am verily persuaded the Lord hath more truth and light yet to break forth from His holy word."

Over the years the Lord has richly blessed this nation with the light of his holy Word. We have come to a point in our history where some are calling this a post-Christian nation. We may indeed have become post-Christian in culture but we still have lots of people who name the name of Jesus Christ as Lord in this land. It's time for us to do what the people of Israel did in this passage: fall on our faces and weep for broken promises. It is not God who broke His promise. Yet we need a new weeping, the weeping of fresh consecration to the Lord Jesus Christ. We need to become people who weep out of longing to see God's Spirit stir us to new life. The Bible tells us that when we do that, then we may weep some more, but the weeping will be tears of joy. We long for that. We may not see the fullness of the transformation in our lifetimes. We may not see a mass revival that so many of us are praying for. But maybe we will begin to see the tears forming in our children's eyes that are the tears of joy that we pray for. For us, it may be enough to weep for the Lord in repentance—and cry out that God restore us. That may be enough to transform *Bochim.*

8

ENSURING RELIGIOUS LIBERTY

*Obama Care, Ronald Reagan, and
the Crisis of Conscience in America Today*

We were told this would not happen. We were told to just let the bill pass and read it later. Well, we are reading it now. And the fine print doesn't look good for religious freedom. Perhaps you have heard about last Sunday's "pulpit protest" by Roman Catholic priests around the nation over the administration's mandated health care program which will require Catholic institutions like universities, hospitals and seminaries to "toe the line" regarding national health care mandates; notably, the requirement to provide insurance that will promote contraception and ultimately abortion. The protest is unprecedented by the U.S. Conference of Catholic Bishops. But make no mistake. This is not a Catholic issue only. It is not a contraception issue. *It is a religious liberty issue.* It is an American issue.

Phoenix Bishop Thomas J. Olmsted was spot on when he preached, "We cannot, we will not, comply with this unjust law. Our parents and grandparents did not come to these shores to help build (America) ... Or to have the posterity stripped of their God given rights..."

Put this Presbyterian down as saying, "Amen" to that Catholic bishop.

As the chief executive officer of one of America's largest protestant seminaries, I can tell you that the Obama health care mandate is already having an enormous impact on our ministry. Yet until this latest revelation, our problems have mostly been financial. In a word, this thing is going to be extraordinarily expensive. Now, unless there is a wholesale repeal of this Act or unless there is dramatic and immediate steps taken to curb the government's prying into the consciences of religious institutions like our seminary, or other similar religious establishments that appeal to a Higher Law than Man's, we will have a constitutional crisis on our hands. Those are heavy words. But this is a weighty matter.

It is interesting that Ronald Reagan's 101st birthday is going to be celebrated as this crisis unfolds before us. He had something to say about how government-mandated medicine steals liberty. Back in 1961, then actor and General Electric spokesman Ronald Reagan warned America: "One of the traditional ways of imposing statism or socialism on a people has been by way of medicine..." Reagan went on to describe how a secularist government would use national health care to advance other leftist agendas. He also went on to quote a founder who warned against the loss of liberty through gradual intrusion of a meddling government: James Madison warned, "Since the general civilization of mankind, I believe there are more instances of abridgement of the freedom of the people by gradual and silent encroachment by those in power than by violent and sudden usurpations."[226]

If liberty and freedom were a government issued right, then it would have the wherewithal to take it back. But liberty and freedom, as our founders declared, come from God. To meddle with

---

226 James Madison, speech in the Virginia ratifying convention on control of the military, June 16, 1788 in: *History of the Virginia federal convention of 1788*, vol. 1, p. 130 (H. B. Grigsby, ed. 1890)

those rights of conscience is to return to the controversies of human rights that gave rise to this nation. Unless these violations of religious rights are curbed now, ruin will be brought upon this nation.

It is time for Americans to speak up for religious freedom while there is still time. Thank God the Catholic Bishops and priests did. We all must. For you can't lose just a little liberty. You lose—we lose—all of it when we lose any of it.

9

LEGIONNAIRES AND JESUS

Earliest Memories of the Fourth of July

My clearest memories of Independence Day are my earliest memories of Independence Day: of sitting next to my Aunt Eva, who adopted this orphan boy, in the third pew back to the preacher's right in our small, little country church in Southeastern Louisiana. There I remember seeing a posting of the colors by old men, young men—turnip farmers, shade tree mechanics, hardware clerks, and barbers, who strained against old age to stand military erect, proud, and strong of heart. They wore American Legion hats, from WWI, and the younger ones, the fathers of my friends, from WWII and Korea. I don't remember words, though I can see them speaking in my mind's eye, like a silent newsreel of "our boys fighting at the front." I do remember that they saluted the American flag, as they stood in formation at the front of the church. And I do remember some of them with a trail of a tear running through up and across and into the creases of their aging faces. That is when I would look up at Aunt Eva and see the tears in her eyes, too. Sensory experience, we are told, make impressions. Impressions make memories. Memories make life. So that is how I recall the Fourth of July. It seems to me that the more distant the interval of time, the deeper the memory of such experiences—deeper yet no less vivid; more intense, in fact. I remember that as the Legionnaires, fathers, grandfathers, brothers, and sons, stood in front of our quaint church, the pastor prayed over them, and we sang something like "O God Our Help in Ages Past.' There was a solemnity about it. No cheering. There was more of a sense of thanksgiving to God for conveying His Fatherly protection to us through these farmers and mechanics and clerks and barbers. There was a connection between the Pilgrim's pride and the Church and the promises and prayers that we were told were made long ago that was somehow entrusted to us. Some might think I am creating a "Christian America" in sentiment if not theology. But that is not what I remember and certainly is not what I suggest. The Fourth of July, as a child, was not about a Christian America we celebrated, but American Christians who claimed their land for God and His Son, Jesus Christ. And in that, they were no different than the pilgrims who came here and at least some of the Christians who signed that Declaration of Independence. And that day, that Fourth of July, gave rise to the longest standing democracy in the world where freedom to worship according to one's own conscience is as sacred as the American Legion heroes who recessed with the colors singing "Onward Christian Soldiers" as the minister gave the benediction.

10

MY POLITICALLY INCORRECT BARBER

WFB and the Certitudes of Christian Conservatism

A funny thing happened on the way to getting my hair cut: I ran into a former Georgian (as in Russian), now full-fledged American "with an attitude!" That is dangerous in anyone's book, but when you put scissors and a straight razor in his hands it is outright suicidal to be in his chair! But there I was. It was innocent enough. I had been looking for a good "old-timey" barber for some time, one that puts hot lather on your neck and behind your ears and shaves you with a straight razor [and clips your eyebrows and ears! Ladies, leave the room! Plus, no *Cosmopolitan* magazines on the table], when I found "Петр"—that is, "Peter."

Peter has now cut my hair enough (three times) that he knew that I was a minister. He is a bold believer in Christ, having escaped Soviet rule under Reagan to come to America to be a free Christian. He told me that he loves America. Whatever you do if you go to Peter's barbershop, do not say anything bad about Ronald Reagan or Margaret Thatcher! Peter claims that it was their influence that brought down the Statist, tyrannical, dictatorial rule of the Soviet Union. He points to those two leaders as the ones who should be credited with the demise of the most brutal system of government in world history. He could not stop talking about how brave Reagan and Thatcher were in telling it like it was. The

Soviets were evil. Period. ("So much for the fashionable historical revisionism of Reagan–Thatcher bashing of 'enlightened' Europeans and their American-wanna-be-followers," I thought.)

Well, Peter went on to tell me his remarkable story; now, really, a new kind of American story. He learned the English language from missionaries. He studied American history. He claims the Pilgrims and Puritans as "his people." Why? They were, as Reagan used to put it, "Freedom men." Moreover, they were believers in Jesus Christ. Peter is a Pentecostal. He seeks to share the Gospel with as many people as God allows while cutting hair. I think he is very effective, especially when he is doing the straight razor part. As we talked he told me several things that reminded me of a book I am reading. ISI Publications has released a brilliant biography of William F. Buckley, Jr. The book, by Lee Edwards, is called *William F. Buckley Jr.: Maker of a Movement.*[227] If you are a Buckley fan, and I am, then this is the one to have (OK, you must have *God and Man at Yale*[228]). It was just before I walked into Peter's barbershop that I had been reading about Buckley's "certitudes"[229] that marked out true conservatism: "The Communist experiment [is] the worst abuse of freedom in history" and "the socialized state is to justice, order, and freedom what the Marquis de Sade is to love."[230]

Of course, WFB said many more things in later years about what marked out true conservatism including the remarkable

---

227   Lee Edwards, *William F. Buckley Jr.: The Maker of a Movement* (Wilmington, Del.: ISI Books, 2010).

228   William F. Buckley, *God and Man at Yale: the Superstitions of Academic Freedom* (Chicago: Regnery, 1951).

229   Edwards. 90.

230   These remarks were delivered by WFB at the Plaza Hotel, hosted by Herbert Hoover, General Douglas MacArthur, and Admiral Lewis Strauss, on the occasion of *National Review*'s fifth anniversary. See Edwards, 90.

affirmation, "I will use my power as I see fit...I mean to live my life an obedient man, but obedient to God, subservient to the wisdom of my ancestors; never to the authority of political truths arrived at yesterday at the voting booth."[231]

So I am thinking through the certitudes of—not just conservatism, but a distinctively evangelical Christian conservatism—when I encounter my Tea Party barber! Here is the thing: his list of certitudes was quite convincing coming from someone who had personally endured the persecution of Communism (his family stayed on the move because his father was an underground preacher and pastor) and has known the insidious authoritarian statism of the Soviet Union.

He paused after clipping up one side (but not the other) and began to tell me these words (approximately):

> I am very concerned about our country. It is starting to look like the country I came from (I challenged him, and he backed off to say that it was nowhere close, but he asked, "Could it not happen here too if we are not vigilant?")! I like Reagan. I like Bush, especially the 'W' one. He protected us well. These men are for freedom and against more state. We need less state, more personal freedom; less taxes, more wise use of money to build up the military to protect us. We need less intrusion into our lives. So I am worried. I see statism all over again with this president. These guys (and he meant the present administration I assumed) forget that this nation was founded by Christian men (and so we then talked about Whitefield and Edwards and the influence of godly preachers on the founders, even those who may not have been "evangelical"). They came from England and other places, like the Netherlands, to be free to worship God as they chose. They chose Jesus mostly. That made this nation Christian in many ways. It gave us God's blessing. Now, there seems to be a push to have more

---

231 Ibid., 71.

freedom to practice homosexuality than to practice Christianity (yes, he was upset!). If we continue this course, we will end up like the Soviet Union and God will not bless us. This nation is great because this nation believed in God and many, many followed Him and put His Word in our government and prayer in our classrooms and started universities to promote biblical knowledge. Faith in God is what makes America great.

He was getting pretty riled up. He had started cutting again, but he still had to shave the back of my neck. I moved in the chair just a bit, out of fear. I was listening but I was worried about that straight razor...

This is wrong what we are doing. Government health care when people don't want it, new taxes, and the National Day of Prayer outlawed by a judge! No to Billy Graham's son at the Pentagon! All wrong! Sarah Palin is right. (He didn't mention on what in particular! She is just "right," he says.) She speaks strongly about freedom and is not afraid, kind of like Thatcher to me. I like her. We need more people to stand up and speak for freedom from government in America.

So, I listened to him until way past the time he cut the hairs off of my ears (usually the final act in the drama of a man's haircut). Then I got up, asked God's blessing on him, paid him, tipped him, and went on my way. But I think I know the certitudes of Christian conservatism a little better because of Peter:

Stand up for Christ in the public square while we have the right to do so.

Stand for others to practice their religion. Their free exercise of religion is grounded in the freedom of evangelical Christianity that is not fearful of the presence of other religions, but welcomes an open forum (as long as it is truly open, in other words, when Christians are invited to the table!).

Stand for human freedom against state control of the individual.

Stand against statism and intrusion into the affairs of the Church, including the biblical norms for morality.

Don't just talk about being a Christian, be one openly, not belligerently (which is antithetical to being a Christian), but be prepared to stand up for Jesus Christ at any cost.

Stand up to speak the truth about America's founding fathers and the Christian foundations of this nation. No, they weren't all believers. Yet is there any debate over the fact that the founders were under the influence of the Pilgrims and First Great Awakening that preceded them by only a few years? The Supreme Court has declared in times past that we are a Christian nation. Now we are told that we are not. Well, now is the time to stand strong and speak of those founders who did trust in Christ, who sought to shape this nation after the governance they found in the Bible.

Be on guard against intrusion into personal liberties by new laws being passed that tell us that they "help us"; we don't need it— American values mean taking care of our own, not the government taking care of us.

Keep the American pioneer spirit alive: we can do things better than the government can, except law enforcement, military, roads, and protecting and advocating free trade for Americans around the world, which is why we have a government "of the people."

Be on guard against the insidious emergence of elite ruling classes rather than distributed power through the states and the local communities and families, especially families.

Keep prayer and God in all facets of public life, or ignore God at our peril.

Love the Lord and love your neighbor.

Read the Word of God privately, grow in grace and knowledge of Jesus Christ, pray for others, including those who despise you, and those with whom you disagree, and practice family devotions.

Pray for our leaders daily by name and for their families. It doesn't matter who they are, what party they are, or what they are advocating (I can pray for the person and pray against his/her policies and also pray that I be given wisdom and insight to know what is good and what is not, according to the precepts of the Word of God).

Be a soul winner, like my barber.

I had hair down my back, which I hate, but I am still going back to him. After I got home, and after I took my post-barber-shop shower, I dressed again, then went back to reading the new Buckley biography and found the next sentence to be the fitting end to the conclusions drawn from my barber: "Such a program...[speaking of the establishment of these certitudes of a true conservatism] is enough to keep conservatives busy, and liberals at bay. And the nation free."[232]

May it be so, WFB. May it be so, Peter. God bless you my friend. I'll see you next time. And if you don't mind, talk about faith and politics *after* you shave my neck!

And God bless America!

---

232 Ibid., 71.

11

"ACTING IS NOT EVERYTHING. LIVING IS."

Irene Dunne and Neil Postman

When the late, great Neil Postman (1931–2003) wrote that we were *Amusing Ourselves to Death* (1985)[233] he spoke of a generation that we all know too well. Our money, our priorities, our talk, our time and thus our lives, are consumed with Hollywood celebrities' regrettable, public emotional problems, the latest commercials that have become the currency of conversation far too often, and of the latest cat video. I am sorry, but I do not like cat videos. But in each of these issues that seem to consume us, in which we live victoriously through the tragedy and comedy of others' lives, we may very well forfeit our own lives.

Irene Dunne knew that. And she did not forfeit her life. Irene Dunne (1898–1990)[234] has been called "the greatest actress to never win the Academy Award."[235] I have seen that quote several times in speaking of her. And that certainly is my opinion. I challenge

---

233 N. Postman, *Amusing Ourselves to Death: Public Discourse in the Age of Show Business* (Penguin Books, 2006).

234 Most of the facts of this article on Irene Dunne were gleaned from the fine biography of the late actress, W. D. Gehring, *Irene Dunne: First Lady of Hollywood* (Scarecrow Press, 2006).

235 "Irene Dunne's Birthday Tribute on TCM," (2011). http://fan.tcm.com/_Irene-Dunne39s-Birthday-Tribute-on-TCM/blog/5653047/66470.html?as=66470 (accessed September 4, 2012).

you: watch Irene Dunne in *My Favorite Wife* or in *The Awful Truth* or the moving *Penny Serenade* and show me a more talented actress–singer–comedienne. Watch *I Remember Mama*, but watch it with a handkerchief nearby. Her performance in that one movie far surpasses much of what I see today in the work of Oscar-toting actresses. She was strikingly beautiful, enormously gifted for drama, musicals, or comedy (an art where I think she was one of the best and most underrated). I still think no one could really keep up with the presence of Cary Grant like Irene Dunne. Indeed, it could be argued that at times Cary Grant seemed to be trying to keep up with Irene Dunne! But it was never competitive for her. That always was clear. She proved with her life that she was not bridled by ambition. Maybe she transcended becoming just another pretty starlet because, in her early days, she was never a chorus girl. She used to talk about that. She came to theater and acted and didn't have to take the chorus line route or the director's private office route. She was better than they were. She knew herself. She didn't need to sell her life to share her gifts.

She was the daughter of a Louisville riverboat man, a U.S. steamboat inspector. He greatly influenced her and shaped her self-confidence identity. Some have said that her humor came through her father. Maybe the rides up and down the river on the steamboat, hearing her father's stories shaped her humor. After her father's death, and from this came her pathos, she moved to Madison, Indiana. It was in Indiana, under the mentorship of her concert piano teacher mother, that she grew in her calling. Like so many of our greatest, Irene Dunne was a Midwestern actress in the same vein as Jimmy Stewart and Ronald Reagan. Indeed, watch a Jimmy Stewart line famously delivered and then study the delivery techniques of Dunne. Very interesting! Description? Plain, clear, unpretentious, and a soul tethered to home, not to an allusive dream. That always comes through to me.

Growing up, her home was filled with music, and it rubbed off on this young lady. She studied voice. She had a captivating operetta singing voice that was happily featured in several of her films. She tried out and didn't make the Met. And we are all thankful for that. For one closed door led to other open doors in theater and eventually movies. But here is what really grabs me: Irene Dunne just stopped. I mean...she acted. But then she stopped. She got married to a dentist, Dr. Francis Griffith, and stayed married to him until he preceded her in death. They had one child, Mary Frances, who became their little girl in 1938, from the New York Founding Hospital, run by the Sisters of Charity of New York. She stopped acting to focus on being a mother and a wife. As she put it, "I drifted into acting and drifted out. Acting is not everything. Living is."[236]

She spent the remaining years of her life dedicating much to the Roman Catholic Church and to Republican causes. In 1985 she was given a lifetime achievement award through the Kennedy Honors, by President Ronald Reagan, an old friend. This Hollywood beauty was never a Hollywood bimbo. She was a smart, professional actress who gave us much in her gifts. But she didn't live *for us.* She lived, according to her own demonstrated life, for God and for others. Her own trust helped many in the Roman Catholic communities. Today the Irene Dunne Guild continues to serve the broken and the needy. Her legacy is not her acting, but like James Stewart (the James M. Stewart Good Citizenship Award is a prestigious Boy Scout award that is an example of his continuing commitments to the Boy Scouts of America) and other celebrities who use their platform to help others, her Christian values remain her legacy.

---

236 J. C. Tibbetts, K. Brownlow, and J. M. Welsh, *American Classic Screen Interviews* (Scarecrow Press, 2010). 36.

And that happened at the decisive point when she could have kept going, kept amusing us all; but she just retired from acting to "living." She is the antidote to *Amusing Ourselves to Death*. We need more like her.

Neil Postman once wrote, "I don't think any of us can do much about the rapid growth of new technology. However, it is possible for us to learn how to control our own uses of technology."

Irene Dunne taught us how to do that. With sparkling eyes, a mischievous grin, an all-American midwestern delivery, she sang and acted and laughed her way into American film history. But then she controlled her own destiny. She put down the remote. She put up the games. She *lived*.

So in between living, check out one of the most talented actresses in American film and enjoy. Even be amused—but not "to death."

Neil Postman books I recommend are

> *Amusing Ourselves to Death* (1985)
> *Technopoly* (1993)
> *The Disappearance of Childhood* (1994)
> *Building a Bridge to the Eighteenth Century* (2000)

Irene Dunne films that are a *must see* include

> I Remember Mama (1948)
> The Awful Truth (1937)
> Love Affair (1939)
> Penny Serenade (1941)
> My Favorite Wife (1940)

12

NOW WHAT?

Some Thoughts after the
Election on Lessons and Expectations

On the other side of the election, what can we learn? What can we expect?

For the believer, our lessons and our expectations are grounded in the Word of the Lord. Our hope for our nation is grounded not in electoral victories, but in "victory in Jesus" ruling and reigning in the hearts of people who will then move in politics, in entertainment, in economics, in every facet of life out of the core of a soul in love with Christ and broken for the souls of lost sinners.

> TO THE CHOIRMASTER: WITH STRINGED INSTRUMENTS.
> A PSALM. A SONG. Psalm 67:

May God be gracious to us and bless us and make his face to shine upon us, *Selah* that your way may be known on earth, your saving power among all nations. Let the peoples praise you, O God; let all the peoples praise you! Let the nations be glad and sing for joy, for you judge the peoples with equity and guide the nations upon earth. *Selah* Let the peoples praise you, O God; let all the peoples praise you! The earth has yielded its increase; God, our God, shall bless us. God shall bless us; let all the ends of the earth fear him!

The old pastoral master, Matthew Henry, wrote, "The success of the gospel brings outward mercies with it; righteousness exalts a nation. The blessing of the Lord sweetens all our creature-comforts to us, and makes them comforts indeed."

Ah, but that such sweetening would come upon us today! And yet it can according to these Gospel promises embedded in this great Word of God.

In Psalm 67, the Psalmist cries out on behalf of the people who are languishing for lack of praise, "May the peoples praise you, O God." His heart beats not only for his local congregation, his own city as it were, but for the whole world, for he says, "May all the peoples praise You." This is truly a world missions Psalm.

I went to sleep, recently, reading of the last days of the great missionary to the Indians, David Brainerd. His heart increasingly beat, not only for the Indians of the Susquehanna Valley and the Connecticut River valley, but also for those all over the world who did not know Christ. He was appalled that the affections of believers were so unconcerned by virtue of lack of prayer for the world. He died thinking of the coming of the kingdom of God, and that the sufferings of man, which he had witnessed in the indigenous pagan societies here in North America, might be dispelled by the beauties of the truths of the Gospel of Jesus Christ.

Jonathan Edwards joined with this young man in his passion. Concerts of prayer began, linked to other parts of the world (even then), which lasted for seven years. Christians banded together to pray for revival that would propel the Gospel to the ends of the earth. Indeed, the first Great Awakening is linked to a dying 29-year-old Presbyterian evangelist with a consuming passion to see the nations, all of them, brought happily and productively under the Lordship of his Savior, Jesus Christ.

Euphoria swells in the hearts of many today as we hope and pray for a change in government policies which will better reflect the government we find in the Bible. I join in that hope. But our economic and political future is tied, not to a party or to any governmental change, but to God. Our hope for recovery lies in the Gospel. I admit that I have no expertise in economic markets *per se*, or in politics for that matter, but anyone, even the simplest homemaker like my Aunt Eva that reared this orphan boy, knew that good things follow the glory of the Gospel. We knew that in our own lives on our own little hardscrabble South Louisiana farm.

From Psalm 67, we can know that where the Gospel goes, God brings showers of blessings. Among those many blessings are truths that set men free. Among those blessings are the liberation of the human soul, of the construction of a human government and free enterprise, and the compassionate love of Christ that reflects the Gospel. The land itself "will yield its harvest" and "God will bless us." Amen and amen!

Bring it on Lord! Bring it on for the world! Bring on a sense of dependence upon those recently elected men and women that they will know that without God we are sunk. Let their first action upon being sworn into office be to go to their knees and cry out for repentance on our nation, for unction, power and divine wisdom from on high, and that God would use our people to reach others who need Christ. To be a politician is to be a missionary. To be a mechanic is to be a missionary. All Christians must be concerned about those who do not have the Gospel, from their own people to the Peoples of the ends of the earth.

Coming back from Cape Town 2010, my heart is stirred by my own lack of prayer for the nations, and I want to change. I want to pray. I want to be one with those who are suffering for Christ. I want to be one with the Church around the world. And I want God to come down in my own nation and shake us so that we see our true condition: no election or government can do what God can do if we will but seek His face.

I ask God to stir the Church up in the West to be concerned again for the conversion of the nations. Let us leverage everything we have, including our time and our prayers, to see that Christ is made Lord of this earth in our generation. And let us remember that the land here will yield its harvest as our true economic recovery is linked to repentance and revival.

God have mercy. Christ have mercy. Lord, let us rain down Gospel truths on our land that we may be all the more encouraged to use that wealth to spread the Gospel of Jesus Christ to the ends of the earth.

Let us join with Brainerd and Edwards in seeking God in concerts of prayer. It is planting time again. We need a Great Awakening in order to know true recovery. That is our lesson. This is our expectation after the election.

13

ON THE DEATH
OF SOMETHING CALLED

Being Christian in America

We have come to a new time in our nation, a time when Christianity is being widely announced as on life support in America. But I do not believe it. Oh, I believe in the falling numbers of true believers, of the closing of churches every week in America, of the fog of immorality, as Peter Marshall described the America of his day which sounds like the America of our day, and the rampant ungodliness that has us calling right wrong and wrong right. I believe that the watery, insipid religion called liberal Christianity is deathly anemic, and the feckless fundamentalism of moralism and justification by good reputation may indeed be dying, as sure as the seeker-sensitive, dogma-denying cults of consumerism and entertainment may be sick unto death, but I, for one, encourage their deaths. I would rather the playing field be leveled between pagans and bold, Christ-believing, grace-embracing, cross-magnifying disciples of the sinless Lamb of God, the Man, Christ Jesus, than to have players like that representing, or seeming to represent, the Christ of the Scriptures. I still believe that Almighty God reigns. I believe that the sinless life of Jesus Christ saves, the sacrificial death of Jesus Christ atones, and the bodily resurrection of Jesus from the dead seals it all as absolutely true. I believe that the Holy Spirit moves over the dead soul of the most vile sinner and transforms him into a saint. I believe that the Lord is building HIs Church, His Body of assembled saints, from all over the world, and I expect that more and more people of our generation will be gloriously swept into this kingdom of Christ. And if C. S. Lewis was right, that in the end there will only be Hinduism and Christianity, for Hinduism swallows up all other religions, and Christianity rejects all other ways to God but through Jesus Christ, then I am confident that Christianity will be victorious in the history of men. For God made man. And Man fell from God in his choice to sin. But the rest of our history is the story of the unrelenting love of God to redeem that sinful Man. And Christ is God's Son and God's provision for Man's sin. Jesus is God in the flesh who came to identify with Man and save us through an unmerited grace offered to all who will call upon His name, the name of Jesus, and that is the underlying power of Christianity. As Augustine said, what God has required, to repair this damaged relationship between Creator and Creature, God has provided. That message, which is nothing but the Gospel, when left to stand as it is, will always come out on top. It did in the first century world, with that age's veritable cafeteria of religions available to the consumer of faith, and it shall do the same today. And because God is God, and Jesus Christ remains the most compelling figure in human history, and because the soul of Man longs for restoration with God and with each other, I am most optimistic. Something called Christianity may be dying in America. But I believe America is dying for a true Christianity. It is our happy cause to see to it that we not let America down; no, that we not let our Savior down who calls us to the noble work of proclaiming the plight of Man and the power of God in Christ to this generation. So let the Church, then, be the Church. Let Christ be Christ. And may this bold, gracious and supernatural Christ of the Bible be unleashed with all of His glory upon the sin sick souls of

Americans. And let the fires of revival come down from on high and devour the false gods of this age, including every pretender to the faith of the apostles, the saints, the martyrs, and the billions of humans who have found new life through Jesus Christ, the resurrected and reigning Lord of life.

14

SAME-SEX MARRIAGE, THE RESPONSIBILITY OF CITIZENS, AND BIBLICAL ILLITERACY

Chipping Away at the Foundation of a Society

Another state legislature approves same-sex "marriage." Another chip in the foundation of civilization. Another moment closer to a death sentence for a nation, and not even ObamaCare will be able to stop it. But the trials that we face in this nation, and in the West, are not about healthcare or even a constitutional crisis, but a crisis of ethics and morality. Legislatures concoct bills to allow for violations of the Law of God because they either do not know the Law of God or they oppose it or they are simply apathetic toward it. Governors sign these laws for the same reason. And the yoke of moral bondage is then placed back on the children and grandchildren of our citizens. But the process of passing bills into law, in this case codifying what the Bible and thousands of years of human civilization clearly abhors, reveals the fatal flaw that our founders warned could happen: uninformed or unconcerned citizens placing people into office who do not meet necessary conditions to serve—the first condition being moral. The government of the United States was not devised on a whim, as Senator Smith told the leadership at the National Religious Broadcaster's dinner this year. Madison, Washington, Adams, and the

others, whatever their differences on religion (there was compara-
tively little space between them), were firm in their conviction
that the representative government of the U.S. could work, but,
and this is a large condition, only if the citizenry was committed to
electing representatives with religious (and they referred to at
least the broader tenets of Judaeo–Christian religion) morals that
could exercise wise moral (and they for the larger part meant biblical) decisions in their stead. Thus John Adams would write:

> ...[W]e have no government armed with power capable of con-
> tending with human passions unbridled by morality and reli-
> gion.... Our constitution was made only for a moral and religious
> people. It is wholly inadequate to the government of any other.
> (Source: John Adams, The Works of John Adams, Second President
> of the United States, Charles Francis Adams, editor (Boston: Little,
> Brown, 1854), Vol. IX, p. 401, to Zabdiel Adams on June 21, 1776.
> See Wallbuilders.com. Former Senator Gordon H. Smith of Oregon,
> now CEO of the National Association of Broadcasters, declared
> that the governmental system of the United States was erected in
> an era when absolute monarchy, and monarchy by divine right
> ideas, was all the rage in the world. The U.S., alternatively,
> grounded a system of government in such a biblical representa-
> tive fashion that King George III once remarked in exasperation
> that the experiment in self governance was a "Presbyterian par-
> son's rebellion!"[237] But the government of this nation, founded on
> the idea of representative governance, requires an "activation
> code" to work. That code is the wise moral choices of a people
> who know the difference between right and wrong. That is why
> the Northwest Ordinance, the first major legislation signed into
> law by President Washington, was passed by the first Congress: to
> provide government funds to establish Christian "schools and the

---

237 Source: Douglas F. Kelly, The Emergence of Liberty in the Modern World:
     The Influence of Calvin on Five Governments from the 16th through 18th
     Centuries (Philipsburg, N.J.: P&R Publishing, 1992), p. 131.

means of education" in the far territories that would support the "religion, morality, and knowledge" of citizens that "necessary to good government and the happiness of mankind." Their conviction? Only those who know the divine laws of God revealed in His Word, the Bible, can intelligently elect a candidate who will uphold those laws in office. Without that one critical element, the government runs sluggish at best, and at worst, is infected with a virus that destroys sacred and indispensable elements of morality that hold the body of our nation together. This is also what President Washington meant when he charged a nation in his farewell address, "It is substantially true, that virtue or morality is a necessary spring of popular government." (Source: George Washington, Address of George Washington, president of the United States... Preparatory to His Declination [Baltimore: George and Henry S. Keatinge], pp. 22–23. In his Farewell Address to the United States in 1796. See Wallbuilders.com). Rogue legislatures and courts that are defying the laws of God can only be stopped when the people know their Bible. Only a true revival of religion in our nation can stop the insidious regression we are witnessing. And only God can do that. As Christians, we need to pray, now more than ever, for the "moral code" that runs this nation to be reactivated. For a government of the people, by the people, and for the people begins with one person who quite frankly knows his Bible.

15

THE PRESIDENT'S EVOLUTION AND OUR CULTURE'S DEGRADATION

A Call to Prayer and a Plea for Revival

Dear Friends and Colleagues,

Often we cannot fully grasp the historical significance of events as they happen. The 24/7 news feeds into our homes can desensitize us to even the most remarkable of events. Yet the announcement of a United States President (and Vice President) publicly endorsing same-sex marriage is to support that which God explicitly condemns. It is shameful and a reproach to decency and honor and a sad commentary on the regrettable departure of our national leaders from the biblical heritage that has guided our country. The President's announcement came hours after another of our states voted to protect the God-ordained institution of marriage and was thus particularly painful for citizens in North Carolina and further deepened the obvious cultural divide in our nation. I join many other Christian leaders, churches and ministries asking God's power for revival to come upon our country as we face this latest assault on the law of God. While we pray for our President and his family, we ask the Lord to bring repentance and Spirit-wrought renewed faith to him and all. Oh, that we might seek Him and live!

Now more than ever, we at Reformed Theological Seminary must be vigilant in our sacred calling to raise up godly pastors and other servants of the Church who will courageously, boldly and compassionately declare Jesus Christ's Word to our people. That Word brings abundant life and eternal life. May God have mercy for the sake of His Church and stir us all to prayer like never before. Then, this remarkably sad moment for our country would have brought about something good.

16

"THE MORAL FORCE OF THE PULPIT"

Puritans and Catholics Together...?

John Wingate Thornton wrote, "To the Pulpit, the Puritan Pulpit, we owe the moral force which won our independence" (*Political Sermons of the American Founding Era, 1730–1805*, edited by Ellis Sandoz [Indianapolis, IN: Liberty Fund, Second Edition], x). Can the same be said today? Or has theological timidity or a distorted view of the role relationship of the Church and the Magistrate muted the prophetic voice of the Reformed and evangelical Church today? Apparently, it has not muted the Catholics.

I want to share a video produced by a Catholic advocacy group that pinpoints the nonnegotiable, central values which support all the other issues that are being raised in this political season. This video is one of the most compelling presentations of the basic biblical teachings that form the foundation of a sane civilization: the sanctity of life, sanctity of marriage, and religious liberty. It puts economy and jobs in the right perspective. May we who are Reformed preachers and Christian ministries have the same courage as Roman Catholic Cardinal Dolan and his increasingly vocal parishes and ministries to speak up for the essentials. Even a cursory reading of the sermons of our spiritual forefathers in the 1700s shows a similar prophetic voice from the pulpits to the people in the pew and those serving the Magistrate. Oh, that we might raise up a holy army of those who preach—John the Baptist-like—into the cultural confusion of our day. Yes, we preach that souls may be saved first and always. But we give that message with the warnings to all that to deny Christ and to disregard biblical truth is to head towards destruction (à la Romans 1).

Our biblical–theological–ecclesiastical differences notwithstanding, I believe that if the Puritan preachers first promoted religious liberty (and thus the other liberties that naturally flow from that one primal fountainhead), then the Catholics may now be the ones putting themselves on the front lines to preserve it. Good for them. And may the Reformed churches rise to preach the Gospel of Christ to this nation, with "all that He commanded" for life and godliness. "And you shall know the truth and the truth shall set you free." (John 8:32 ESV) That Word is needed to be preached now more than ever. That is the force which wins and preserves souls unto abundant life and eternal life.

17

THE WORLD UPSIDE DOWN
IN THE MIDDLE EAST

*Can We "Attain the Unattainable" and
See Democracies Arise in a Region of Despots?*

The World Turned Upside Down was the title of Sir Christopher Hill's history of the English Civil War. The title was borrowed from Scripture (Acts 17:6). Today, as then, our world is also being turned upside down. From Tunisia to Egypt to Libya, the Middle East is quaking. Not since the fall of the Berlin Wall has the world witnessed such far-reaching geo-political reconfiguration,on as well as human tragedy and hope mixed together. The question on the minds of of senior military and foreign service officialsworld leaders in Washington and London, Paris and the Hague, is "What's next?"

There is a profound great uncertainty among many pundits that the people in the Middle East cannot govern themselves, having become so dependent upon despots and rogue dictators. for millennia. I have even heard reasonable people opine that the ability to govern democratically is a uniquely Western European concept and thus and out of reach for beyond tribal, autocratically-ruled peoples of the Middle East.

I reject that idea. History shows demonstrates that the only reason why that our Western nations have been endowed with free forms of government democracy is because these such expressions of liberty are built on the bedrock of the Bible. Before Jesus taught that you shall know the truth and the truth shall set you free (John 8:32), Germanic and Gaelic Barbaric tribes roaming across the European continent Europe and British Isles would have given the worst Middle Eastern dictators a run for their money.

What is needed in these desperate days in the Middle East is a firm resolve such as Ronald Reagan displayed firm resolve when he looked at the situation of people living behind the iron curtain. under the Soviet Union. According to Dr. Paul Kengor, in his book *The Crusader: Ronald Reagan and the Fall of Communism*, "Reagan not only hoped for Communism's demise; he often predicted it. More so, his administration went beyond hoping for the end, and... went so far as to design and implement action, policies and even formal directives intended to reverse the Soviet empire and win the Cold War." Reagan simply believed that people could, as Kengor recalls, "attain the unattainable," through the power of truth.

Freedom was from God and intended to unleash the potential of all men everywhere.

The role of the Church in the twenty-first century will be to speak prophetically, respectfully, but clearly to all to the nations of the West and to the freedom-hungering peoples of the Middle East that liberty comes from the Lord.

Reagan said, "It is time for the world to know our intellectual and spiritual values are rooted in the source of all strength, a belief in a Supreme Being, and a law higher than our own." The It is the love of Jesus Christ that sets people free and liberates human beings to discover their potential in every area of life. Only such faith can "attain the unattainable," set human beings free, bring democracy, and turn the world right side up.

Oh God send revival to the Middle East. Let a movement of Your Holy Spirit wash away the hatred, the bitterness, the religious oppression, and division. Come Lord Jesus. If revival comes, if the Middle East is changed we will know it is Your work. And many will believe again. Amen.

18

"TINKER, TAILOR, SOLDIER...PASTOR"

How Two Cold War Foes Became Pastoral Friends

The picture would have been impossible to imagine for the two men before.

When I was granted a Top Secret clearance under the Naval Security Group, part of the National Security Agency, it would have been (spiritually as well as practically) delusional to think that one day I would be a pastor serving a system of seminaries preparing other pastors. I was an American spy—in military intelligence— trained to "listen in" (literally) to a former Soviet block country.

The Rev. Dr. Sasha Tsutserov, a former KGB agent spying on American missionaries and now Director of Moscow Evangelical Christian Seminary, equally had no idea that he would, after the Berlin Wall fell and the Soviet empire crumbled, discover a new life as a believer and then as a pastor who served a seminary to prepare other evangelical pastors. Yet as I was beginning my ministry, my former adversary, Dr. Tsutserov, was being converted to evangelical Christianity by those he spied upon. He would soon be studying for his Ph.D. at St. Andrews University (at the same time as Prince William and the future Duchess of Cambridge were there, which caused him to remark, "This may have been a little uncomfortable for the British MI6"). After obtaining his doctorate he returned to Russia with a vision to advance the Gospel he once sought to destroy.

Now, Dr. Tsutserov, as an ordained evangelical minister, expresses his vision by leading one of the largest seminaries in Russia. As I now serve as the next Chancellor of Reformed Theological Seminary, our unlikely paths converging in my study seemed surreal, except that this is just the way the Gospel of Jesus Christ seems to work. Paradoxes and transformations like this are but ordinary reflections of the powerful pattern of the Cross of Jesus Christ at work in the world. But I have to tell you—when it happens it is still breathtaking. That God would bring two former top-secret antagonists together as Gospel allies in the Kingdom of God is just the way the Lord brings honor and glory to Himself and proves that the Kingdom of God is greater than all other realms and is, in fact, a Gospel conspiracy at work in the world today.

I learned more. Sasha told me that from 1917 until 1997, the Soviet Communist empire was responsible for the murder of more than 200,000 pastors, seminary presidents, professors, missionaries and other Christian leaders. They imprisoned more than 500,000 others, many in unspeakably cruel conditions. Thus, the seminary is now seeking to offer a new generation of Christian leaders for the growing evangelical church in Russia. Sasha is seeking God in prayer to replenish his nation with a new generation of pastors, and I am seeking His presence and power to revitalize our nation with a new generation of pastors. We want to work together in some way, giving expression to the unity of Christ in the world. I pray that we can. We need to learn so much from the Russian Christians who have suffered. Maybe we can share some things, too.

As we talked, we learned that we were also both orphans. We are both musicians (he a real one as a classically trained violinist, and I as, well, a Martin guitar picker). And of course we were both top-secret linguists and agents for our respective nations. Yet both of us were called out of that life, not to yet another SIS mission, like in the John le Carré novel, but to Christ's Gospel mission. The author of *Tinker, Tailor, Soldier, Spy* characterized his main character, George Smiley, as "one of the meek who doesn't inherit the Earth." I don't know how meek these two old spies are, but we do fully expect King Jesus to inherit the earth. That is what we work for now.

Our two-hour meeting, remembering what was and dreaming of what could be, concluded with a thought that was so obvious I had to say it: "We were once enemies. We are now brothers, in the Lord, in the pastoral ministry, in seminary leadership, and in our united desire to bring reconciliation to the world."

19

TWO SPEECHES

Remembering D-Day through Eisenhower and Reagan

THE "IN-CASE-OF-FAILURE" NOTE WRITTEN BY EISENHOWER ON JUNE 5

Today I want to post Eisenhower's letter that was never read and then post another, by Ronald Reagan, that was read fifty years later. One was given because the other was not. And that is another story of D-Day that bears remembrance. It is a story of leadership and strategic analysis and downright human courage that bears repeating in every generation facing the forces of evil and oppression. Our world faces enormous forces of evil today. And we are in desperate need of Eisenhowers and the men who fought with him, who weighed the risks and the costs and outcomes and determined that God-given freedom is always worth it. May our stories be retold as well.

In the tension of the decisive moment, the only mistake made was the date: Eisenhower scribbled "July 5." It was written on June 5, 1944, one day before Operation Overlord would forever be recalled, simply, poignantly, and thankfully, as "D-Day."

"In Case of Failure" by General Dwight David Eisenhower

Our landings in the Cherbourg–Havre area have failed to gain a satisfactory foothold and I have withdrawn the troops. My decision to attack at this time and place was based upon the best information available. The troops, the air and the Navy did all that Bravery and devotion to duty could do. If any blame or fault attaches to the attempt it is mine alone.

President Reagan's Speech at Pointe du Hoc, Normandy

We're here to mark that day in history when the Allied peoples joined in battle to reclaim this continent to liberty. For four long years, much of Europe had been under a terrible shadow. Free nations had fallen, Jews cried out in the camps, millions cried out for liberation. Europe was enslaved, and the world prayed for its rescue. Here in Normandy the rescue began. Here the Allies stood and fought against tyranny in a giant undertaking unparalleled in human history. We stand on a lonely, windswept point on the northern shore of France. The air is soft, but forty years ago at this moment, the air was dense with smoke and the cries of men, and the air was filled with the crack of rifle fire and the roar of cannon. At dawn, on the morning of the 6th of June 1944, 225 Rangers jumped off the British landing craft and ran to the bottom of these cliffs. Their mission was one of the most difficult and daring of the invasion: to climb these sheer and desolate cliffs and take out the enemy guns. The Allies had been told that some of the mightiest of these guns were here and they would be trained on the beaches to stop the Allied advance. The Rangers looked up and saw the enemy soldiers—at the edge of the cliffs shooting down at them with machine guns and throwing grenades. And the American Rangers began to climb. They shot rope ladders over the face of these cliffs and began to pull themselves up. When one Ranger fell, another would take his place. When one rope was cut, a Ranger would grab another and begin his climb again. They climbed, shot back, and held their footing. Soon, one by one, the Rangers pulled themselves over the top, and in seizing the firm land at the top of these cliffs, they began to seize back the continent of Europe. Two hundred twenty-five came here. After two days of fighting only ninety could still bear arms. Behind me is a memorial that symbolizes the Ranger daggers that were thrust into the top of these cliffs. And before me are the men who put them there. These are the boys of Pointe du Hoc. These are the men who took the cliffs. These are the champions who helped free a continent. These are the heroes who helped end a war. ...

Gentlemen, I look at you and I think of the words of Stephen Spender's poem. You are men who in your 'lives fought for life... and left the vivid air signed with your honor'... Forty summers have passed since the battle that you fought here. You were young the day you took these cliffs; some of you were hardly more than boys, with the deepest joys of life before you. Yet you risked everything here. Why? Why did you do it? What impelled you to put aside the instinct for self-preservation and risk your lives to take these cliffs? What inspired all the men of the armies that met here? We look at you, and somehow we know the answer. It was faith, and belief; it was loyalty and love. The men of Normandy had faith that what they were doing was right, faith that they fought for all humanity, faith that a just God would grant them mercy on this beachhead or on the next. It was the deep knowledge—and pray God we have not lost it—that there is a profound moral difference between the use of force for liberation and the use of force for conquest. You were here to liberate, not to conquer, and so you and those others did not doubt your cause. And you were right not to doubt. You all knew that some things are worth dying for. One's country is worth dying for, and democracy is worth dying for, because it's the most deeply honorable form of government ever devised by man. All of you loved liberty. All of you were willing to fight tyranny, and you knew the people of your countries were behind you.

Source for the "In Case of Failure" letter:
Dwight D. Eisenhower Library, Abilene, Kansas
Pre-Presidential Papers
Principal File: Butcher Diary
1942–1945
ARC Identifier: 186470

20

WALL STREET, VON BALTHASAR, AND HOMECOMING DINNER

Three Streams Converge

Three streams of thought are converging in my mind this morning. There is one stream that is swallowing up the others and forming a grand river of hope. In these days we need hope.

One stream is the current financial crisis in this country. I am no economist. I know little of the inner mechanisms of Wall Street. I am like every other man and woman in this country, and trust, perhaps with abandonment, that the controls set in place by government, the impulses inherent in the free market, and the business sense gained by decades of experience in the American system of finance will keep us afloat and even allow us to prosper. Whether my assumptions are now proven naive is a matter for me to consider. But the real thing that I, and all of us, must remember this morning is that this is just a little stream. Hans Urs von Balthasar's words ring true: "History is concretely put together from an infinite number of finite moments..." (*Engagement with God*, 57).

This present concern is like a 24-hour news cycle. It rises and it will fall. In the meantime, it will hurt some people, and for that, our hearts break. But "when the lines of life are seen from end to

end" this is a finite moment in an infinite number of finite moments. This is a time to remember the prayer of Moses:

> LORD, Thou hast been our dwelling place in all generations. Before
> the mountains were brought forth, or ever Thou hadst formed the
> earth and the world, even from everlasting to everlasting, Thou
> art God. Thou turnest man to destruction; and sayest, Return, ye
> children of men. For a thousand years in Thy sight are but as yes-
> terday when it is past, and as a watch in the night. (Psalms 90:1–4
> Authorized Version)

As we live out this crisis we must do so in the context of eter-
nity. We must do so in the context of God.

That leads me to the second stream flowing through my soul
this morning. Hans Urs von Balthasar was a Roman Catholic contemporary of Karl Barth. Our theological differences notwithstanding, his views are worth exploration. In *Engagement with God: The
Drama of Christian Discipleship*, Von Balthasar presupposes that
discipleship is lived out by those who have been gripped by a grace
he could not imagine and by a drama that has now entered the
world through Jesus Christ. As we await His return, the drama of
discipleship involves a grace of God that "is prior to all our involvement, undertaken for God in the world, and for the needs of the
world for His sake" (p. 47). Von Balthasar sees history as a living
history, as well as a dying history, a history marked by entropy,
decay and death. The life of Jesus, at work in the believer, has burst
upon the scene, not only in extraordinary ways, but also in ordinary ways (family, work, feasts, funerals, friends, enemies, comedy
and tragedy), almost unseen by the world. This enables us to face
down the culture of death: "For the real object of the Christian's
hope is to overcome the boundaries of death that cross the stream
of human history at every moment, as to all appearances it flows
onward on its course." (p. 58)

This stream, the drama of discipleship, now flows like white water rapids into the murky, stagnant water of human crisis, whether this present financial crisis or my family crises or your health crisis, and overtakes it. It changes it. The scum of despair is gladly disturbed, though it resists movement. Then, the streams have not just merged. The stream of the drama of Christ alive in the world, through the lives of His people, now becomes a new river. This gives us hope. This is God's everlasting being made manifest through the drama of life, death, resurrection, ascension, and the new heavens and earth hopefulness of Jesus Christ in us. The murky disappears in the cheerful, refreshing streams of God. There are no longer two streams, but one.

My final thought is of another stream, this new stream that is being formed out of these two streams: the final stream of the Church. This past week I encountered that stream in a powerful way. I preached at Walnut Hills Presbyterian Church in Bristol, Tennessee. The church, gathered out of the hollows of the East Tennessee mountains, formed out of the life of Jesus in the lives of Scotch–Irish, Welsh, and English farming stock at the beginning of the twentieth century exists in splendor today. As I preached their 75th Homecoming service, I watched the faces of the people singing the songs of ascent as they went up to the Mount of God in Christ-centered worship. I saw tears forming and some trailing down cheeks as I explained the grace of Christ that transforms the broken. I heard their pastor's own story of faith, of how God led him there, of how he marvels at their love, and how he wants to lead them to serve the community. He said, "At the end of five years I don't care if we have one more member. I care that our present members have grown more in Christ. I care that the community knows that we love them. And the elders agree."

After the service, we all walked up the hill to the Fellowship Hall. There we enjoyed a wonderful Southern "Homecoming" meal. When I was a boy we had these Homecomings, down in the piney woods of southeastern Louisiana. We called them "Dinner on the Grounds" because that is how they were served. Part way through the service half of the women slipped out to prepare the food (just like they did this past Sunday). This did not disturb the preacher but gave him urgency in his message! I have eaten a lot of fried chicken and deviled eggs and sweet potato casseroles on sagging paper plates as fire ants gathered around me for their own feast. I remembered those times under the ancient live oaks, where the tangled Spanish moss hung over the bright red and white check-ered plastic table cloth covered tables. I remember the stories, the laughter, the tobacco spitting deacons and the Civil War-veteran-like old men who stayed their distance from the women who did all of the work. I remembered these common things where God was alive in them through it all.

As I saw their Homecoming, ate their delicious food, heard their stories, saw their women, their men, watched as ten-year-old boys wrestled on the front lawn of the church while little girls in frilly pink and polka-dot dresses watched and scolded them, I thought that this is the Body of Christ like leaven in the world, bringing in the Kingdom of God. Imperceptibly, incredibly, and splendidly. There in that place, in that time, at that Homecoming, I remembered that God is from everlasting to everlasting. I remembered Von Balthasar's "drama of discipleship" observations.

This morning, as this last stream of thought came, the murky river of human troubles became the white-water rapids of disciple-ship, and finally flowed into the beautiful, crystal clear and calming brook called the Church, flowing from the fount of the Covenants

of God through the mount called Calvary into the world and moving to the river that runs through the city of God.

From everlasting to everlasting Thou art God. The finite finds
meaning in the Infinite.

21

WE LOANED YOU THEIR MINDS—NOW YOU ARE REQUIRING THEIR SOULS?

*Pedagogical and Spiritual Crimes
on the American University Campus*

"Where is the wisdom we have lost in knowledge? Where is the knowledge we have lost in information?"

Dr. Michael M. Jordan, Prof. and chair of English at Hillsdale College, recently wrote that "The Bible is the wellspring of Western literature, art, and science. To ignore this great book in our studies is a pedagogical crime, and active spiritual and cultural suicide."[238]

Yet for most public and private universities in the West, Jordan's pedagogical crime and cultural suicide became part of the core curriculum years ago. The result is that in a effort to coddle secularists in the faculty lounge and in the state houses, not to mention the Federal Loan Program, centers of higher education became four-year, white collar trade schools. Curriculum changes that ousted the Bible and the Great Books became all the rage. Without the Bible and the Great Books which flowed from them—enriching not only literature, but also all the arts and sciences, and in short,

---

238 Michael M. Jordan, "Great Books, Higher Education, and the Logos," *Modern Age: A Quarterly Review* 53, no. 1 & 2 (2011).

all that it means to pursue a Western Civilization education—the pedagogical crime was committed. As usual, the proverbial frog in the boiling kettle was executed slowly and never knew his fate. So it is with the forfeiture of genuine learning and true freedom that follows it on so many of our campuses.

Never mind that it is impossible to read Augustine, Chaucer, Erasmus, Donne, Milton, Mark Twain, John Steinbeck, Faulkner, and Robert Penn Warren unless one has an understanding of the Bible. It was Warren himself who once told other writers, "All models, budding or otherwise, should read and mark their Shakespeare, also their Bible. These are the two greatest founts for writers."

The rejection of Shakespeare, not to even mention the outright attack on the Bible, is now a *fait accompli*. One would think that this accomplishment would be enough for liberal educators. Except for a notable few (one thinks of Grove City College, Hillsdale College, St. John's College among the several prominent Great Books schools), who "cling to their Shakespeare and Bibles"(and are actually educating students), a vast number of our universities and colleges have long ago traded "Intro to Old Testament" for "Survey of 19th-Century Gender Studies." Alas, the "crime" has been codified, and the "criminals" have Ph.Ds.

Now there is a new crime afoot: it is called "denying religious freedom" to voluntary Christian organizations on campuses (who, by the way, offer students the older, classical study in Scripture which allows them to actually read university texts with understanding). In a matter of weeks, reports of threats from SUNY at Buffalo and Vanderbilt University to require student-led Christia n campus ministries to adhere to the universities' broad, pluralistic mandate (opening the way for atheists, agnostics, homosexuals, drug users, and a host of other practices and their unrepentant practitioners that the Bible condemns to lead a Christian ministry they do not even believe in) or face being kicked off the campus. So much for the concept of the University as a place of free expression of ideas. This latest trend has moved from cultural suicide to religious homicide by the searching out and effective termination of groups like Intervarsity Fellowship, Campus Crusade for Christ, and Reformed University Fellowship, to name only a few.

Years ago William Butler Yeats described what would happen if intellectual–spiritual–cultural cohesion were dissolved. In his "The Second Coming" (1919) Yeats described the consequences which we are seeing now: "Things fall apart; the center cannot hold; / Mere anarchy is loosed upon the world." T. S. Eliot in his "The Rock" (1934) also described the educational system we have found ourselves in now: "All our ignorance brings us near to death, but nearness to death no nearer to God. Where is the wisdom we have lost in knowledge? Where is the knowledge we have lost in information?"

The answer to Eliot's poignant question is now our disorder. The gradual but deliberate loss of religious freedom on our campuses is becoming clear: eschew the Bible; therefore, trash the "code" (the Scriptures) which allows our youth to read with understanding (not to mention live with wisdom); and then banish the last vestige of faith by using open-mindedness as a cloak for the intellectual crime. This is the appalling answer that Eliot could not even conceive.

Cunning. And chilling. But here is the thing: we are now cutting ourselves off from the classical education which gave rise to reason and virtue; virtues like freedom. Maybe an army of donors and alumni withholding their financial gifts will send a message: "Leave the Christian ministries alone! Without them we will have no place for our children to hide from the liberal assault on true education we wish your $45,000 annual tuition would provide! We loaned you their minds, but are you now requiring their souls?"

22

STATISM, FRANKENSTEIN'S MONSTER, AND THE ROAD TO SERFDOM

A Biblical–Theological Reflection on the
Supreme Court Decision on the Healthcare Law

I deas have consequences—and unintended consequences.

Dr. Gerard Casey, of the University College, Dublin (Ireland) recently wrote, "Religion and politics have long been intertwined, but in an age of growing government authority, the connection between religion and the state is particularly important to consider."[239]

This is, in my pastoral opinion, an incredible understatement.

The Supreme Court decision regarding the constitutionality of the Affordable Healthcare Acts ("Obama Care") is one such case. Its merits, deficiencies, nuances and implications will be debated between legal scholars for decades and, no doubt, between the political parties for months, and between news pundits of all ideological stripes for, possibly, hours, maybe even days. Yet, the deeper realities that have touched our lives, crafted our national consciousness and, at the risk of melodrama, sculpted the "very soul of our nation"

---

239 Gerard Casey, "Religion, the Market, and the State," in T. Woods, *Back on the Road to Serfdom: The Resurgence of Statism* (ISI Books, 2010).157.

for centuries, often remain undetected. Mary Shelly's *Frankenstein* (1818)[240] may be helpful at this point. Her classic novel was not just a great Universal classic horror movie, but a profound early 19th century statement on unintended consequences in ethics in a changing world. As a pastor, I want to help people consider the "monsters" in their decisions. I have seen many saddened souls living, barely existing, with those unintended consequences from bad decisions: decisions that led to unintended consequences like tearful battles in family court to rebellious adolescents to alcoholism and even suicide. "Frankenstein's monster," or the unintended consequences, are not all traced to a singular bad decision. More often the monsters arise, as in Shelly's classic, from a series of bad ideas that lead to the inevitable, horrendous checkmate; and the unleashing of the Creature.

I have no credentials beyond that of an armchair-quarterback-concerned-citizen to analyze the Obama Care SCOTUS decision. But I do want to offer a pastoral–theological reflection on what I see as a precipitating event in a series of bad moves that can lead to being stalked by an unnatural, Godless and uncontrollable beast that we appear to be creating. Again, my interest is the monster: unintended consequences. I believe that our "Frankenstein's Monster" is *Statism*: a perpetual philosophical lie that redemption comes from a centralized political collective that will lead us to a Utopia we inherently desire. The desire for a better place is not wrong. It is, as I say, inherent. It is a familiar longing in all of us. The choice of a redemption to get you there can destroy you or save you. That choice of the road to redemption is called "worldview."

---

240 Shelley, Mary. *Frankenstein, or The Modern Prometheus* (New York: Oxford UP, 1994).

Statism is a worldview.[241] It is a very bad and dangerous worldview that grips much of the world today and promises to feed that inherent human desire for a better place, that *Utopia*, if you will, with a Faustian devil's deal if ever there was one.

Statism denies the biblical worldview of Creation–Fall–Redemption.[242] Here is a bite-size review of the worldview that has been the glue, sometimes unseen, often forgotten, that has held Western Civilization together. The Bible teaches that God created the world. Man disobeyed and fell into sin, and is in bondage to that sin, and the world itself is fallen with it, all needing redemption. Redemption comes from God, and Christianity, my own faith, and the faith that we teach at our seminary, the faith that is enshrined in the very architecture of the nation's capitol as well as embedded in our foundering documents and proclaimed by so many of our founders themselves, comes through Jesus Christ and through the truths of His Word, the Bible. Jesus Christ claimed that to know Him is to know Freedom ("You shall know the Truth and the Truth shall set you free," and "I am the Way, the Truth, and the Life"). He is then, according to His testimony, the way to the place we instinctively desire to go. There is no *Utopia*, but there is a Kingdom of love that is here, available to all who receive it, and is also a kingdom on its way in the form of a new heaven and a new earth. That faith, explicitly stated in Christian doctrine, is taught in similar ways as the writings of the Hebrew Old Testament prophets, whether Moses or Malachi, were taught. *Statism*, as Austrian economist F. A. Hayek pleaded in his landmark title, *The Road to Serfdom* (1944), is the

---

241 See F. A. Schaeffer, *A Christian Manifesto* (Crossway, 2005). 114.

242 See, for instance, P. S. Heslam and A. Kuyper, *Creating a Christian Worldview: Abraham Kuyper's Lectures on Calvinism* (W.B. Eerdmans, 1998); J. W. Sire, *The Universe Next Door: A Basic Worldview Catalog* (Inter-Varsity Press, 2009).

antithesis of the worldview of Christianity. As he begins his chapter on "The Great Utopia," he exposes the rotten-core worldview of Statism: "What has always made the state a hell on earth has been precisely that man has tried to make it his heaven."[243]

Having left his native country in 1931, which eventually collapsed itself under the monster of Statism and eventually handed itself over to the shackles of totalitarianism and National Socialism, he became a professor at the London School of Economics. He believed that European people were making a deal with the devil by accepting the State's offer of promising a trade of personal liberty would lead to a collective security. He argued that Britain, as early as 1944, was in danger of a selfsame Statism that could lead to devastating consequences. His arguments were, at length, exported to America as he immigrated here to teach at the University of Chicago. Though "he being dead yet speaketh."[244] Hayek's call to be wary of the "outsourcing" of personal security and responsibility for State control and planning of our lives is the bedrock issue we are facing today as a people. I say again, as a minister and theologian, I am most concerned that the recent issues in healthcare and national debt and growing entitlements are lifting the curtain to reveal a mad scientist at work creating a monster that will not be silenced but by many sorrows. The voices of Shelly and Hayek are important, but they are yet lesser voices of warning echoing a greater voice to every man, woman and child:

---

243   F. A. Hayek, *The Road to Serfdom: Text and Documents*, edited by Bruce Caldwell (Chicago: The University of Chicago Press, 2007 edition of the 1944 original), 76. Hayek began this chapter with the quotation cited by German poet, Johann C. Hölderlin.

244   The Epistle to the Hebrews 11:4. Authorized Version (AV).

Stand fast therefore in the liberty with which Christ has made us free, and be not entangled again with the yoke of bondage. (Galatians 5:1 AV)

Independence Day[245] is a good time to remember that America was founded by those whose worldview exposed the lie of Statism and chose freedom and then were willing to pay the price to keep it. Their selfless sacrifice for that liberty brought about consequences that have been a blessing unto this day. Such is the tradition of the Magna Carta and English Law. Such is the tradition of Western Civilization. Such is the aspiration of the human heart wherever and however a people are gathered into community—North, South, East, or West. We all desire that essential liberty granted to us by God.

It is never too late to reclaim that liberty again.

---

245 This essay was originally released for July 4, 2012, in the U.S.A.

23

THOUGHTS ON 'THE RISE AND FALL...' IN NEW ENGLAND

And Why I Am Still Optimistic

I write this as I sit at Groton Long Point, our tenth-year anniversary since discovering this wonderful jewel in New England. Through the auspices of a kind benefactor, our family has been able to retreat from pastoral ministry to renew physical and spiritual energies but also to think. When sitting on the porch of "A House by the Sea," a most suitable name for this lovely cottage, one may, indeed, think and think widely and, as the cool Atlantic breeze comforts your skin, think deeply, or maybe—others will have their own opinion—deeper.

Today I am to be thinking about a paper that I am going to deliver to the Evangelical Theological Society in San Francisco in November, but I cannot stop thinking about a book I saw today, and the notions that owned me as I looked upon it. You see, we had made our usual excursion to the Book Barn,[246] in Niantic, Connecticut—as splendid a bookshop as I have ever experienced—and my eyes fixed on the title of a volume that I have in my own library, *The*

---

246 It is worth the effort to go there if you are anywhere near New Haven. You will never go to a more interesting bookstore in your life! http://www.bookbarnniantic.com/

Rise And Fall of the British Empire.[247] This book, playing off of the title of Edward Gibbon's masterpiece, *The Rise And Fall of the Roman Empire,*[248] reminded me of the characteristics of old empires that arose and great nations that fell (which reminded my why I must acquire *Vanished Kingdoms* by Norman Davies). In this "Arab Spring" we can't help but think of Libya and Egypt and the sand storm of change eroding the power in despotic capitols of the Middle East that once, only months ago, seemed invincible. We can all think of those sad features of an empire that has fallen: there is a surge in irresponsible spending and the consequent beaurocratical growth and unsatiable hunt for more revenue to sustain the status quo; extraordinary use of military force to conserve gains or to protect against increased threats (so often, the threats may be attributed to the fact that enemies perceive a pathological weakness in the great country) and, at the same time, there are often budget cuts to the military that endanger the nation's capacity to safeguard the *Pax Romana* (27 B.C.–A.D. 180)[249] *or Pax Britannica* (1815–1914)— or, maybe, *Pax Americana*—in an unforgivingly hazardous world. One also is reminded of that one, invariable common characteristic in the fall of all of the great civilizations: an internal free fall into

---

247   Lawrence James, *The Rise and Fall of the British Empire*, 1st U.S. ed. (New York: St. Martin's Press, 1996).

248   Edward Gibbon, *The Rise and Fall of the Saracen Empire*. [Being a Reprint of the 50th, 51st, and 52nd Chapters of *The Decline and Fall of the Roman Empire*. Edited by A. Murray.] [Another edition. 1873]

249   Pax Romana. (2011). In *Encyclopædia Britannica*. Retrieved from http://www.britannica.com/EBchecked/topic/447447/Pax-Romana (accessed August 26, 2011).

moral depravity, however that depravity may be manifest.[250] But a preacher is always held to suspicion in tackling that one, so I will leave it for historians to decide. But can you tell me of anyone who talks of a moral strengthening at the very time of an empire's fall? One may argue about the details of each of these characteristics and even add many more reasons for a fuller discussion, but the larger matter is undeniable.

This is when I sat down on an old sofa between shelves. I was sobered by the notion that I could be living in such a time. I had to admit that wherever we are on the continuum of history, in our nation, few see us on the "rise" side of that equation. It was not necessary for me to chronicle the distastrous consequences of our nation when we have exchanged our godly heritage for a pot of secular stew. That was not the sense that began to simmer. History will show whether or not this is the last great chapter. "But of that day and hour knoweth no *man*..."[251] So I immediately began to think of what I pray will be the difference between where we are and where we can be in the days to come. I, for one, would prefer Ronald Reagan's intuitive optimism that appeals to our better angels, and that contagious national spirit that persistently pronounces that our best days are yet to come. That would be my response in the face of such overwhelmingly depressing shelves of "rise and falls!" And my gloomy spirits began to evaporate past the dusty shelves and up to the ceiling of that book barn. Yet if, I

---

250   It is admitted that the morality of Rome and Britain are strikingly dissimilar in their manifestations, but the impiety of sexual peversion in the one and what some may pinpoint as imperialistic irreverence for the subjects of the Empire of the other are both based in a moral failure in some way. For an examination of the factors leading to national decline, see Norman Davies, *Vanished Kingdoms: The Rise and Fall of States and Nations* (New York: Viking, 2012).

251   Matthew 24:36, King James Version.

thought, this optimism is to be justified by reality—and I believe it shall—then something *must* happen. The "something" that must happen is what happened a decade or so before the American Declaration of Independence and the founding of our nation. There was, indeed, in those days, in the colonies, the presence of all of those three features that I mentioned of the decline of a civilization. There were increasing and often needless skirmishes with local Indians. There was, of course, the notorious problem with taxes from the mother country, and historical evidences of an increasingly profligate lifestyle among the colonists. Adding to all of this, there was a formality that was settling into religion. Taken together, these spreading cracks in the young society led to a combustible state. This was a great fork in the road for the young American civilization. One could imagine what would've happened to the idea of the American experiment had these deplorable situations not been addressed and resolved. In fact, however, mercifully, they were dealt with. The First Great Awakening of the 1730s and 40s must be considered a turning point in American history; the turning point that not only dealt with the problems of the society at that era, but also those activities that actually prepared a nation to be born in the decades that followed. I will grant the position, first of all, of those among us who believe that this "awakening" was merely a religious excitement; some stirring of human religious sensitivities linked, perhaps, to unshakable Puritan strands of their forefathers, with all of the Calvinistic guilt which some attribute to that ever-present thread in our fabric as a people; or for that matter, the impressive rhetorical gifts and skills of a remarkable cadre of preachers. I will grant you that position, even if I do not believe it. I do so because I believe that you can point to even those things and still see that *something* happened of enormous historical consequence that changed the course of human affairs for the better.

That I believe that the First Great Awakening was a true movement of Almighty God in the lives of the colonists, and that my belief characterized as my own unconscious attempts at making sense of a mad world, cannot repudiate the historical certainty of it, or disregard an amazingly uncommon connection between this mass spiritual awakening and the American Revolutionary war and the founding of the nation that followed. For, as the great British historian, Dr. Paul Johnson, reminded us in his *History of the American People*,[252] America is a preiminent nation in the history of nations whereby one may observe, document, and point to the influences that led to her establishment. The Great Awakening, under the glorious preaching of the Rev. Jonathan Edwards at Northhampton, Massachusetts, and the Rev. George Whitefield of England, remain an irrefutable factor in the series of factors that led to the establishment of the United States of America. Therefore, granting even the most skeptical analysis of the higher history and lower history of this period, one cannot escape the facts: there were problems in society, there was a religious awakening in society which positively impacted those problems, and there was a new nation born in the years after these remarkable events. As has been stated so

---

252 Paul Johnson, *A History of the American People*, 1st U.S. ed. (New York: HarperCollins Publishers, 1997).

succinctly, "Thus, the Great Awakening brought about a climate which made the American Revolution possible."[253, 254]

Now to my point—a remarkably simple point to state, but an entirely supernatural point to bring about: *if it happened before, it can happen again.* To be explicitly Christian about the matter, if the sovereign God of redemptive history did it before, our God can do it again. Even if what we are talking about is the Puritanical–Calvinistic religious remnants at work in our national conscience, like

---

253   Roger Shultz, "A Celebration of Infidels: The American Enlightenment in the Revolutionary Era," *Contra Mundum Fall*, no. 1 (1991).

254   Shultz, note 10: "For the influence of the Great Awakening, particularly on the Revolution, see Alan Heimert, *Religion and the American Mind From the Great Awakening to the Revolution*" (Cambridge: Harvard, 1966). See also Robert Bushman, *From Puritan to Yankee* (Cambridge: Harvard, 1967); Ruth Bloch, "Visionary Republic." See also Jonathan Edwards, *Some Thoughts Concerning the Present Revival of Religion in New-England and the Way in Which It Ought to Be Acknowledged and Promoted, Humbly Offered to the Publick, in a Treatise on That Subject. In Five Parts; Part I. Shewing That the Work That Has of Late Been Going on in This Land, Is a Glorious Work of God. Part II. Shewing the Obligations That All Are under, to Acknowlege [sic], Rejoice in and Promote This Work, and the Great Danger of the Contrary. Part III. Shewing in Many Instances, Wherein the Subjects, or Zealous Promoters, of This Work Have Been Injuriously Blamed. Part IV. Shewing What Things Are to Be Corrected or Avoided, in Promoting This Work, or in Our Behaviour under It. Part V. Shewing Positively What Ought to Be Done to Promote This Work.* By Jonathan Edwards, A.M. Pastor of the Church of Christ at Northampton. [Two Lines from Isaiah] (Boston: printed and sold by S. Kneeland and T. Green,, 1742). http://galenet.galegroup.com/servlet/ECCO?c=1&stp=Author&ste=11&af=BN&ae=W029462&tiPG=1&dd=0&dc=flc&docNum=CW118695958&vrsn=1.0&srchtp=a&d4=0.33&n=10&SU=0LRF&locID=29002; Joseph Tracy, *The Great Awakening: A History of the Revival of Religion in the Time of Edwards and Whitefield* (Boston: Tappan & Dennet, 1842). Cedric B. Cowing, *The Great Awakening and the American Revolution: Colonial Thought in the 18th Century*, The Rand Mcnally Series on the History of American Thought and Culture. (Chicago: Rand McNally, 1971)

some inexplicable but undeniable, even unwanted, hormone, then I would say, "Give me the injection!"

The situation we face may be compared to the mighty Mississippi River, making its way past Memphis and Baton Rouge, on down to its mouth below New Orleans. The U.S. Army Corp of Engineers does its best to build levees to contain the natural desire of "Old Man River" to wind westward, but inevitably there are breaks in the levee. No matter how powerful and ingenious we may be, we cannot stop, ultimately, the terrestrial powers all around us. So, too, there are powers beyond the earthworks of our own strength and cleverness that can reroute the mighty Mississippi River-like flow of the history of time. This "Old Man River" of a civilization inclines downward. The law of aging, rundown and entropy is unrelenting on our best and most ingenious claims to the future. Those who attribute natural causes to the Great Awakening will not be comforted by such nature as they look into the future. They see an inevitable demise of our nation. And if all I had to go on were the flow of history, the cause and effect of man and sin and time and nature, then, I, too, would be, of all men, most skeptical. But I am not.[255]

Ceslaw Milosz was an atheist turned Christian. The great Polish poet who witnessed the unimaginable horrors of the twentieth century finally reconciled with the God of his childhood. He began to see, with the eyes, albeit grey eyes, of a believing poet, that there was hope. From the cold, colorless Socialist regimes of his homeland, like the junk-yard-high-rise-Proletariat apartment buildings that grew like poison weeds after the devestation of the War; a man

---

255   Even the end of this world is not for me the end, but the turning of a page to a new heaven and a new earth. Even if I see a collapse of our society on the horizon, I see yet a greater and infinitely better future just beyond it.

began to dream again. Once, as was expressed in *First Things* in a wonderful piece about this man, Milosz was in his Roman Catholic parish in Berkeley, California, when he came face to face with the reality of hope in Christ. In his poem, "With Her,"[256] the old poet, then in California, heard the reading of the Gospel of Mark in his home parish, and the Gospel power of that reading, about Jesus raising a little girl to life, became the hope he needed so far removed from his home. We listen as he writes: "A reading from the Gospel according to Mark/About a little girl to whom He said: '*Talitha, cumi!*'"[257] "Then," states the article, "with an unselfconscious humility, the poet witnesses to how he has received these words. He writes, 'This is for me. To make me rise from the dead/And repeat the hope of those who lived before me.' Here Milosz is exactly a Christian—the Scriptural word is received as a word for him in that moment, together with all those who have believed before him."[258]

I like the way Diogenes Allen put it, "Jesus' resurrection has changed everything."[259]

To read of the life of Reagan is to understand that this simple truth, learned in Tampico, Illinois, in the Christian Church there, was the ground of Reagan's optimism.[260] It should be the reason for

256 Czeslaw Milosz, *New and Collected Poems 1931–2001* (New York: Ecco, 2001).

257 George B. Perkins and Barbara Perkins, *The American Tradition in Literature*, 11th ed., 2 vols. (Boston: McGraw-Hill, 2005).

258 O. S. B. Jeremy Driscoll, "The Witness of Czeslaw Milosz," *First Things* (2004). http://www.firstthings.com/article/2007/01/the-witness-of-czeslaw-milosz—25 (accessed August 29, 2011).

259 Diogenes Allen, *Theology for a Troubled Believer: An Introduction to the Christian Faith*, 1st ed. (Louisville, Ky.: Westminster John Knox Press, 2010).

260 See, for example, Paul Kengor, *God and Ronald Reagan: A Spiritual Life*, 1st ed. (New York: Regan Books, 2004).

ours. This, then, is the ground of our hope for an American renewal. This is the reason that each of us should be driven to our knees in prayer, in repentance for our follies, our ingratitude for such bountiful blessings, and in pleading for another Great Awakening.

I rose, with some struggle, from the dilapidated, old cushion, in between the narrow shelves holding multiple volumes of used *Rise and Fall of the Third Reich* and some other books on warfare, and made my way to the Book Barn's door, which opened to a fine view of a thriving garden.

24

INTENDED CONSEQUENCES

Dispensing Plan B Pills to Abort Plan A

N ew York City Department of Education is now in the contraception business. But who really is surprised?

The "Plan B" "CATCH Plan" pill can now be administered to students of any age or grade without any parental involvement. This should not be shocking to anyone. The NYC school district already dispenses several other birth control pharmaceuticals as well as condoms. The Department of Education has, for some years now, required classes on proper placement and wear of the contraceptive devices. Yet 7,000 school girls were with child last year. The *New York Post* reported that 64% of those received The abortions. Is abortion supposed to relieve our concerns? That is a success story according to some. At least children weren't born. The Mayor of New York City, Michael Bloomberg, reminded us, at his press conference on this initiative, that having children at a young age is a difficult situation for all.

Thank you Mr. Mayor. I am sure that Plan B will not make things better.

The practice is objectionable from a medical perspective according to Dr. Manny Alvarez, Chairman of the Department of Obstetrics and Gynecology and Reproductive Science at Hackensack University Medical Center in NJ, and a host of other physicians. In fact, Dr. Alvarez says that such medications are "life threatening."

Alvarez does not believe that this will stop the greater issue of pre-marital sexual relations but would accelerate it, leading to the further spread of venereal disease. Yet, somehow, one gets the distinct impression that making moral stances on human sexuality, even among children, is hardly on the minds of the Mayor or the NYC Department of Education.

It is on my mind—and my heart.

The radical, moral anarchy that has lurked in the hearts of men since the fall was given license in pseudo-intellectual circles of the early twentieth century by the likes of Margaret Sanger, the mother of Planned Parenthood ("motherhood" being an admittedly ironic and cruel metaphor for this malicious woman and her menacing creation). Her influence was coupled with Marxist–Socialist movements in the 1960s and birthed far-reaching ethical and social changes that we have yet to recover from. That which was forbidden was soon, however, codified by the United States Supreme Court in *Roe v. Wade*. Warnings made by those like President Ronald Reagan in his book, *Abortion and the Conscience of a Nation* (1984), about the national consequences of such immorality (immoral not only on the standards of both the Bible and the Western Civilization that was erected through the Old and New Testaments, but creation itself), should be renewed. Life is holy. Sexuality is the spark of life and human bonding that is intended by the Almighty, supported by His creation, for those in a consecrated God-ordained covenant of marriage (between one man and one woman). Respect for human life is a supreme act of reverence for life's Creator. Such respect will produce respect for the act of marriage. And such respect will produce modesty in women and nobility in men and appropriate restraint; modesty and nobility being the very essence of a civilized people. Yet immorality has bred immodesty and disrespect for God, His gift of marriage and sexuality, and thus, humanity itself.

Can it be reversed? I cannot fathom how wide-sweeping transformation of this nation's moral condition can come about short of spiritual revival. Yet the nation has known the undeserved blessing of God before. Perhaps we have our Pilgrim forefathers and mothers for that. Their covenant with God and the prayers of devout people may be our only hope for getting out of this "Plan B" nation we are living in now. We have never been this far along the downward spiral of sin and shame, but as a believer in Jesus Christ I retain hope. As a pastor, I must decry this recent decision of a major school district, sure to spread to other parts of the nation, as the height of ungodliness which will, undoubtedly, produce infinitely more harm than good. The action is indicative of a confused people. As I pray to God to have mercy and send revival, I plead with right minded people to condemn this sordid mess and call it what it is: a misguided, immoral attempt to stop the cycle of sin and shame that they cannot even understand. For the sake of common sense and self survival as a people, if you will not speak for the sake of God, New York parents must take back, not their schools, but their children! They are yours, my friends, not the Mayor's or the School Board's.

Yes, we have lost our way. The sexual revolution's unintended consequence was the killing of the unborn. The unintended consequence of that is that those who survived the sinister scalpels of Planned Parenthood over the last three decades are now themselves producing children outside of marriage. They are living out the immoral choices of their parents and grandparents. The only way to fix it, say the muddle headed proponents of policies like the

NYC Department of Education, is to dispense Plan B drugs. Why? I will tell you why: Because Plan A is not an option to them. Yet Plan A remains our only true hope for redemption of this sin-sick society. And Plan A is God's Word and God's Way which leads to God's blessings.

We can have no Plan B and still have a future as a people.

SECTION FOUR

SPEAKING OUT THROUGH SERMON AND CRYING OUT IN PRAYER FOR A NATION

1

AN ELECTION DAY PRAYER

For God's Glory and the People's Good

As we approach the November national elections in the United States of America, I have written a prayer for our nation. To do so is to keep in step with our founding forefathers and mothers who treated elections as great moments of spiritual renewal and possibilities. Churches were often filled to hear "election day sermons" from clergy whose job it was to point the people to their God-given responsibilities. They encouraged their congregations to cast the ballot for those who would most nearly preserve the blessings of a God-given freedom that contributed to national morality, economic health, and protection against enemies foreign and domestic.

I have no other motivation in this prayer but that God would bestow His very blessings on the people of this nation in this, our great hour of need. I make this prayer not as a minister of the Gospel of Jesus Christ, nor as merely the servant of a great theological seminary, nor as an officer and chaplain in the United States Army Reserves, all of which I am. No, I make this prayer as one believer filled with a foreboding sense that unless God comes down and moves among us in these days, we will not escape judgment and we will not know the divine covering that we need to endure the war against us: both the real warfare that is taking our sons and daughters from without, as well as the spiritual warfare that is destroying us from within. Yet for the demonstration of God's mercy and grace in days past, I make this prayer with absolute confidence that God hears and answers. I pray with great optimism for the future, for it is surely a future in the hands of a sovereign and just God.

Let us pray.

Almighty God, our heavenly Father, who guards, protects and governs all of Creation with perfect oversight, unfathomable grace and unapproachable justice and righteousness; Thou, whose ultimate gift of protection for our lives, grace abounding for our souls, and divine justice for our sins was given through Thy Son, Jesus Christ our Lord and Savior; we come to Thee before this coming election day in our nation, the country Thou hast given unto us, even the United States of America.

We recall, O Father, how so many of our founders cried out to Thee as one people for Thy blessing and how their prayers were answered with Thy providence and favor. Yet we confess with pierced and mourning hearts our own sinful negligence and lackadaisical attitudes towards sin and Hell, holiness and Heaven, that we have not come to Thee as we ought. We remember how our forefathers and mothers covenanted together for the sake of the Gospel of Thy Son. We recall how they consecrated their lives and fortunes to Thee for the advancement of the Kingdom of Jesus Christ to the ends of the earth, and how they did not count suffering something to be avoided for the sake of all righteousness. In our memory of those men and women of God, our fathers and mothers in the faith, and given that these, our spiritual forebearers prayed for us, their posterity, to keep the Gospel, and to bring that godly influence to this nation, we plead for Thy forgiveness. Forgive us of our private, personal, corporate and national sins before Thee, O Christ! Where have we to go but to Thee? What chariot or horse, what army or navy, however brave and honorable, can deliver us from our enemies, but Thee, O Father? In what economic power can we boast before the living God, who owns the cattle on a thousand hills, and who will not put up with our ingratitude forever?

Yet in Thy eternal mercy through Thy Son, Jesus Christ, be our fortress and shield, O Lord! Protect us from national catastrophes and the terror that would seek to strike at the heart of our people. Remember our weak frame, O Lord, and remember the blood and righteousness of Thy Son, O Father, and preserve this nation. Preserve us through the means that Thou hast ordained for our governance: through the power of the sword given to the armed services of this nation. Therefore, in remembering this provision, we are bound to pray for the soldiers, sailors, airmen, guardsmen, and Marines of this country that Thou hast made great before the world. We also are bound to pray for all policemen and firemen, doctors and nurses, lawmen and representatives of the court, first responders to life, health and property, and all who risk their lives for the sake of common grace and common good. Bless them, O Lord, with their families, and cause them to know the applause of heaven over such humanity that imitates Thy grace and protection, even as they would know the gratitude of a thankful nation.

O Lord, we also lift up those who serve our nation in elected offices. These are "ministers" doing Thy work and deserving our honor and obedience and our prayers. Guard the lives and bless the families of our President, Barack Obama, and of our Vice President, Joseph Biden. Keep the Speaker of the House and the leader of the Senate in Thy perfect care. Strengthen our justices and the courts of our land. Bless that noble institution for good with wisdom from on high. Guard their lives, O Father. Give them wisdom. Give them wise counselors who are under the influence of Thy Word. Strike from our government thoughts and ideas that are contrary to Thy Word and overrule our folly through whatever means is best for our elected leaders and our people.

Do bless also our people, O Christ. Help us to recall our heritage as people seeking to replicate the government we find in Thy sacred Word, that of self-governance. Remind us of how Your people, O Lord, were governed by elders and deacons elected by the people. Remind us how the people were to choose only those who cultivated and exhibited noble and holy lives in both their personal and professional undertakings, as far as one was able to do so by Thy grace. We desire such representatives, O Lord! Grant that we, the people, may exercise wisdom, discernment, and seriousness of mind as we cast our ballots for these, our representatives. Give us candidates from among the people who have the people's best interest at heart and not their own. Keep us from wolves in sheep's clothing, who would devour the people's wealth, the people's creativity, the people's independence, and the people's God-given rights to life, liberty and the pursuit of happiness through unwise and hurtful laws. Grant that in keeping away such self-serving public officials, we may be blessed with a renewed trust in the people's government and, thus, a renewed esteem for the offices of public service that, according to Thy Word, deserve to be held in great honor.

Give us an election day, this November, O Lord, in which we may rejoice in righteousness, be astounded by true humility in the lives of those who are elected, and be encouraged by the humbled hearts of those who are removed from office or denied office by the vote of the people. Bless this Election Day, O God. We in America need Thee more than ever. We have learned that we have nothing apart from Thee. We are humbled before the nations and before the throne of Heaven. Have mercy, O God. Have mercy, O God. Have mercy and send Your Spirit even in these days of national election.

Remember the covenants of our mothers and fathers, O Lord, who prayed that this nation would be used of Thee for the advancement of the Gospel. Remember their prayers and now hear the prayers of their children as we cry out before Thee for genuine revival! Thou didst send a powerful movement of Thy Holy Spirit in the Church before the days of the Revolutionary War when we were given Jonathan Edwards and George Whitefield and countless other faithful ministers and godly people. When we were at war among ourselves, during the War Between the States, both sides encountered an outpouring of Thy Spirit. So now, O

God, in this time when radical religious madmen aim to decapitate our nation, kill innocent people, and destroy a way of life that leads to peace; and when our own sin eats away at our core as an unseen but real and deadly virus, visit us, astonish us, and humble us with a magnificent display of Thy glory. Let the Church know of the power and presence of the resurrected and reigning Lord Jesus Christ. May souls be saved and lives be transformed through the faithful exposition of the Word of God by dedicated ministers called out and prepared by Thee. Bless us with a spirit of prayer, not only for ourselves, but also especially for those who do not know Thee. Make us once more a nation of missionaries, O Christ. Let us humbly learn from Thee among the nations of the global east and south who are experiencing Thy divine visitation and then join with them in the march to evangelize the world. Let us renew our commitment to the Covenant of Grace so that we may once more hate sin and love Thy law, extinguish the raging fires of sensuality in our culture, and regain that godly disposition of reverence and modesty in our relationships. Let us drink of Thy grace that we may draw from thy holiness. For the sake of the very preservation of this nation, grant us grace to know genuine nobility in our men, heavenly virtue in our women, and sweet innocence in our children.

Thus we pray, O Father, not for a party spirit but for Thy Spirit. We pray not for a victory that leads to good for some, but a victory that leads to good for all. We pray for a government that exults in what is right before Thee and unleashes the people in a creative marketplace where all to which we put our hands glorifies Thee! We pray for a victory that leads to true freedom for all men and a new sense of refreshment that will bring us to the "old paths" of faithfulness to Thee.

Lord God, our heavenly Father, will You be pleased to pour out Your blessings on America? Bless her as in days past. Bless her for the good of the Gospel and the strengthening of Thy Church. Bless her to be a blessing to the world and a model of biblical government that we may lead peaceable lives before Thee and extend that peace, through freedom and mercy and justice, to a world in need. We ask this in desperation, for we have no other Name to go to but to the Name of Jesus, our Lord and our Savior. Amen.

2

LET THE SHEPHERDS
LEAD THE WAY

Thoughts on Election Day Sermons

There is a tradition in our nation of preaching Election Day Sermons, and this American tradition is one that is based upon the teachings of Christ and should not be abandoned. Yes, we have learned that putting your trust in politics will lead to disaster. Equally disastrous would be ignoring God's clear warnings concerning the responsibilities of God's people in this world.

I want to share these thoughts especially with pastors who will stand in the pulpits of our land in these days when our people will elect their leaders.

Historian Joel Headly wrote,

These [Election] sermons were as much a part of the stately and imposing ceremonies as the election itself. The clergy were not a whit behind the ablest statesman of the day in their knowledge of the great science of human government. The publication of these sermons in a pamphlet form was a part of the regular proceedings of the assembly, and being scattered abroad over the land, clothed with the double sanction of their high authors and the endorsement of the legislature, became the text books of human rights in every parish. (As quoted from an article by Tim Ewing)

Forgetting the works of God is a very dangerous business. Impatience with God brings disaster. As our nation faces an election, those of us who preach the unsearchable riches of Jesus would do well to join in that great American Puritan and Reformed tradition of Election Day Sermons. In it we are called, as we read about in Psalm 106, to recall the mighty deeds of the Lord and declare His praise (v. 2) from the pulpit. If we who are shepherds do not guide our flock to remember God in the founding of this nation and in the covenant our forefathers made with God for this land, then our grandchildren's children will rise up and say of our generation, "But they soon forgot His works; they did not wait for His counsel"(v. 13).

Yes, and it will be said of us, He gave them what they asked (v. 15). Shepherds guide. Shepherds lead. Shepherds point out the way. In Psalm 106 shepherds recall, before the people, how God saved them for His name's sake, that He might make known His mighty power (v. 8). Why do we not recall John Winthrop on the Arbella recounting his City on a Hill sermon (1630)?

Why do we not recall that first winter and the provision of God to our forefathers? Or should we not point out the sins of our fathers that led them to wander from God's way? They in turn received "what they asked" and were led into a "wasting disease" as when our forefathers abandoned the system of every man working to feed his own family, rather than working for a collective. Yet this happened and this failed! This short-lived experiment in socialism failed and the people almost starved. Today people play with the ideas of wealth redistribution and deny the biblical injunctions that a man ought to work to eat.

Freedom, the essential character of man, is done away with as we surrender our own good ambitions to feed an inhuman governmental structure. Our forefathers learned from their sins. A government by the people and for the people was formed. This is not meddling in things outside of the church, my Beloved, it is preaching the truth to a generation who has forgotten. Shall we dare gloss over the matter of character in those whom we elect to govern us?

Were the saints in Acts 6 told by the holy apostles to pick out from among you seven men of good repute (Acts 6:3)? In this very passage, Acts 6:3 and the matter of picking our leaders, we find the biblical injunction of not only representation (which we must cherish as a God-given right that governments have taken from the people when the people have abrogated that right of electing their own leaders), but also responsibility in choosing those who will lead us!

Quite clearly we find the biblical view that our leaders should be men of godly character. "But," I hear someone saying, "Paul is talking about the church! This is not about civic leaders." Do you think, then, that in our relationship with God as a people that we should elect ungodly leaders? The Word of God in Proverbs 29 tells us, "When the righteous increase, the people rejoice, but when the wicked rule, the people groan." (Proverbs 29:2) "If a king faithfully judges the poor, his throne will be established forever. When the wicked increase, transgression increases." (Proverbs 29:14, 16)

Did not Israel suffer under Saul's oppressive rule? Did not the very kingdom of David, under whose governance Israel enjoyed her golden years all the way through his son Solomon (who prayed for wisdom and did receive it, though he sinned in many ways), split in two when Rehoboam disdained godly counsel to become a "servant" to the people (1 Kings 12:6–7)? Instead of listening to this from the "old men" (v. 8)...the king gathered his cronies around him who told him to lay a heavy yoke on the people (vv. 10–11). Over and over again, we see the outcome of ungodly leadership.

Yes, in answer to a popular rhetorical question that arose a few years ago, character does matter!

It matters whether a man supports laws that promote abortion. Concerning the questions before us in this election, it does matter where we go to church, who we associate with, what our marriage is like, how we have reared our children, who we gather around us as advisors, and how we listen to those advisors. All of these things and more should be laid out before our people. We must guide the precious flock of Christ, and we must speak as prophets to the nation, not just in how to rear their children and how to get along with their wives, but also how to come into the voting booth.

Or we will, as shepherds, in the name of supposed "separation of church and state" halt on the matter of preaching this part of the whole counsel of God. God forbid! For what is at stake, not only now in this presidential election, but in every election? What is at stake, among other things, is our faithfulness to the covenant that our fathers made with God that this nation should be a light, a Gospel light, to the world. What is at stake is also the ability of the Church to go forward with the Gospel without the unwanted element of governmental intrusion into the Church, or, in the last and most heinous case, martyrdom.

> "But don't we fare better when the Church is up against the wall? Isn't it true that the blood of the martyrs is the seed of the Church?" Yes on both counts. But that is not what you really want for your children, is it? Indeed, we are told to pray for a peaceful government "that we may lead a peaceful and quiet life, godly and dignified in every way. This is good, and it is pleasing in the sight of God our Savior, who desires all people to be saved and to come to the knowledge of the truth. (1 Timothy 2:2, 3)

This is our calling, dear pastors! This is our calling, seminarians. This is our calling, lay leaders, elders, and vestrymen. Our calling is, contrary to the ideas of some who prefer peace over truth, to advise the flock on the biblical injunctions concerning our responsibilities in self-government. But after we have done all, and the lot is cast, the matter is in the hands of the Lord. We pray for our president no matter his party or our choices.

That is another biblical injunction, to pray for all people, for kings and all who are in high positions (1 Timothy 2:1, 2) because these leaders are "God's servant for [our] good." (Romans 13:4) Indeed we must be subject to the governing authorities, for there is no authority except from God, and those that exist have been instituted by God. (Romans 13:1) Then, on November 5th, however the lot was cast, God will be on the throne. The Gospel mandate of the Church will not depend on this man or that man in Washington, but on the sovereign Lord who is building His kingdom and will not be stopped until the kingdom of this world has become the kingdom of our Lord and of His Christ. (Revelation 11:15)

Thus, as we do what we are called to do, in our relationship with God and with man, in worshipping Him on the Lord's Day in the sanctuary, as well as serving Him on election day in the voting booth, Christ Jesus reigns forever and ever.

> Thou Great I AM, Fill my mind with elevation and grandeur at the thought of a Being with whom one day is as a thousand years, and a thousand years as one day,
>
> Let me live a life of dependence on Thyself, mortification, crucifixion, prayer.
>
> Almighty God, who, amidst the lapse of worlds, and the revolutions of empires, feels no variableness, but is glorious in immortality.

Turn my heart from vanity, from dissatisfactions, from uncertainties of the present state, to an eternal interest in Christ.

Give me a holy avarice to redeem the time, as I pray for all of our candidates and their families, study the issues, the character, the principles of Your Word and the principles that they embrace, and exercise the gift of self-government as a gift from Thee.

Then let me do my duty and leave the matter to Thee.[261]

---

261   A prayer based on and adapted to this message from the *Valley of Vision* "The Infinite and the Finite" [pp. 190–191].

3

JACKALS AMONG RUINS

A Charge to the Seminary
Community of Reformed Theological Seminary

INTRODUCTION TO THE READING

There is a quiet killer roaming our land. In our day, many ministers of the Gospel, and many Christians in general, have fallen. Mostly they fall from sexual sin. Some fall from love of money. But a tragically innumerable sum of them will fall from the quiet killer of ministry. What is it? *We turn to the inerrant and infallible Word of the living God for our answer.*

Scripture Reading
Ezekiel 13:1–4

The word of the LORD came to me: Ezekiel 13. "Son of man, prophesy against the prophets of Israel, who are prophesying, and say to those who prophesy from their own hearts: 'Hear the word of the LORD!'" Thus says the Lord GOD, Woe to the foolish prophets who follow their own spirit, and have seen nothing! Your prophets have been like jackals among ruins, O Israel.

1 Timothy 4:6–16

If you put these things before the brothers, you will be a good servant of Christ Jesus, being trained in the words of the faith and of the good doctrine that you have followed. Have nothing to do with irreverent, silly myths. Rather train yourself for godliness; for while bodily training is of some value, godliness is of value in every way, as it holds promise for the present life and also for the life to come. The saying is trustworthy and deserving of full acceptance. For to this end we toil and strive because we have our hope set on the living God, who is the Savior of all people, especially of those who believe.

Command and teach these things. Let no one despise you for your youth, but set the believers an example in speech, in conduct, in love, in faith, in purity. Until I come, devote yourself to the public reading of Scripture, to exhortation, to teaching. Do not neglect the gift you have, which was given you by prophecy when the council of elders laid their hands on you. Practice these things, devote yourself to them, so that all may see your progress. Keep a close watch on yourself and on the teaching. Persist in this, for by so doing you will save both yourself and your hearers.

> The grass withers, and the flower falls, but the word of the Lord remains forever. (1 Peter 1:24–25 ESV)

On this Convocation Day, I want to bring a message of warning and a message of hope for our seminary community, which I am entitling "Jackals Among Ruins." First, let us pray:

> Spirit of the Living God, illumine Thy Word before the eyes of our spirits, that seeing You by faith, we may believe, and believing, we may follow. Through Christ our Lord. Amen.

INTRODUCTION TO THE SERMON

The quiet killer of the prophets of old who were judged by God was, according to Ezekiel, their choice of curriculum. They taught what was in their own spirit. Thus the people were being fed ideas and being given images that were formed not from the mind of God but from that place that Calvin called the factory of idols, the mind of man without God. Thus they were, according to Ezekiel, jackals among ruins. These were the figures of dog-like creatures, alone, separated from the blessing of God and His Word, and laughing and barking and foaming at the mouth over the carcass of a king-dom which was no more. Like savage beasts, they ripped the last vestiges of men's souls from them through teaching that came not from heaven but from earth. This is a devastating image of the false prophets. Thus Calvin would write of this episode in Israel's history, referring to the jackals also as foxes: "But when the Israel-ites were wandering exiles, and attention to the law no longer flourished among them, it came to pass that foxes, meaning their false prophets, easily entered."

One can only imagine Ezekiel, who began his book by declaring that it was "the thirtieth year," no doubt referring to the year that he would have begun service as a priest, feeling the pain of all of this. How much better it would be if the people were being fed the Word of God, worshipping in the familiar courts of the Temple of God. But it was also the "fifth year of the exile of King Jehoiachin" who was taken by Nebuchadnezzar's unstoppable forces in 597 B.C. (2 Kings 24:8–12). Thus, Ezekiel, instead of serving God in the temple at the time of his ordination, instead of serving God's proposes in the place where God's presence was solemnly commemorated, sat with the other prisoners in exile, along an irrigation canal southeast of Babylon called the Chebar, far from the city called holy. But as he would learn, he was not far from God. For God came to Him in a whirlwind. And God ordained him to be a prophet to the rebellious people of Israel. But this holy man of God had a "Word from Another World," as Robert L. Reymond has termed a phrase. And he spoke that Word, not his Word but God's, not only to the rebellious people-at-large, but specifically, here, to the beastly preachers of Israel. They had forfeited their ministries by preaching what they wanted, what arose from their own spirits, their hobby horses, their causes, not God's.

And so, too, St. Paul, in his epistle to Pastor Timothy, who was to carry on the church planting and church revitalization work at Ephesus, warned against the preachers who would "depart from the faith." And in doing so, the Great Apostle warned Timothy to having nothing to do with "irreverent, silly myths." What were these? They were surely the Judaizing myths of a rabbinic religion that had nothing to do with the faith of Abraham, Isaac and Jacob, but were manmade impositions on the consciences of human beings which brought Babylonian-like bondage to human beings, not freedom and new life. The killer of truth in Ephesus would not be as much the public scandals involving the deacon running off with the Director of Music's wife, but irreverent rabbis running off with their mouths! The quiet killer of Ephesus would be preachers who were, if we were to take just the opposite of Paul's warnings, untrained in godliness (v. 8), lazy in the ministry (v. 9), and whose hope was set on things other than the "living God," the Savior Jesus Christ (v. 10).

The quiet killer of ministry is preaching and teaching the things that are not of God and His Word. The quiet killer of ministry is putting our efforts into causes and movements which do not promote that which will save ourselves as well as our people. And when we have neglected the ordinary means of grace—Word, Sacrament, and Prayer—then our people will languish, our churches be weakened, the unconverted neglected, the Great Commission ignored. In short, our people will fall into ruin. And the leaders of such churches will become like Jackals among those ruins.

Few would deny that Western secularized Europe, Britain, and sadly we must say, the United States, look like the spiritual ruins of a faith that once was. And today we know of scandals and scandalous spiritual leaders who are jackals among the ruins. Some of us might call the jackals antinomianism or legalism, or perhaps Mormonism or the new Mysticism, or, following Paul who named Hymenaeus and Philetus as famous heretics, we might call the jackals by more personal names like Joseph Smith, Mary Baker Eddy, Charles Taze Russell, or Jim Jones. And you would be right, I think. But could such religious beasts arise from our ilk? Could these roaming hounds of Hell begin to sniff out human souls in evangelical seminaries? And if so could they then reproduce their pups and let them loose in our day to bay senseless words in the pulpits of our land and wander upon the already Babylonian-like spiritual landscape of our nation?

It happened in the Golden Age. When was that? Many of us in the Reformed and Presbyterian faith think of seventeenth-century English Puritanism as the golden age of Christianity. And in many ways it most certainly was! It was the day of the Westminster Assembly of Divines who produced in their 1,163 numbered sessions what are surely the crowning confessional statements of the Word of God since the days of the Apostles: The Westminster Confession of Faith, a Larger Catechism, and a Shorter Catechism, a Directory for Public Worship, as well as the lesser studied Form of Government. And it was not only their doctrine but their lives which would cause us to agree with the saintly Robert Murray M'Cheyne (1813–1843):

Oh for the grace of the Westminster divines to be poured out upon
this generation of lesser men.[262]

This was the time of Richard Baxter (1615–1691) at Kidder-
minster and John Owen (1616–1683) at Oxford. This was the productive time when Emmanuel College at Cambridge was a veritable
factory of Puritan divines whose hearts and minds were aflame with
the glories of Christ and His Word. The doctrines of grace flowed
like the oil over Aaron's beard and could be heard in the preaching
of Scots like Samuel Rutherford (1600–1661), Welshmen like Christopher Love (1618–1651), and Englishmen like John Bunyan
(1628–1688), the famous Baptist of Bedford, as well as long-serv-
ing, faithful English pastor in the *fins*, William Gurnall (1617–1679)
the Anglican rector of Lavenham. Great books were written in those
days. Great men and women of prayer emerged in those days. But
as the barnacles of Hell would attach themselves beneath the great
Gospel ship that sailed through Northampton in the Great Awakening in New England during Jonathan Edward's day, so they attached
themselves to the edges of the golden 1640s of Puritan ascendancy
in Westminster. We remember the glaring examples of false teachers like the infamous Laud. And so, Archbishop William Laud (1573–
1645), in the opinion of Patrick Collinson was "the greatest calam-
ity ever visited upon the Church of England."[263] We remember that
the Church of England was removed, and while the Presbyterian
government that replaced it might be preferable to many of us, the
Church of England formed an institution which held together the
'center" of Christianity, and even Reformed Christianity, in that
day. Thus, as the center collapsed, the fringes were set free. And

---

262   R. M. M'Cheyne, *The Life and Remains, Letters, Lectures, and Poems of the
Rev. Robert Murray Mccheyne* (R. Carter & Brothers, 1856), 125.

263   P. Collinson, *The Religion of Protestants: The Church in English Society,
1559-1625* (Clarendon Press, 1984), 90.

seventeenth-century Puritanism came into ascendancy even as sectarian groups such as the Quakers, the Levelers, the Ranters, the
Diggers and other mystical, heretical groups began to emerge.[264]
These groups were usually either neo-Montanists,[265] advocating
extra biblical, continuing revelation, which led them into heretical
claims about the Person of the Godhead or of Christ or about
prophecies concerning the end times, or they were anarchists, who
used the Kingship of Jesus to advocate the overthrow of all governments. It is not an overstatement to say these groups came upon
the land like locusts. So in the very era when the unsurpassed
Westminster theology was being taught, heresy and anarchy seemed
unstoppable. Into this veritable cauldron of false teaching and pris-
tine biblical theology came a man named Vavasor Powell. This
Welshman was possessed of natural gifts as a preacher and especially as a teacher. An Oxford man, this former teacher was also
gifted in leadership and vision. When he was converted under the
preaching of the godly Walter Craddock (1610?–1659) and the writings of Richard Sibbes (1577–1635) and William Perkins (1558–
1602), he began an itinerant ministry that led him ultimately to
becoming rector at Holy Trinity in Dartford[266]. There he also became

---

264 See the full story of the proliferation of the sects in the classical C. Hill,
     *The World Turned Upside Down: Radical Ideas During the English Revolu-
     tion* (Penguin Books, 1991).

265 Montanism was an "apocalyptic movement of the 2d cent. It arose in Phry-
     gia (c.172) under the leadership of a certain Montanus and two female
     prophets, Prisca and Maximillia, whose entranced utterances were
     deemed oracles of the Holy Spirit" according to "Montantism" *The Co-
     lumbia Encyclopedia*, 6th ed. New York: Columbia University Press,
     2001–07. www.bartleby.com/65/. [July 25, 2008]. See also the article,
     by David F. Wright, "Why Were the Montanists Condemned?" at http://
     www.earlychurch.org.uk/article_montanists_wright.html.

266 M. A. Milton, *The Application of the Theology of the Westminster Assem-
     bly in the Ministry of the Welsh Puritan, Vavasor Powell (1617-1670)*
     (University of Wales, 1997), 100.

a chaplain to Parliament during the English Civil War. When the Westminster divines set up a committee[267] to study how to get the Gospel to Wales and to do what we would call "church planting," the Committee looked to this extraordinarily gifted man, Vavasor Powell. The Committee met on the 11th of September, Session 704 of the Westminster Assembly, and 18 divines signed Powell's certificate to preach in Wales. The number included no less than Jeremiah Burroughs (1600–1646),[268] whose devotional works on contentment[269] and worship[270] rank as first class contributions to the Church from this era (and I hope you get to read them) as well as Powell's fellow Welshman, the famous Presbyterian pastor of St. Lawrence Jewry in London, Christopher Love (1618–1651).[271] So Powell was sent out by the Assembly to do both church planting and revitalization in Wales. But alas, as he was separated from the orthodox Presbytery of London and set free to earn the title of "the metropolitan of Wales," Mr. Powell became influenced by the sectarian movements of his day. And the one association which most scholars have linked him to was the Fifth Monarchy Movement.[272] This movement believed that they were fulfilling the cause of

---

267   Ibid. 109.

268   Ibid. 105.

269   J. Burroughs, *The Rare Jewel of Christian Contentment by Jeremiah Burroughs. (1685)* (BiblioBazaar, 2010).

270   J. Burroughs and D. Kistler, *Gospel Worship, or, the Right Manner of Sanctifying the Name of God: In General, and Particularly in These 3 Great Ordinances: 1. Hearing the Word, 2. Receiving the Lord's Supper, 3. Prayer* (Soli Deo Gloria Publications, 1648).

271   D. Kistler, *A Spectacle Unto God: The Life and Death of Christopher Love (1618-1651)* (Reformation Heritage Books, 2003).

272   B. Capp, *Fifth Monarchy Men: A Study in Seventeenth-Century English Millenarianism* (Faber & Faber, Limited, 2008); P. G. Rogers, *The Fifth Monarchy Men* (Oxford U.P., 1966); and L. F. Brown, *The Political Activities of the Baptists & Fifth Monarchy Men in England During the Interregnum* (American Historical Association, 1913).

Christ by supporting anarchy, removing all human governments, and thus ushering in Daniel's fifth and final kingdom, or monarchy, that of Jesus Christ Himself. They were a millenarian group whose theology became mixed up in politics, always a dangerous and combustible mixture. And Powell was friendly to them, there can be no doubt. Indeed, on one of his return trips to London, when he was filling the pulpit at Blackfriars Church, the pulpit of late, venerable William Gouge (1575–1653), the oldest member of the Westminster Assembly when they convened, Powell gave a sermon.

It was December 16, 1653, the day that Oliver Cromwell (1599–1658) was named Lord Protector of all of the British Isles. And Vavasor Powell preached to old Mr. Gouge's congregation and asked them to go home and ask themselves if they wanted Jesus Christ to rule over them or Oliver Cromwell.[273] Cromwell did not take that comment very well, and Powell was locked up immediately. So here was a man who would debate the heretics of the day, who championed high Calvinism against Arminians of the day, who was so gifted that he caught the attention of men like John Owen, who wrote the preface to one of Powell's books, and yet would become involved with the fringe political movements of his day, and began to focus on anarchist, radical millenarian ideas, that pitted him against his own heretofore allies. And Vavasor Powell forfeited his ministry. He was locked up by the Puritans.

When Charles the Second returned, he released a number of prisoners but considered Powell so dangerous to the populace that he left him there. And Powell grew sick in prison. And there in the horrible conditions of the Fleet Street Prison, Vavasor Powell, the fiery evangelist and radical millenarian, returned, through the sanctifying powers of a cell and time alone with God and God's

---

273   Milton, *Vavasor Powell,* 4.

Word, to become a pastor. It was said of him that he transformed
his cell into an academy and his guards into parishioners who
were catechized by Powell and sat under his preaching each Lord's
Day. Indeed, he became so pastoral in his outlook and behavior,
that the officials let this once dangerous lion of Wales out each
Sunday to preach in the streets of London. He wrote beautiful letters to the little churches in Wales, some of which he had founded.
He wrote some marvelous hymns and devotional books, one of
which, "Bird in a Cage Chirping," contains remarkably tender and
pastoral passages on Christian suffering. In short, this man forfeited the years of his ministry in fringe groups only to recover his
ministry in the last years of his life. He died in his cell in 1670 and
was buried in Bunhill Fields Cemetery in London in what is now an
unmarked grave. I went there and remember reconstructing the
day of his funeral service, and with the help of the cemetery
worker that day, located the place where his remains lay. I will
never forget the words of that worker that day, as the sunset and
the shadows fell upon the whole scene. He said, in unmistakable
Cockney, "I 'ave no idea why ye would want to look fer this 'ere
bloke; this ground is filled 'ith nuttin' but rebels and the dregs of
society." As he said that to me, I looked over his shoulder to see the
tomb, on one side, of John Bunyan. Over his other shoulder, I saw
the tomb of Susannah Wesley.

"Yes," I said, "but I suspect this whole cemetery will erupt with
glorified saints on the day when Christ comes again." He shook his
head, and we parted.

And thus Powell's legacy is mixed. But the lessons of his life
are clear for our ministries, for our studies, for our lives. They may
be summarized in two words: *focus* and *avoid*.

Focus
Focus your ministry on the Word of God, not this movement or

that movement, or political involvement or speculative theological ideas or academic or professional peer groups or even accrediting groups. They exist to help serve our mission and our mission does not serve them. As we would learn from Ezekiel, we must not "follow our own spirit" or our own vision, but God's. For our seminary, let us focus on the central vision of the coming Kingdom of God and the need to pray for laborers for God's harvest. And thus let us focus on preparing men for the pastorate and men and women to become missionaries and other Christian leaders. And in all things let us focus on doing it with a sound methodology given to us in the Word of God, of faithful men teaching faithful men who will be able to teach others also.

Avoid

And as St. Paul teaches us, we must avoid the irreverent, silly myths, which sometimes attach themselves to the true, good old ship of the Gospel. We make our way through a world where truth and error are often being mixed, where those who would seek to minister to people in Post modernity may be prone to become one with the bad ideas they are first sought to address, or those who would seek to recover the good traditions of the past become entangled in ritualism which ruined them. And thus they who would have preached the Gospel of Christ faithfully through dependence upon the Word, Sacrament, and Prayer, begin to preach out of the poison well of their ideas or the ideas of others. They not only forfeit their ministries. They become "jackals among ruins."

Remember the words of Paul: "Keep a close watch on yourself and on the teaching. Persist in this, for by so doing you will save both yourself and your hearers." (1 Timothy 4:16)

As I begin my time with you as your president and as the newest faculty member, and as we welcome our new students, our returning students, as well as each of our fine staff, I pray that we will remember that, as Charles Hodge would tell his new students at old Princeton, "You will learn nothing new here." You will, we pray, learn nothing new here. Unless it is the newness of the truth of the Gospel fresh upon your soul. And I do pray that you will receive from the repository of two thousand years of Gospel ministry the essential teachings that will help you to stand and preach or teach or minister faithfully. And I pray that we will all recommit our lives today to the inerrant and infallible Word of the Living God, to dependence upon the Holy Spirit, and to focusing on the life and Person and sacrificial death on the Cross of our Lord Jesus Christ as well as His glorious resurrection from the dead and ascension into heaven, where he reigns now, and from hence He shall return to judge the living and dead, and usher in a new heaven and a new earth. And in all of this, I pray that you who are beginning your studies here at RTS Charlotte will love Jesus Christ more at the conclusion of your studies than at the beginning. And then shall our seminary be used of God to train up shepherds of Christ who shall scatter the jackals among ruins, and raise the Cross of the Savior that all who will look upon the One on that Cross and repent of their sins, trusting in the finished work of Christ alone, will be saved.

In the name of the Father, and of the Son and of the Holy Spirit. Amen.

Let us pray.

O blessed Savior, sent of the Father, and impressed upon our hearts today, from Your Word by Your Spirit, we are prone to wander. We are prone to speak out of our own imagination, our own vision, and when we do we become like these jackals among ruins, seeking our own way, leaving the people destitute of Your Word and its mighty blessings. Today we ask, in this new semester, in the new time for our seminary, and in each of our lives, that You would show us where we have neglected Your Way for the world's way, reveal how we have relied on our strength and not

Your strength, and unveil the awful sins of pride and presumption and minimization of the glorious Gospel of grace, so that, stripped of the things that separate us from You and each other and limit our usefulness in the Kingdom of God, we may, with renewed spirits, follow Thee, Lord Jesus, all the way home. Bless our seminary, anoint our ministers as they teach, bless our students as they learn, and help our staff to be so united in our love for You and our heart for this mission that Your glory would be exalted in this place and your mission in the world would be fulfilled, at least in part, by what You do here with us.

And so surrounding our hearts to You O Christ we pray now that we may know nothing but the Cross, preach nothing other than the Gospel of God's grace, and follow no other One but the One who lived the life we could never live and died the death on the cross that should have been ours, and rely on no other means of grace—no other way to You and Your Kingdom—but what has been revealed in Your Word.

I commend this seminary, this new semester, all of our faculty and staff and each of our precious students to You and to the Word of Your grace. In Jesus' name. Amen.

4

DEADLY DIVISION AND DIVINE DELIVERANCE

How to Overcome the Greatest Obstacle in Global Theological Mission in the Church Today (1 Corinthians 3:1–9)

[The following was delivered to the Lausanne Consultation on Global Theological Education at Gordon–Conwell Theological Seminary.]

Spiritually the Lausanne event in Cape Town, South Africa, was transformative. I saw my new calling as the servant of a seminary to now be more of a missionary than before, and that excited me. I saw our seminary, with many others, as complementary movements of God in our generation to raise up a new generation of pastors grounded in the Word of God and with a white-hot passion for missions across the planet. I will never forget the closing ceremony and that processional with all the tribes and tongues of the earth in diverse unity moving through a saintly sea of five thousand believers who were caught up in a worship service that must surely be a reflection of the sublime worship going on in heaven now. I was moved by Archbishop Henry Luke Orombi's message. I was stunned with the Holy Spirit's impact on so many by the testimony of the little Korean lass who told of her heart's desire to return to North Korea to share Christ. I was not the same when I came home, and I hope I will be transformed more and more into this vision of the one and the many.

There was a virus in Corinth. And that virus threatened that global crossroads city of its day and thereby threatened the redemptive work of Jesus Christ across the world. So Paul writes this letter to discuss the disunity. And his letter was and is the God breathed Word from heaven that gives life to all who will read or hear. And that is good. For we all have a virus. It is either the sin of Adam untouched by the blood of Jesus or it is the residual of that sin still flowing through our minds and hearts and cultures and institutions. The virus is there. And it can shut down ministry, as it was doing in Corinth.

Paul's diagnosis of the disease and his treatment in chapter three, verses one through nine, are essential to every believer but has particular import for those engaged as servant–leaders in God's mission in the world today. In this passage, God has given us a Spiritual diagnosis and cure for the virus that creates division in the Church. Since all of us suffer in one way or another from that ancient Adamic virus, and since most of us would even have testimonies of the feverish consequences wreaked on our bodies as a result of this dark spot on our souls, we have every reason to pay attention to this passage: for our lives, our souls, and as we gather together in this special place for this special purpose, for the mission of global theological education.

There are two aspects of this passage that need our attention if we would know this heavenly diagnosis and treatment and cure for division.

The first aspect before us in the passage is most plain:

1. Because there is a virus of sin, there is a possibility for deadly division that threatens the mission of the church (vv. 1–4).

Look at the passage. Paul moves, in this extraordinary epistle, from explaining spiritual realities and being able to discern them to now practicing that deep spiritual discernment himself. His first concern is the division that is threatening to undue the mission of this global church. Consumed as this culture was with sexual immorality, politically correct idolatry, and systemic abuse and corruption at every level of society, the Church of Corinth was not only suspect but infected. And the infection was a double dose. Not only were they were infected by the residual of sin in their lives because of the very nature their condition—but they were also being infected by the viruses of the vile and wicked generation around them.

This is our case as well. We are not only struggling with sin in ourselves, in our churches, in our seminaries, because of the residual deadly virus in our souls, that left over Adamic strain that produces death, but we are subject to the virulent viruses that abound in our culture. The list in Corinth of sexual immorality, idolatry, and corruption of powers sounds like our own today, whether in the Majority Christian world or in old Christendom. It is present everywhere, for it is the very out working of fallen man.

But consider what this infection does in our lives as we look at the text.

The virus stunts our growth.

In verse 1, Paul calls them brothers and sisters—they are not pagans, you see. He says that they are "in Christ" in verse one, yet look: they are "infants in Christ." They are more characterized as "people of the flesh," that is the desires of the flesh and its earthly

rule over their members, than "spiritual people." Paul had seen
this when he had to give them "milk, not solid food" (v. 2), and
even after some time, they remained in that condition and were
unable to be fed the deeper truths of God's Word. We must recognize that unless there is a treatment of the virus within, it will continue to wreak havoc in our very system. Our lives, our churches
and our institutions will be unable to cooperate in the partnerships
we spoke of yesterday, for we will be too childish in our selves to
exercise a maturity needed to form alliances for Gospel effectiveness. More than that, selfishness will reign in our stunted condition. We will be what J. I. Packer called spiritual dwarfs in his book,
Quest for Godliness.[274] I know this condition well. I lived it for most
of my years growing up. I knew enough of the Gospel to know I
was a sinner and needed a Savior and that Jesus Christ was the
God–Man to take that sin, but I lived like Hell. I once had a Mormon
tell me, after I was witnessing to him, that he would listen to me
when my life reflected the Christ I was seeking to proclaim. Until
then, he told me, your witness is just an argument that you seem to
enjoy. But there is nothing in your life to tell me that you really believe. "Mike," the young sailor told me in our barracks, "you need
help." When you are reprimanded by a Mormon for your faith in
Christ, then it is not good. And it was not good! Mike Milton was a
sham. I was worse than a Corinthian. But what if I kept going in
that condition? What if I went to seminary, served a church, got
some head knowledge, and then led a ministry in that unchecked
condition? Is that possible? You know that it is. And you know that
my condition would have infected others from the pulpit. And you
know that global theological education is subject to the viruses
that are stunting the growth of our leaders and infecting the same

---

274   James I. Packer, *A Quest for Godliness: The Puritan Vision of the Christian
Life* (Wheaton, IL: Crossway, 1994).

in our students. I am saying that this is a deadly possibility for many seminary leaders and church leaders today. Stunted growth in sanctification, in growth in grace and knowledge of Jesus and His Word is a present, deadly reality. The stunted growth creates a human-centric praxis if not theology, which brings division in the church. Children who are not mature can be quite self-centered. And their self-centeredness creates division on the playground. There is division in the Church and the possibility of division that hinders the work of God because there is a shallowness, a self-centeredness and contentment that refuses to stretch forward in discipleship. In our circles it can manifest itself in denominational or institutional aggrandizement or theological prejudice and isolationism. This can and most certainly will bring deadly division. Yet the virus has other effects.

The virus strangles our perspective.

When a virus enters a system, for instance, a neurological system, it can, as doctors tell me, begin to systematically rewire the most delicate parts of the whole, creating neurological anarchy. This may not be true for me physically, but I have known spiritual anarchy! I have known the Corinthian viral effect of going from spiritual immaturity to spiritual pride! This is what happened to these people, and it is what can happen to us. The virus, unhindered by the means of grace, brings about a pride that seeks to elevate personal experience over corporate unity and health. Thus, the famous Corinthian parties arose: the "Paul party," and the "Apollos party," and the "Cephas party," and finally, the party which sought to trump them all, "the Christ party!" Now who wants to try to compete with that party, huh? Ah, the filthy stupidity of it all!

"Are you not merely human?" Paul surmises in 3:4. Why did he say that? For he had just talked about spiritual realities being discerned by spiritual beings. The souls of the Corinthians were not only stunted in spiritual growth but were being strangled in spiritual perspective. And yet we know that there are churches and seminaries and institutions that are not unlike this. There are seminary presidents and parish ministers and deans and professors and some of us today whose souls may be fighting this deadly virus. Professional jealousy and ungodly competition and unfair assessment of others and judgmental attitudes towards those who should be "esteemed as higher than ourselves" (Philippians 2:3) can and do hinder the God-given mission of global theological education as a preeminent part of our Lord's redemptive purposes in the world. And the rest of 1 Corinthians chronicles the devastating consequences of this virus if it is not attacked by a strong response. But thank God there is a response, and Paul shows it to us in verses 5–9!

2. Because there is a remedy—there is a power for divine deliverance that energizes the mission of the church (vv. 5–9)!

Paul's tone in the text is still testy, but he is an apostolic endocrinologist who is moving from diagnosis of the infected hormonal system at Corinth to the patient physician bringing the remedy. And that remedy is as divinely powerful and effective for us today as it was for these spiritual infants then.

What is the power for deliverance? And can the deliverance also bring a renewed vision for the Church and its mission? I believe the text says it can.

Divided believers may be delivered from division through a model of servanthood among the leadership (vv. 5–9).

Paul said that he was nothing and Apollos was nothing, They were simply, in verse 9, fellow workers. The fact that one had come to Christ through Paul and another through Apollos was a result, in verse 5, of God's sovereign choice, not Paul's choice or for that matter the believer's choice. God did this, and He alone deserves glory and honor. In this, Paul demonstrates the servanthood that the Corinthians needed. This is the servanthood spirit we need as we lead our seminaries and our churches and, in particular, as we prepare the next generation of pastors and missionaries. We live in a day of cults. I have seen it in India as well as in Indiana, in Cardiff as well as Cape Town, and it is in Seoul as well as Singapore: the cult—of the celebrity cleric. It is alive and—bad. Majority Church or Minority Church means nothing when it comes to the ego of a preacher! An inflated sense of super hero preacher and scholar is not tied to any ethnic group or any part of the world. It is a human problem that we as God's pastors and scholars must put to death! And when that cult is demolished by the Christ-like servant of God who ministers out of a healthy understanding of God's sovereignty, then the idolatrous tables of self-selling are turned over in the "temple," and not only is the pastor or scholar as free as St. Paul, but the believers and the churches and the institutions we serve are set free as well.

Divided believers may be delivered through a demonstration of complementary ministry (vv. 6–9).

Paul will say that one plants and another waters. Indeed, he tells the divided church in verse 8 that the two are one. In verse 9 they are "fellow workers"—complementary colleagues ministering with different gifts at different places in the life of the Church to advance the Kingdom of God. Now, this is the centering place for us. I have heard churches argue that they do not need a community of scholars and Bible teachers who focus on preparing pastors. They can do that. I have heard seminaries say that they are more important than the local church. As a long time pastor, I can tell you that does not cause me to want to recommend your seminary to my missions committee! Indeed, the parish ministry is in need of theological education and theological educators are in need of the parish ministry. The pastor and the scholar, the church planter and the senior minister of the downtown, historic congregation, the young, the old, North, South, East, West, all need each other, and we all need Christ. And that is the remedy. When we show a complementary expression of giftedness in our global mission, as seminaries and churches and mission agencies, we model what it is for believers to also come alongside each other in their lives. We glorify Christ with our humble service and offering of our diverse gifts for His One Kingdom.

THE GIFT OF WEAKNESS

A lady told me not long ago that her cancer was a gift from the Lord. She said that had she not had the cancer, she would not have known God's grace in such a new and deep way. She would not know the joy of service in weakness and the blessing of seeing God's strength. Weaknesses, whether a virus or a cold or a spiritual dark night of the soul, remind me of my mortality, of the Church's work going forward with or without me, and that Christ is building His Church, not I. This liberates. This brings a new health. If you are a servant of the Church it brings health to others, too.

I also hope it brings a new unity with each of you as you, too, realize that we need each other and we are dependent upon the Lord. I cannot do it alone. I never could. Now I know that in a new way. And I think this is what Paul wanted Corinth to know. This is what God wants us to know. This is the Church that God wants us to be.

Then will divisions be mended as deliverance is found in Jesus Christ, our Reconciler and our Redeemer.

In the name of the Father, and of the Son, and of the Holy Spirit. Amen.

WHEN GOD COMES DOWN

Isaiah 64

The greatest threat we face as a nation is an unawareness of our own condition. So many in our nation fail to realize that we really are at war.

What a Pentagon official told me could be said about the Church. Many have settled into a mindset that Ephesians 6 and the battle in the spiritual realms for the souls of men is just not relevant today. We seem more concerned about the latest trends in technology in worship or the latest controversial book or the hippest new preacher than we are in the reality that the devil, the flesh, and the world conspire against our souls. If we ever doubted that we are in a spiritual battle, the past few days of outright assault on religious liberty should have awakened us. And if that is not enough, just look at the worldliness of our people.

There needs to be prayer for revitalization in the West; support for revival in the Rest. It is good in inaugurating a missions conference to begin, then, with a holy dissatisfaction.

And so we begin with Isaiah 64:1–12. Isaiah has seen the throne room of God. He has seen God's glory. He has not only a sacred encounter (in Isaiah 6) but a divine calling. He can never be the same. In a way, he can never be satisfied with pious platitudes or shallow solutions or earthly answers. He wants God to come down. It is God's message to His Church today.

> This is the inerrant and infallible Word of the living God.
> Oh, that You would rend the heavens!
> That You would come down!
> That the mountains might shake at Your presence—
> As fire burns brushwood,
> As fire causes water to boil—
> To make Your name known to Your adversaries,
> That the nations may tremble at Your presence!
> When You did awesome things for which we did not look,
> You came down,
> The mountains shook at Your presence.
> For since the beginning of the world
> Men have not heard nor perceived by the ear,
> Nor has the eye seen any God besides You,
> Who acts for the one who waits for Him.
> You meet him who rejoices and does righteousness,
> Who remembers You in Your ways.
> You are indeed angry, for we have sinned—
> In these ways we continue;
> And we need to be saved.
> But we are all like an unclean thing,
> And all our righteousnesses are like filthy rags;
> We all fade as a leaf,
> And our iniquities, like the wind,
> Have taken us away.
> And there is no one who calls on Your name,
> Who stirs himself up to take hold of You;
> For You have hidden Your face from us,
> And have consumed us because of our iniquities.
> But now, O Lord,
> You are our Father;
> We are the clay, and You our potter;
> And all we are the work of Your hand.

Do not be furious, O Lord,
Nor remember iniquity forever;
Indeed, please look—we all are Your people!
Your holy cities are a wilderness,
Zion is a wilderness,
Jerusalem a desolation.
Our holy and beautiful temple,
Where our fathers praised You,
Is burned up with fire;
And all our pleasant things are laid waste.
Will You restrain Yourself because of these things, O Lord?
Will You hold Your peace, and afflict us very severely?

Isaiah 64:1–12

The grass withers and the flowers fall, but the Word of the Lord will stand forever. Let us pray.

Lord, You wrote these words for Your people. Open them to our hearts this evening. Open them to this congregation, these pastors, these elders and deacons, these men, women, boys and girls; that we may be fruitful in Your kingdom; that we may know what we are to do; that we may be saved; and that many others would be saved as well. In Jesus' name I pray. Amen.

INTRODUCTION TO THE MESSAGE

Once you experience revival, you will never forget it.

I remember having gone to my first trip to Albania to preach there. It was right after the wall fell. There was revival in the air. I was coming back home through London. I was in a black cab going to my hotel, passing monuments of a glorious Christian past, and yet people were passing by them as if they were passing by a Starbucks. I began to unload on the cab driver about how at the top of the Bank of England there is an inscription that says, "The earth is the LORD's, and the fullness thereof; the world, and they that dwell therein." (Psalms 24:1 KJV)

I asked him, indignantly, "Do you know where that comes from, my friend?" Before he could answer, I told him, "That is from the Psalms! Or don't you know where the Psalms are located? That is the Bible, my friend! This entire city and civilization was built on the foundation of that Word, and just look at the people passing by! One day these will all crumble for lack of spiritual upkeep and then you will know!" I paused, out of breath. He looked at me in the mirror, giving a look of open-mouth wonder, and asked, in his Cockney way, "You wouldn't be a padre would ye?"

Isaiah had been on a mission trip of sorts. He had been to the very throne room of God. He came back with a message that could be summarized as "repent and believe and follow God." The cab drivers of Jerusalem knew he was likely a padre too. God, told him, however, that his divine message would go unheeded. Yet Isaiah reveals that he had a heart for the people and he had a heart for God. Jim Kennedy used to tell me, "Michael, to be a minister you must love God, love people, and love His Word. Without any one of those things you will never be useful for the Lord." Isaiah seemed to have all three working. And in Isaiah 64 he has looked upon the godly foundations of Israel crumbling under the increasing weight of sin and neglect of their faith in God. And so he begins not by trying to change laws, but trying to change himself into a praying man. He calls down God. He believes that without God there is no hope.

Our nation needs hope. Our churches need hope. And so we do. In 1961 then-actor and GE spokesman, Ronald Reagan, said that if government intrusion went unopposed we could find ourselves, in our sunset years, telling our children what American used to be like when men were free. We are already there in telling our children what it was like when biblical Christianity was a primary presence in our nation. For we see our nation at a point where many of us don't recognize it. Many are concerned that the foundations, erected by our forefathers, are crumbling under the weight of secularism, relativism, increasingly antagonistic relations between unbelievers and believers, and worse than all of that, apathy among those who name the name of Jesus.

Isaiah 64:1–12 describes what I need to do and what God will do in this nation today to see the spiritual foundations restored and have a realistic hope for a real recovery.

WE NEED A HOLY DISSATISFACTION

> Oh that you would rend the heavens and come down, that the mountains might quake at your presence... (Isaiah 64:1 ESV)

When I read God's Word in its whole, I come to understand that the Word of God begins with a burden. The burden is God's burden for His own creation. Man was unable to keep God's law and fell away from his Creator. This grieved God. According to Ephesians 1, God saw this before the foundation of the world and took steps to remedy the problem. After the fall, the rest of Scripture is a record of God working out His covenant of grace; that is, God, by grace, doing for man what man could not do for himself. It is a record of God ordaining that He would come down to fulfill the requirements of His own law and to pour out His divine wrath for sin upon Himself as a propitiation for the sins of man. God was burdened for His own creation.

So the vision of the Bible begins with a burden. Therefore, I would say that if it is to be biblical, any outline for a church's vision must begin with a burden. When we come to understand that burden, when we have a heart and a passion for something that grieves us, that pains us, that creates desire, we then have a vision. A biblical vision is a divine solution that lifts the burden.

So I begin this series of messages on a vision for our church by locating in God's Word the burden that He has given me for our time. I turn to Isaiah 64, for Isaiah was a man with a burden for God's glory in his own generation. In this passage we may first come to understand the definition of this burden. We see this when we encounter the prophet's words, "Oh, that."

Job uses this phrase more than anyone in Scripture. He cries out from the deepest part of his soul, "Oh, that my words were written! Oh, that they were inscribed in a book!" (Job 19:23)

David uses the same opening in his exasperation over the sin of the wicked: Oh, that men would give thanks to the Lord for His goodness,

> And for His wonderful works to the children of men! (Psalm 107:21)

> And Isaiah the prophet cries out, "Oh, that You would...come down..." (Isaiah 64:1b).

"Oh, that" is a holy dissatisfaction with the way things are in comparison with who God is. The prophet has seen God, experienced His glory, known His salvation, desired that Israel know Him, and was, thus, dissatisfied.

There is evidence throughout the Bible that Christians are to be dissatisfied. We are enjoined to be content, but it is to be with our circumstances, not with God's glory!

Moses had a burden. When he first had a burden for his Hebrew brethren, he took matters into his own hands and ended up herding goats in the back forty of Midian. But then God came down in a burning bush, and when Moses took his rod and marched into Pharaoh's court, that man had a burden for God's glory.

Paul knew God's glory in grace and could never be content with ordinary religion. He would sacrifice all, count every gain as rubbish, put himself at risk, and take on any earthly power. For what? That he might know Christ and the power of His resurrection. Paul was a burdened man. He was burdened for God's glory. He had experienced Christ and thought the world unworthy until every knee would bow and every tongue confess that Jesus is Lord to the glory of the Father.

The Reformation could be traced to a holy dissatisfaction in the soul of the Germanic priest, Martin Luther. That paper with the 95 theses that he nailed to the Wittenberg church door was a sign of his holy burden for God's glory and God's grace to flow over the land.

There is a song I remember singing with Christians in Wales when I studied there. I brought it back, and when I planted a church in Kansas City, I used to gather our core group and sing this and remind them that this is why we were planting a church, because we were desperate for God to come down!

> RESTORE, O LORD,
> The honor of Your name,
> In works of sovereign power
> Come shake the earth again;
> That men may see
> And come with reverent fear
> To the living God,
> Whose kingdom shall outlast the years.
> Restore, O Lord,
> In all the earth Your fame,
> And in our time revive
> The church that bears Your name.
> And in Your anger,
> Lord, remember mercy,
> O living God,

Whose mercy shall outlast the years.
Bend us, O Lord,
Where we are hard and cold,
In Your refiner's fire
Come purify the gold.
Though suffering comes
And evil crouches near,
Still our living God
Is reigning, He is reigning here.
Restore, O Lord,
The honor of Your name,
In works of sovereign power
Come shake the earth again;
That men may see
And come with reverent fear
To the living God,
Whose kingdom shall outlast the years.[275]

This is Isaiah's cry exactly. This was Luther's and Calvin's and Whitefield's and Edward's, and it is ours tonight. Any mission to our nation, for our family, for our own lives to be right with God, must begin with a burden, a holy dissatisfaction. "Oh, that" is the soul cry of a person or a church who has known the grace of God, who has come to know the joy of surrendering his life to the compassionate Christ, and who is discontent until God is glorified and worshipped and enjoyed.

God is calling us to see and experience His own burden in our generation. We must be like Isaiah and say, "Oh, that God would come down" in our community. There are people here who need Christ. Oh, that God would come down to our nation. Oh, that God would come down to the Muslim people; to the African people; to

---

275 "Restore," by Graham Kendrick and Chris Rolinson, Copyright 1981, Thankyou Music.

Hispanics in Los Angeles; to smug, comfortable, pretend Christians who are not living to give God the glory.

I pray for a church with a burden for the glory of God.

Isaiah's "Oh, that" reveals his holy discontent, but the unfolding passage reveals more. We move from what I need to do to what God will do.

WE NEED FOR GOD TO COME DOWN

I am saying that Isaiah is telling us three responses to this necessary dissatisfaction: There must be a prayer for revival, a position of repentance, and a Plea for Remembrance. Let me explain.

1. When God comes down, there is prayer for revival (vv. 1–4).

Isaiah is dissatisfied. Isaiah is burdened, and the relief that he seeks is genuine revival. The entire passage is a prayer for revival. Especially from verses 1 through 4:

> Oh, that You would rend the heavens and come down, that the mountains might quake at your presence—as when fire kindles brushwood and the fire causes water to boil—to make Your name known to your adversaries, and that the nations might tremble at your presence. When You did awesome things that we did not look for, you came down, the mountains quaked at your presence. From of old no one has heard or perceived by the ear, no eye has seen a God besides You, who acts for those who wait for Him.

Oh the passion in this passage! The prophet's holy dissatisfaction moves him to prayer: his prayer focuses on God supernaturally coming down to the earth, which is in dire need of His presence and power. Not that Isaiah expects that when God comes down in revival there is a catastrophic reaction on earth, mountains burning, forests aflame, the rivers boiling over. Imagine the

Japanese earthquake, the California forest fires and the deadly Indian Ocean tsunami all at once! And the effect? This unmistakable
presence of God creates terror in the hearts of those who oppose
God and His name is magnified in the earth. Revival happens, and
this is what it looks like. It is outside of our control. It is an act of
God. It is clearly all about God's timing, not ours, for Isaiah says
that God acts for those who "wait." But the waiting yields climactic
revelations. It turns the world upside down. It converts the worst
offender, and entire nations are impacted.

Beloved, our only hope is for God to come down in revival. And
what this passage teaches us is that such transformative power,
the power that brought Jesus to earth, that turned the cross from
an instrument of shame into a symbol of salvation, and made the
tomb a sign of hope, is the power that saves us from ourselves.
Pray, then, for this in our lives, our families, our nation, and our
world. "O God rend the heavens and come down!"

In 1992 it was my pleasure to preach throughout Albania. Communism had fallen only days before I arrived. I was to do street
preaching in Skanderbeg Square, the main square in the capital
city of Tirana. I asked my Albanian friend where I should stand. He
smiled a sort of mischievous smile and said, "Stand there." I saw
what appeared to be crumbled concrete. Then I saw it. It was a
toppled statue of Joseph Stalin. I stood on the crumbled remains of
an edifice to a madman who sought to destroy the gospel. From
those remains I proclaimed the gospel. I saw the hunger for God in
people who crowded around to hear God's Word. I saw God coming down and transforming souls. When you see the glory of God in
revival and then you see the cold, dead formalism of so many in
our day, you are burdened. And when you see revival you will
never forget it. I love this quote from Duncan Campbell about the
revival he witnessed in his country:

This is revival dear people! This is a sovereign act of God! This is the moving of God's Spirit, I believe in answer to the prevailing prayer of men and women who believed that God was a Covenant-keeping God, and must be true to His Covenant engagement.[276]

Paul Johnson, in his wonderful book, *History of the American People*, notes that American history is a history of revival. I look upon our nation; our need; our evangelical churches so often going from one faddish program to another to try to grow members, to use marketing and psychology to build buildings; and I want to cry out, Oh, that God would come down! We need genuine revival, a moment of God that transcends our natural abilities and makes everyone know that God has come down.

Will you continue as you are? Or after encountering God in this passage will you pray? Will you have such a holy dissatisfaction that our predicament becomes prayer for God to come down? There is no other answer to the redemptive goals of Christ in the Church than for God to carry them out through His Holy Spirit coming upon us. There is no other solution for our national and global problems other than a prayer for God to come down and cause us to tremble before His presence.

When God comes down you can be sure there is a prayer that is calling Him. But we see a second result of Isaiah's holy dissatisfaction that leads to this prayer:

Dear Lord, you came to us in Your Son, and we find ourselves in desperate need for You to come again: to comfort, to give hope, to bring Your presence to overwhelm the evil around us. We cry out for a revival in Your Church and the Spirit of Christ to transform our world today. As we wait for Your appearing, we wait also for your power to be displayed in Your people. Come Lord Jesus. Amen.

---

276 http://www.firesofrevival.com/trevival/hrevival.htm

2. When God comes down, there is a position of repentance (vv. 5–7).

There is a bad idea out there about passivity in Christianity. If we walk an aisle; if we say a prayer; if we simply adopt an attitude of prayer, then that is "enough." Yet Isaiah teaches us that there must be a militant rebellion against sin itself. There must be an observable response in the life of the believer to God. Isaiah says, "You meet Him who joyfully works righteousness, those who remember you in their ways."

Yet this new way of working what is pleasing to God begins with a wholehearted hatred of our sin and a confession of our condition:

> Behold You were angry, and we sinned; in our sins we have been a long time, and shall we be saved? We have all become like one who is unclean, and all our righteous deeds are like a polluted garment. We all fade like a leaf, and our iniquities, like the wind, take us away. There is no one who calls upon your name; who rouses himself to take hold of You; for You have hidden Your face from us, and have made us melt in the hand of our iniquities.

Any hope for our lives, for our nation, for our world—and there is great hope because of Jesus Christ our Lord and His grace—begins with repentance. That is, literally, making a turn from everything else to God. Isaiah is so serious about this repentance that he names the sins. Often Paul in the New Testament will name sins. So must we. But to examine our sinful life before a holy God causes God to come down and change us and make us new people.

I remember a childhood friend named Sandy. Sandy was a bully. He was a year older than I and was known principally for his almost uncanny command of an ever-growing volume of curse words. I've never heard a more filthy mouth. But another kid began to pray for Sandy and invited him to church. There was a new preacher at our church, and it was an excuse for Sandy to go. Well, Sandy was saved, and he changed. He eventually led his entire family to Christ. He was called to the ministry and is today a greatly used preacher in the Southern Baptist Church. The point is that Sandy became as aware of his sins as others were! And as his heart was changed, his speech and behavior were changed. He began to take hold of God. He began to work righteousness. His militant response to sin, of repenting and transferring his trust wholly to Jesus Christ, caused God the Holy Spirit to come down into his life. He was a new man.

We must have a burden for God's glory in North America today. We are tired of vulgarity on the airwaves of our nation, horrified by abortions being given legal protection, struck with righteous indignation over our great Christian churches ordaining unrepentant sinners to the pulpit, offended by the sexualizing of everything and the open attack by Madison Avenue on our children's innocence. But are we burdened because we have a burden for God's glory in our land?

We must surely be a church burdened by the ugliness of sin in our generation and by the bondage and pain and brokenness that go with it. We long for reformation of our land. We pray that God would come down and do something in the hearts of our countrymen, that God would supernaturally renew the minds of our family and our community so that we can walk in righteousness before God and Man.

3. When God comes down, there is a plea for God to remember (vv. 8–11).

But the question comes then, how can we be saved? Indeed, this is Isaiah's question in Isaiah 64:5:

"Shall we be saved?" (ESV)
"How then can we be saved" (NIV)?
"And we need to be saved" (NKJV).

Our answer is found in Isaiah 64:8:

But now, O Lord, You are our Father...

When we pray, repent, we also call on God to remember His covenant. This is what Mary did in her Magnificat when she said that in the coming of Jesus God had remembered His covenant. She is one of the best covenant theologians in the Bible!

In that one statement we have our hope. We fix our eyes on the very nature of God as He reveals Himself to us. He is our Father. The fatherhood of God assures us that He will answer our prayers.

God as Father desires our salvation, our healing, and the transformation of our world more than any of us could. This is the testimony of Scripture:

...while we were still sinners, Christ died for us. (Romans 5:8)

...God was in Christ reconciling the world to Himself, not imputing their trespasses to them.... (2 Corinthians 5:19)

For God so loved the world that He gave His only begotten Son.... (John 3:16)

Benjamin Warfield of old Princeton taught that the emphasis of John 3:16 is on the love of God in comparison to the wickedness of the world. He "so loved the world." God's love is greater than our sin. His grace and mercy are greater than our little rebellion.

This tells me that when I am burdened for God's glory in revival and reformation, I am wanting what God wants. Yes, and more, my prayers are bound to be answered. For God's own nature, His fatherhood, assures me that He will come down.

Jesus assures us of this truth when He says, "All that the Father gives Me will come to Me, and the one who comes to Me I will by no means cast out." (John 6:37)

Look also at Isaiah 64:9:

...do not remember our sins forever...

He didn't. God, before the foundation of the world, made a sacred pledge with Himself, a covenant of grace, that He would assume the sins of His people Himself. Thus, on Calvary's cross, the central act of cosmic history was conducted. I quote Paul:

God made him who had no sin to be sin for us, so that in him we might become the righteousness of God. (2 Corinthians 5:21)

Our burdens are lifted at Calvary. And therein is our hope; our answer; and the vision of our lives, our churches, and our families. The love of God in Jesus Christ gives us optimism in our day. God will be successful. We may begin the work of prayer, of preaching, and of witness in our day. We may not see the salvation *en masse* that we long to see, but God's kingdom will be successful. He will bring them all in. This gives us unbounded assurance and joy over our work as a church. We are on the winning side.

CONCLUSION

Isaiah 64 draws us into a surprising beginning together. Our mission in the world, for God, can only be met by God. Thus, there is a prayer for revival, a position of repentance, and a plea for God to remember His covenant in Jesus Christ. Then we shall be saved. Then the vision of Isaiah, that the earth would be so affected that nations would be converted, will come to be. We are at war. Christ is our victory. There is none other. Our holy hope is at the foot of the cross.

I once preached a message on the soul's desire for God. After the service an elder came to me and said, "I go to church. I pray. I do everything a good Christian is supposed to do. But when you talk about desiring God, I'm lost. When you talk about panting for the presence of God, I have no idea what you are talking about. I know the catechism, but I don't know about this passion for Christ or this love for Him. Can you tell me what's missing?" What was missing was a true awareness of God's glory, of his sinfulness, and of God's love and grace in Jesus Christ at Calvary's cross. I am happy to say that he came to know that love and grace. To know Him is to love Him and desire Him. To desire Him is to long for Him, to be burdened for His crown rights as King of kings and Lord of lords in our generation.

I quote the words of Martyn Lloyd-Jones on the matter of praying for God's burden to see God's glory:

> We say our prayers, but have we ever prayed? Do we know any-thing about this encounter, this meeting? Have we the assurance of sins forgiven? Are we free from ourselves and self-concern, that we may intercede? Have we a real burden for the glory of God, and the name of the Church? Have we this concern for those who are outside? And are we pleading with God for his own name's sake, because of his own promises, to hear us and to answer us? Oh, my God make of us intercessors.[277]

My dear friends: don't leave this place until you come to know your sin, your need, His holiness, but also to know His love in send-ing His own Son to die for your sinful condition. When you know Him in that way and you look out on a world of brokenness and sin

---

277 D. Martyn Lloyd-Jones, Revival (Wheaton, IL: Good News Publishers/ Crossway Books, 1987) 198.

and shame—across the ocean, across the nation, across the city, and yes, across the living room of your own home—then your soul will be burdened to cry with Isaiah, "Oh, that God would come down...."

Prayer:

Oh that my heart would be burdened for Your glory in this generation; Oh that You would send Your Spirit to renew and revive me and your church to take the Gospel of the cross to this generation!"

6

THE KIDNAPPING
OF OUR CHILDREN

And How to Get Them Back

Childhood is a divinely protected season of life. That is what Jesus declared when He said,

> ...But whoever causes one of these little ones who believe in me to sin, it would be better for him to have a great millstone fastened around his neck and to be drowned in the depth of the sea. (Mark 9:42, ESV; see also Matthew 18:6 and Luke 17:2)

The Evil One will be thrown into the lake of fire, drowned in the depth of the sea of eternal flames, because of his direct attack on children. Satan masquerades in our culture as one who would help children, but we must be careful. There is not a devil under every bush, but there is a devil behind every attempt to kidnap childhood.

I used to require all of my assistant pastors to read Neil Postman's *The Disappearance of Childhood.*[278, 279] The late professor of communications at the University of New York used common grace,

---

278 Postman, Neil. The Disappearance of Childhood. Vintage, 1994.
279 Revelation 19:20 "But the beast was captured, and with him the false ..." 2004. 19 Aug. 2012 http://bible.cc/revelation/19-20.htm

for he was not a believer,[280] to see that childhood was, in essence, created by Jesus Christ with these very words, reclaimed, I would say, from the Fall, and subjected to re-entry into darkness when a man or woman or a community rejects the light they were given in God's Word. Thus, Postman felt that while the Reformation, with its emphasis upon the Word, reclaimed childhood, postmodernity and the new "image based" society seeks to steal it. The picture of the little cover photograph of a little girl—she looks to be eleven or so—with twenty-year-old makeup is a shocking image in itself pointing to the professor's thesis. These words do not do the book justice. Read it for yourself. Yet it is enough to say that our society, by rejecting God and His Word, by rejecting the commandment of God to have no other images, for images provoke the idol factory of the mind and the idols must be then be fed. The image gods are fed with immodesty at the first and then, finally, by utter moral failure and corruption until finally the child is consumed.

Christ's words are so focused on children because He seeks to love them. They are also the model of what our faith should be. "...For to such belongs the Kingdom of God."[281]

Society is kidnapping our children through *ungodly education, careless and often intentional withholding of the truth,* and *immoral imagery.* This is being done not only by the world, but, shockingly, sadly, and contemptibly, by those who claim to be followers of Christ.

---

280   "20/20 Hindsight." 19 Aug. 2012 http://www.nytimes.com/ books/99/11/14/reviews/991114.14lindlt.html

281   "Luke 18:16 But Jesus called the children to him and said, "Let the ..." 2004. 19 Aug. 2012 http://bible.cc/luke/18-16.htm

UNGODLY EDUCATION

The educational systems of this present age are beastlike Apocryphal forces that are ravaging and devouring the sweet souls of our children by teaching them that there is no God. While our public education system, and so many private educational institutions, claim distance from any singular moral program, they are, in fact, embracing a morality of their own making, or at least of the devil's making. One cannot teach from an ethical or moral vacuum. Either one teaches there is a God or does not. Darwinism, that blight on the pages of nineteenth-century English history[282] and the perfect companion to the Socialism of John Dewey,[283] the "father of American public education,"[284] that expresses itself in fanciful but godless theories of cosmology, and interpretation of history and life from a naturalistic ground, making no room at all for a supernaturalism, not to even mention Judeo–Christianity, steals the heart of the child from where their heart, by virtue of the *sensus divinitatis*, as Calvin called it (the sense of the divine inside of all of us as Paul explains in Romans 1:19–20). This is, as Robert L. Reymond[285] has put it, one of the greatest abominations in our time. Others, even agnostics, do not disagree.[286]

---

282 Wiker, Benjamin. "Playing Games with Good & Evil: The Failure of Darwinism to Explain Morality." *Crisis: Politics, Culture & the Church* (2002).

283 Dewey, John. "The One-World of Hitler's National Socialism." *The Collected Works of John Dewey. The Middle Works* 8 (1924): 1915.

284 Egan, Kieran. *Getting it Wrong from the Beginning: Our Progressivist Inheritance from Herbert Spencer, John Dewey, and Jean Piaget.* Yale Univ. Pr., 2004.

285 In a private conversation.

286 Postman, Neil. *The End of Education: Redefining the Value of School.* Vintage Books, 1996.

WITHHOLDING TRUTH

Yet there are more culpable groups than just institutions operating from faulty frameworks. There are parents themselves, and other family members, some Christian and some not, who are seduced by the idolatrous ideas of this world, who must be questioned at this point. For while one is actively pursuing a program of atheism with our children, the other is neglectful in teaching the things of God. Timothy was to continue in the things he had heard from his mother and grandmother. He had a heritage of faith to call upon in difficult times. Today, too many families have neglected the family altar, the daily ministry of the Word and Prayer in their homes. More than this, they have done so because of the busy-ness of "this present evil age," which demands, like the Old Testament pagan deity, Moloch, to be fed by their very children.

> And thou shalt not let any of thy seed pass through the fire to Moloch. (Leviticus 18:21 KJV)

Yet too many of God's own people present their little ones to the hidden powers of the darkness, to this same devouring demon, by neglecting the teaching of the Word of God, of singing hymns, and Psalms and spiritual songs, of making their home a church, where the little ones will grow in Christ. I do not even indict the ungodly world on this, for they know not God at all. Woe to those who sacrifice their children through neglect of the things of God.

We are called to educate, to teach, train, and rear up our children with the Word of God and in the community of God's people until they ask for themselves, "What does this mean?" and you tell the story of God's deliverance in your own life through Jesus Christ (Deuteronomy 6). Then your teaching will be coupled with your life and with the God ordained progress of faith under the Covenant of Grace, and that child will call upon the Lord. This is the education that must be given. This is the education which must not be withheld. This is to help our children to come to know Jesus Christ as Lord and to fulfill the command of the Gospel in this area. Oh, that some reading this will stop and take heed. Oh that some will draw back from the quenching fires of Moloch and run with their little ones in their arms to the loving Savior who brings life abundant and life eternal.

IMMORAL IMAGERY

Judaism stood apart from the pagan nations in that they were to be people of the word, not making images of God. God Himself would give us the image we needed in the Incarnation of Himself in Jesus Christ. But we were to think thoughts after God, not make images of Him. And so our faith is a word-centered faith, not a religion of images. This is not to say that to think thoughts after God is to avoid painting or sculpture. To the contrary, the Bible has produced those whose art has sought to express the nobility of God and His Word.[287, 288] Yet when the Word is ejected and image is exalted as a primary way of communication there is, as Postman reminded us, a formidable danger. The flesh desires the image over the Word. We *think* that we can control the image. Yet it is a power that if benign would surely not have been so singularly dealt with in the Bible. The image eats away at the Word and once the Scriptural tether is finally severed, we create a god in our own image. We can also unleash the carnal powers of the flesh. That is the danger we face in our day, not only for ourselves, but also most heinously to God, to our little ones.

---

287 Wolterstorff, Nicholas. *Art in Action: Toward a Christian Aesthetic.* Wm. B. Eerdmans Publishing, 1980.

288 Murray, Peter, and Linda Murray. *The Oxford Companion to Christian Art and Architecture.* New York, 1996.

Children are not ready to hear or see the expressions of sensuality at a young age.[289, 290] Their hearts are not formed yet in the
ethics of God. Their minds are not settled on the Gospel truths of
Christ. Their longings are not even recognized, much less [291]met in
Him first, before they are subjected to the immorality of this lustful
age. The media has brought wondrous things to our lives, but there
has been a cost. The cost can be, if we are not diligent, to allow the
merchants of Madison Avenue to sexualize our children's minds.
Nothing could be more reprehensible than a child molester. We
cringe to think of it. Yet too many of us will allow our little ones to
see the most ungodly images and, in reality, become party to the
devilish scheme of destroying the souls of our children. Make no
mistake. Pornography is not the only threat to our children. The
daily dose of merchandizing by sensuality has its effects on our
children.[292] They are being led from us by these images, and their
little hearts and minds are taken from the refuge that is in Jesus.

There is no prevention to such child-stealing like that of the
Christian home and the community of saints called the Church.[293] It
is there that we must guard our children from the monsters who
would steal them. Moreover, we must not keep them from Christ.

289   Ybarra, Michele L, and Kimberly J Mitchell. "Exposure to Internet
        pornography among children and adolescents: A national survey." Cy-
        berPsychology & Behavior 8.5 (2005): 473–486.

290   Hymowitz, Kay S. Ready or Not: Why Treating Children as Small Adults
        Endangers Their Future—and Ours. Free Pr., 1999.

291   Postman, Neil. Technopoly: The Surrender of Culture to Technology. Vin-
        tage, 1993.

292   Barber, Benjamin R. Con$umed: How Markets Corrupt Children, Infan-
        tilize Adults, and Swallow Citizens Whole. WW Norton & Company, 2007.

293   Milton, Michael A. "The Sacred Cycle of Ministry."

We must bring our children to the Lord[294, 295] and let Moloch and his demons be damned by the Spirit of Christ who destroys all who seek to harm His children.

It is time to unmask the evil childhood killers of this age that seek to steal our children's souls. It is time to turn to God in Christ through prayer and through teaching of the Word and living of the Word and to take our children back—better yet, to bring our children forward to Jesus Christ. In Him there is renewal of life, including childhood.

294 Beeke, Joel R. *Family Worship*. Reformation Heritage Books, 2002.

295 Johnson, Terry. *When Grace Comes Home: the Practical Difference that Calvinism Makes*. Christian Focus Publications, 2003.

7

Epilogue

LISTENING TO GOD BEFORE SPEAKING TO MEN

Attentiveness to God's Message to You

Each of us is part of a Greater Story, and behind our stories is a Storyteller calling us home.—Leighton Ford[296]

By faith he [Moses] left Egypt, not being afraid of the anger of the king, for he endured as seeing him who is invisible. (Hebrews 11:13 ESV).

This book has sought to establish a ground for prophetic pastoral and, indeed, Christian speaking into every area of life to declare the Lordship of Jesus Christ. By now you may not agree with me, but you know that I believe the Gospel has something to say about missile defense as much as adultery. I hope I have not been misinterpreted so that one hears me saying that I must speak to every issue in every instance! If you have heard that, please forgive my lack of clarity. I have no obligation to speak to every issue all of the time. I am conscious, as we should be, of the dangers of our calling to speak: "Do you see a man who is hasty in his words? There is more hope for a fool than for him" (Proverbs 29:20 ESV); "Know this, my beloved brothers: let every person be quick to

---

296 Ford, Leighton. *The Attentive Life: Discerning God's Presence in All Things*. IVP Books, 2008, 11.

hear, slow to speak..." (James 1:19 ESV); and, the one that should strike fear into every preacher, "Let not many of you become teachers, my brethren, knowing that as such we will incur a stricter judgment." (James 3:1 NASB)[297]

On this passage clerics and commentators from John Wesley[298] to Matthew Henry,[299] Arminian and Calvinist, have agreed. The business of preaching necessarily involves speaking the very Word of God into the lives of men and their affairs. What could be more dangerous than to speak for a king? Only to speak for *the King*.

Yet we are called. We are taught (it is hoped). We are sustained. We are compelled to speak out the truth of God out of a burden for His glory and the Church's good and the good of others. This burden to speak usually comes with an open door (not necessarily an invitation; John the Baptist had no invitation to speak to the adulterous lifestyle of Herod, but he did have an open door or ministry), not a door to be forced open. To discern that open door as being from God, and to diagnose the situation as being dangerous to the flock of Jesus, or, for the sake of God's glory, dangerous to Mankind who bears His image, is the thorny work of a shepherd, a pastor. That is my point. Through commentaries and scholarly papers and several sermons, I have sought to raise your consciousness to several dangers at bay, and also, as a seminary chancellor, to demonstrate what I believe is an appropriate response. I may or

297 New American Standard Bible © 1960, 1962, 1963, 1968, 1971, 1972, 1973, 1975, 1977, 1995 by The Lockman Foundation, La Habra, Calif. All rights reserved.

298 Albert Cook Outler, Richard P. Heitzenrater. (2012) Explanatory notes upon the New Testament, 298 - John Wesley - Google Books. Retrieved September 12, 2012, from books.google.com/books?id=LVgHAAAAQAAJ

299 "James—Chapter 3—Matthew Henry Complete Commentary on ..." 2002. 12 Sep. 2012 http://www.studylight.org/com/mhc-com/view. cgi?book=jas&chapter=003

may not have succeeded and I leave that to the reader and, finally, to the Lord. But two things are of great concern to me as I complete this book: first, that you are not fearful of the days in which we live; and second, that you not speak before listening.

COURAGE GROUNDED IN REVELATION

For the pastor to speak out against dangers that would hurt the soul of Jesus' flock is not a sign of fear, but of courage. God's Word teaches us about the cosmic struggle between good and evil, and it also teaches us that one is less powerful than the other! Greater is He who is in us than he who is in the world! Jesus told us that there would be trials and affliction, but He also told us that there would be victory through His Gospel power:

> I have said these things to you, that in me you may have peace. In the world you will have tribulation. But take heart; I have overcome the world. (John 16:33 ESV)

Paul reminded us of the war that we are in:

> For we do not wrestle against flesh and blood, but against the rulers, against the authorities, against the cosmic powers over this present darkness, against the spiritual forces of evil in the heavenly places. (Ephesians 6:12 ESV)

Yet the outcome is certain because the Gospel is the ruling motif, not only personally, in our lives, but cosmically, in the world. The things that have come against us have caused us, like the cross itself, to be transformed from the instrument of shame into the sign of salvation:

> What then shall we say to these things? If God is for us, who can be against us? He who did not spare his own Son but gave him up for us all, how will he not also with him graciously give us all

things? Who shall bring any charge against God's elect? It is God who justifies. Who is to condemn? Christ Jesus is the one who died—more than that, who was raised—who is at the right hand of God, who indeed is interceding for us. Who shall separate us from the love of Christ? Shall tribulation, or distress, or persecution, or famine, or nakedness, or danger, or sword? As it is written: "For your sake we are being killed all the day long; we are regarded as sheep to be slaughtered."

No, in all these things we are more than conquerors through him who loved us. For I am sure that neither death nor life, nor angels nor rulers, nor things present nor things to come, nor powers, nor height nor depth, nor anything else in all creation, will be able to separate us from the love of God in Christ Jesus our Lord. (Romans 8:31–39 ESV)

Oh, how we cling to the assurance of our Master as we do His work in this world: "Fear not, little flock, for it is your Father's good pleasure to give you the kingdom." (Luke 12:32 ESV)

So let us take courage from God and His redemptive plan in Christ Jesus as we speak. But let us also take time. And this is where I will conclude this book on being silent no more: by encouraging silence...*much more.*

THE MINISTRY OF ATTENTIVENESS

Not too long ago I had the unforgettable opportunity of sitting for several hours with the preeminent evangelist, Leighton Ford. Our talk centered on our testimonies. Before I left he gave me a book: *The Attentive Life: Discerning God's Presence in All Things.*[300] While one might not, at first, think that a book on prophetic preaching and contemplative reflection has any connection at all, I found that

---

300 Ibid.

it is the best coupling of pastoral concerns. When we are attentive to God we hear His message. When we hear His message we can better discern the discordant voices around us. It is only then that we may speak. I like the way Leighton Ford puts it: "I have found it helpful both at the beginning and at the ending of a day to spend a few minutes in this kind of quietness, saying, 'My soul waits for the Lord,' or 'Be still and know I am God.' I suppose it is like a gentle knocking on God's door to say, 'I am here waiting.'"

Until you have listened in that way, you cannot speak. Until we have been silent before God, listening to His voice, we cannot be vocal. So I end this collection of essays and sermons on being *Silent No More* with a strong urge for silence; silence before the Lord. Only then do we have a license to speak on His behalf.

I came across a wonderful little poem about listening that I felt worthy of quoting at this point:

> The wise old owl sat on the oak,
> The more he listened the less he spoke,
> The less he spoke the more he heard,
> Why can't we be like that wise old bird?[301]

I invite you, then, to mediate with me on some passages that help us to recalibrate our spirits away from the spirits of this present evil age and find the peace of Christ. Then, when we are called to speak, perhaps our voices will better carry the cadence of grace and truth of our Father.

Listen for courage, but above all, listen to make sure it is God talking, not you.

---

301   Author unknown. See Cotner, June. *Bless the Beasts: Children's Prayers and Poems about Animals.* Chronicle Books, 2002, 11.

Pray through these passages. Open your heart to the Lord of life. Let His voice from His Word drive away your voice, or other voices, before you speak.

And do not be afraid. The Lord reigns. His Kingdom will not fail. And you can speak with His authority and optimism if indeed you are listening. There is a story to tell and the Great Storyteller is telling it through His Word and through your life.

So, in this final essay, just listen.

LISTEN FOR COURAGE

- 2 Timothy 1:7—For God has not given us a spirit of fear, but of power and of love and of a sound mind.[302]
- 1 John 4:18—There is no fear in love; but perfect love casts out fear, because fear involves torment. But he who fears has not been made perfect in love.
- Psalm 27:1—The LORD is my light and my salvation; Whom shall I fear? The LORD is the strength of my life; Of whom shall I be afraid?
- Joshua 1:9—Have I not commanded you? Be strong and of good courage; do not be afraid, nor be dismayed, for the LORD your God is with you wherever you go.
- Genesis 26:24—I am the God of your father Abraham; do not fear, for I am with you.

---

302 The verses quoted are from The Holy Bible, New King James Version Copyright © 1982 by Thomas Nelson, Inc.

Psalm 91

1   He that dwelleth in the secret place of the most High shall abide under the shadow of the Almighty.

2   I will say of the LORD, He is my refuge and my fortress: my God; in him will I trust.

3   Surely he shall deliver thee from the snare of the fowler, and from the noisome pestilence.

4   He shall cover thee with his feathers, and under his wings shalt thou trust: his truth shall be thy shield and buckler.

5   Thou shalt not be afraid for the terror by night; nor for the arrow that flieth by day;

6   Nor for the pestilence that walketh in darkness; nor for the destruction that wasteth at noonday.

7   A thousand shall fall at thy side, and ten thousand at thy right hand; but it shall not come nigh thee.

8   Only with thine eyes shalt thou behold and see the reward of the wicked.

9   Because thou hast made the LORD, which is my refuge, even the most High, thy habitation;

10   There shall no evil befall thee, neither shall any plague come nigh thy dwelling.

11   For he shall give his angels charge over thee, to keep thee in all thy ways.

12   They shall bear thee up in their hands, lest thou dash thy foot against a stone.

13   Thou shalt tread upon the lion and adder: the young lion and the dragon shalt thou trample under feet.

14   Because he hath set his love upon me, therefore will I deliver him: I will set him on high, because he hath known my name.

15   He shall call upon me, and I will answer him: I will be with him in trouble; I will deliver him, and honour him.

16   With long life will I satisfy him, and shew him my salvation.

More Scripture Verses

- Numbers 21:34—Do not fear him, for I have delivered him [your enemy] into your hand.
- Deuteronomy 1:21—Look, the LORD your God has set the land before you; go up and possess it, as the LORD God of your fathers has spoken to you; do not fear or be discouraged.
- Deuteronomy 3:22—You must not fear them [spiritual or natural enemies], for the LORD your God Himself fights for you.
- Deuteronomy 31:6—Be strong and of good courage, do not fear nor be afraid of them; for the LORD your God, He is the One who goes with you. He will not leave you nor forsake you.
- Deuteronomy 31:8—And the LORD, He is the One who goes before you. He will be with you, He will not leave you nor forsake you; do not fear nor be dismayed."
- Joshua 10:8—And the LORD said to Joshua, "Do not fear them, for I have delivered them into your hand; not a man of them shall stand before you."
- Judges 6:10—Also I said to you, "I am the LORD your God; do not fear the gods of the Amorites (the ruling principles and idols of the world hostile to God), in whose land you dwell."
- 1 Chronicles 22:13—Then you will prosper, if you take care to fulfill the statutes and judgments with which the LORD charged Moses concerning Israel. Be strong and of good courage; do not fear nor be dismayed.
- 1 Chronicles 28:20—And David said to his son Solomon, "Be strong and of good courage, and do it; do not fear nor be dismayed, for the LORD God—my God—will be with you. He will not leave you nor forsake you, until you have finished all the work for the service of the house of the LORD.
- 2 Chronicles 20:17—You will not need to fight in this battle. Position yourselves, stand still and see the salvation of the LORD, who is with you, O Judah and Jerusalem! Do not fear or be dismayed; tomorrow go out against them, for the LORD is with you.

- Psalm 27:3—Though an army may encamp against me, My heart shall not fear; Though war may rise against me, In this I will be confident.
- Psalm 37:4—The Angel of the LORD encamps all around those who fear Him, And delivers them.
- Psalm 46:2—Therefore we will not fear, Even though the earth be removed, And though the mountains be carried into the midst of the sea;
- Psalm 56:4—In God (I will praise His word), In God I have put my trust; I will not fear. What can flesh do to me?
- Psalm 118:6—The LORD is on my side; I will not fear. What can man do to me?
- Isaiah 35:4—Say to those who are fearful-hearted, "Be strong, do not fear! Behold, your God will come with vengeance, With the recompense of God; He will come and save you."
- Isaiah 41:10—Fear not, for I am with you; Be not dismayed, for I am your God. I will strengthen you, Yes, I will help you, I will uphold you with My righteous right hand.
- Isaiah 41:13—For I, the LORD your God, will hold your right hand, Saying to you, "Fear not, I will help you.
- Isaiah 43:1—But now, thus says the LORD, who created you, O Jacob, And He who formed you, O Israel: "Fear not, for I have redeemed you; I have called you by your name; You are Mine."
- Isaiah 44:8—Do not fear, nor be afraid; Have I not told you from that time, and declared it? You are My witnesses. Is there a God besides Me? Indeed there is no other Rock; I know not one.
- Isaiah 51:7—Listen to Me, you who know righteousness, You people in whose heart is My law: Do not fear the reproach of men, Nor be afraid of their insults.
- Isaiah 54:4—Do not fear, for you will not be ashamed; Neither be disgraced, for you will not be put to shame; For you will forget the shame of your youth, And will not remember the reproach of your widowhood anymore.
- Isaiah 54:14—In righteousness you shall be established; You shall be far from oppression, for you shall not fear; And from terror, for it shall not come near you.

- Daniel 12:2—Then he said to me, "Do not fear, Daniel, for from the first day that you set your heart to understand, and to humble yourself before your God, your words were heard; and I have come because of your words."
- Daniel 10:19—And he said, "O man greatly beloved, fear not! Peace be to you; be strong, yes, be strong!" So when he spoke to me I was strengthened, and said, "Let my lord speak, for you have strengthened me."
- Joel 2:21—Fear not, O land; Be glad and rejoice, For the LORD has done marvelous things!
- Zephaniah 3:16—In that day it shall be said to Jerusalem: "Do not fear; Zion, let not your hands be weak.
- Haggai 2:5—According to the word that I covenanted with you when you came out of Egypt, so My Spirit remains among you; do not fear!
- Matthew 10:28—And do not fear those who kill the body but cannot kill the soul. But rather fear Him who is able to destroy both soul and body in hell.
- Matthew 10:31—Do not fear therefore; you are of more value than many sparrows.
- Mark 4:40—But He said to them, "Why are you so fearful? How is it that you have no faith?"
- Luke 12:4—And I say to you, My friends, do not be afraid of those who kill the body, and after that have no more that they can do.
- Luke 12:7—But the very hairs of your head are all numbered. Do not fear therefore; you are of more value than many sparrows.
- Luke 12:32—Do not fear, little flock, for it is your Father's good pleasure to give you the kingdom.
- Romans—8:15 For you did not receive the spirit of bondage again to fear, but you received the Spirit of adoption by whom we cry out, "Abba, Father."
- Hebrews 11:27—By faith he forsook Egypt, not fearing the wrath of the king; for he endured as seeing Him who is invisible.
- Hebrews 13:6—So we may boldly say: "The LORD is my helper; I will not fear. What can man do to me?"

- Revelation 2:10—Do not fear any of those things which you are about to suffer. Indeed, the devil is about to throw some of you into prison, that you may be tested, and you will have tribulation ten days. Be faithful until death, and I will give you the crown of life.

LISTEN FOR HIS VOICE

And said, "If thou wilt diligently hearken to the voice of the LORD thy God, and wilt do that which is right in his sight, and wilt give ear to his commandments, and keep all his statutes, I will put none of these diseases upon thee, which I have brought upon the Egyptians: for I am the LORD that healeth thee." (Exodus 15:26 *Geneva Study Bible*)[303]

Pay attention to what you hear: with the measure you use, it will be measured to you, and still more will be added to you. (Mark 4:24 ESV)

And the peace of God, which surpasses all understanding, will guard your hearts and your minds in Christ Jesus. (Philippians 4:7 ESV)

Again he appoints a certain day, "Today," saying through David so long afterward, in the words already quoted, "Today, if you hear his voice, do not harden your hearts." (Hebrews 4:7 ESV)

He who has an ear, let him hear what the Spirit says to the churches. (Revelation 3:6 ESV)

Silent no more—yes—but silent before God first.

May the Lord God raise up prophetic preachers of boldness and humility who have listened well. Amen.

---

303 Sproul, R. C., and Luder Whitlock Jr. *New Geneva Study Bible.* Thomas Nelson (1995).

APPENDIXES

Appendix A

DR. MILTON AND REFORMED THEOLOGICAL SEMINARY

D r. Michael A. Milton is the Chancellor and Chief Executive Officer of Reformed Theological Seminary (RTS). The Board of Trustees appointed him as Chancellor Elect in 2011 and his inauguration as Chancellor and CEO was held on 14 September 2012.

Founded in 1966, RTS was established to provide solid pastoral training grounded in a commitment to the authority of Scripture and the theological understanding of the Bible found in the Westminster Confession of Faith and the larger and shorter catechisms. Independently governed by a board of trustees, RTS serves students from over 60 evangelical denominations and churches. It is one of the largest seminaries in the world and is accredited by both the Association of Theological Schools in the United States and Canada and the Commission of Colleges of the Southern association of Colleges and Schools. The seminary has no debt and does not accept any government funding to assure its fidelity to its founding principles.

The first campus was located in Jackson, Mississippi, with additional campuses being established in later years in Orlando, Florida; Charlotte, North Carolina; Atlanta, Georgia; and Washington, D.C. In addition to these campuses, RTS now has extension campuses in Memphis, Tennessee and Houston, Texas, and we offer an online master's degree from our virtual campus that serves students in countries throughout the world. International doctoral programs have been established in both Brazil and Indonesia.

RTS is known for its academic rigor, effective pastoral preparation, commitment to missions and its flexible delivery systems and program accessibility. A bounty of information about our campuses and degree programs is available online at www.rts.edu. Free course lectures and other learning resources are available to all and can be downloaded at http://itunes.rts.edu , and information about Faith For Living , Dr. Milton's Television and Radio teaching ministry, is available at www.faithforliving.Financial support by individuals and churches is not only appreciatively accepted, but is necessary for the ongoing ministry of the seminary. Donations may be sent to RTS, 5422 Clinton Blvd., Jackson, Mississippi, 39209, or gifts may be made online at www.rts.edu/give.

DR. MICHAEL A. MILTON
(BIOGRAPHY)

M ichael Anthony Milton (Ph.D., University of Wales, Lampeter), an ordained minister and longtime pastor in the Presbyterian Church in America, serves as the fourth chancellor and CEO of Reformed Theological Seminary. He follows Dr. Robert C. "Ric" Cannada.

Before his service as Chancellor of RTS, he was the president of RTS/Charlotte since 2007 and continues to hold the James M. Baird, Jr. Chair of Pastoral Theology. While president of RTS/Charlotte, he founded two new institutes (campus ministry and chaplaincy), formed key partnerships for ministry outreach (including a new Doctoral program in church revitalization), and led in the preparation of a new master plan for the campus, which culminated with the purchase of additional acreage for the seminary. These steps pave the way for a campaign of "finish the dream" with housing, an academic center, and a chapel.

Dr. Milton previously served as the senior pastor of First Presbyterian Church in Chattanooga, Tennessee; he has planted two churches and founded Westminster Academy Christian School in Overland Park, Kansas. He completed his pastoral internship under Dr. D. James Kennedy and later served as the interim president of Knox Theological Seminary.

Dr. Milton is the founder of Faith for Living, a multi media outreach, which began airing in Chattanooga. Faith for Living with Dr. Mike Milton is now the broadcast outreach arm of RTS. He has been broadcasting the Gospel since 1992, and now RTS's and Milton's Faith for Living reaches 70,000,000 potential households each week through national networks. He writes theological reflections at http://michaelmilton.org.

Dr. Milton has authored numerous books including *Songs in the Night: How God Transforms Our Pain to Praise* (P&R), *What Is the Doctrine of Adoption* (P&R), and *Hit by Friendly Fire: What to do When Other Believers Hurt You* (EP Books). He is also the author of *Small Things, Big Things: Inspiring Stories of God's Grace* (P&R Publishing); *What God Starts, God Completes: Help and Hope for Hurting People* (Christian Focus Publications); and *Leaving a Career to Follow a Call: A Vocational Guide to the Ordained Ministry* (WS Publishing). He is currently working on a textbook on pastoral theology and two commentaries (Leviticus and Jeremiah). He has written numerous popular and academic articles and has been published in such periodicals as *Preaching Magazine*, *World Magazine*, and *The Journal of the Evangelical Theological Society*. He is also a regular presenter of theological papers at annual meetings of the Evangelical Theological Society. Dr. Milton also produces *Commentary by Michael A. Milton* on matters of Christianity and Culture, which have appeared in newspapers and online publications throughout the world.

Often his sermons are illustrated with songs that he writes, sings, and performs with guitar or piano. His recording, He Shall Restore, was released in 2006 under the label Music for Missions and is distributed through iTunes. He released his second album, Follow Your Call, in 2008, and the third, Through the Open Door (Music for Missions), has just been released. A single, When

Heaven Came Down, was released at Christmas 2011 and is the title cut of a Christmas album due in late fall 2012. *Christianity Today* gave four stars to the latest album and called the music "emotionally moving and musically opulent."

In addition to his civilian ministry, Dr. Milton holds a commission in the U.S. Army Reserves as a Chaplain (Lt. Col.), a ministry that he continues. His military career has taken him from battalion chaplaincy positions in Kansas to Brigade level chaplaincy positions, service in the Office of the Chief of Chaplains, overseas Reserve missions, the deputy command chaplain of the 108th Training Command, U.S. Army Reserves, and presently serving as a writer and instructor at the U.S. Army Chaplains Center and School. In 2010, he was nominated by the Chief of Chaplains of the U.S. Army and inducted as a charter member of the College of Military Preachers.

Serving on several boards and active in a number of civic organizations, he maintains a full schedule of preaching and teaching in churches and seminaries and at conferences. His preaching and teaching has taken him from throughout churches and conferences in America to Emmanuel College, Cambridge, and churches in Wales, Germany, Albania, and to seminaries and churches from India to Mexico.

He is a member of the National Religious Broadcasters, the Evangelical Theological Society, the American Legion, the Reserve Officer Association, and the Fellowship of Evangelical Seminary Presidents.

Dr. Milton and his wife Mae reside in the Charlotte area where he is an avid gardener, reader of history, and a fan of classic British and American movies from the golden era of film.

Appendix C

BIBLIOGRAPHY

Bainton, Roland Herbert. *The travail of religious liberty; nine biographical studies*. Philadelphia: Westminster Press, 1951.

Barth, Karl. *The theology of John Calvin*. Grand Rapids, Mich.: W.B. Eerdmans Pub. Co., 1995.

Bercovitch, Sacvan. *Election day sermons: Plymouth and Connecticut*. New York: AMS Press, 1983.

Bolt, John. *A free church, a holy nation: Abraham Kuyper's American public theology*. Grand Rapids, Mich.: W.B. Eerdmans, 2000.

Buckley, William F. *God and man at Yale: the superstitions of academic freedom*. Chicago: Regnery, 1951.

Calvin, Jean. *Institutes of the Christian religion*. Grand Rapids, Mich.: Christian Classics Ethereal Library, 199.

Carson, D. A. *Christ and culture revisited*. Grand Rapids, Mich.: William B. Eerdmans Pub. Co., 2008.

Carter, Stephen L. *The culture of disbelief: how American law and politics trivialize religious devotion*. New York: BasicBooks, 1993.

Douglass, R. Bruce, and Joshua Mitchell. *A nation under God: essays on the future of religion in American public life*. Lanham, Md.: Rowman & Littlefield Publishers, 2000.

Dreisbach, Daniel L., and Mark David Hall. *The sacred rights of conscience: selected readings on religious liberty and church-state relations in the American founding*. Indianapolis: Liberty Fund, 2009.

Edwards, O. C. *A history of preaching*. Expanded ed. Nashville, Tenn.: Abingdon Press, 2004.

Election Day sermons, Massachusetts. New York: AMS Press, 1984.

Fowler, Paul B. *Abortion: toward an evangelical consensus*. Portland, Ore.: Multnomah Press, 1987.

George, Timothy. *Theology of the reformers*. Nashville, Tenn.: Broadman Press, 1988.

Guest, John. *Risking faith: personal answers for weary skeptics*. Grand Rapids, Mich.: Baker Books, 1993.

Hall, David W. *Election day sermons*. Oak Ridge, Tenn.: Kuyper Institute, 1996.

——. *Preaching like Calvin: sermons from the 500th anniversary celebration*. Phillipsburg, N.J.: P&R Pub., 2010.

——, and Peter A. Lillback. *A theological guide to Calvin's Institutes: essays and analysis*. Phillipsburg, N.J.: P&R Pub., 2008.

Hannan, Daniel. *The new road to serfdom: a letter of warning to America*. New York: Harper, 2010.

Harper, I. R. L. *Christian theology and market economics*. Cheltenham, Glos, UK: Edward Elgar, 2008.

Hart, D. G. *Defending the faith: J. Gresham Machen and the crisis of conservative Protestantism in modern America*. Baltimore: Johns Hopkins University Press, 1994.

Hodge, Charles. *Systematic theology*. Grand Rapids: Eerdmans, 1952.

Holland, DeWitte Talmadge. *Sermons in American history; selected issues in the American pulpit, 1630–1967*. Nashville: Abingdon Press, 1971.

Kelly, Douglas F. *Creation and change: Genesis 1:1-2:4 in the light of changing scientific paradigms*. Fearn, Scotland: Mentor, 1997.

Kengor, Paul. *God and Ronald Reagan: a spiritual life*. New York: Regan Books, 2004.

——. *The crusader: Ronald Reagan and the fall of communism*. New York: Regan Books, 2006.

——. *Dupes: how America's adversaries have manipulated progressives for a century*. Wilmington, Del.: ISI Books, 2010.

——. *The communist: Frank Marshall Davis : the untold story of Barack Obama's mentor*. New York: Threshold Editions/Mercury Ink, 2012.

Kuyper, Abraham. *Lectures on Calvinism*. Grand Rapids, Mich.: Eerdmans, 1931.

_____, and James D. Bratt. *Abraham Kuyper: a centennial reader*. Grand Rapids, Mich.: W.B. Eerdmans, 1998.

Laycock, Douglas. *Continuity and change in the threat to religious liberty: the Reformation Era and the late twentieth century*. Minneapolis, MN: University of Minnesota Law School, 1996.

_____. *Religious liberty*. Grand Rapids, Mich.: W.B. Eerdmans Pub. Co., 20102011.

_____, Anthony R. Picarello, and Robin Fretwell Wilson. *Same-sex marriage and religious liberty: emerging conflicts*. Washington, D.C.: Becket Fund for Religious Liberty, 2008.

Luther, Martin. *A treatise on good works*. Champaign, Ill.: Project Gutenberg, 199.

MacCulloch, Diarmaid. *The Reformation*. New York: Viking, 2004.

Machen, J. Gresham. *Christianity and liberalism*. New York: Macmillan Company, 1923.

_____. *The Christian faith in the modern world*. New York: Macmillan Co., 1936.

_____, and Stephen J. Nichols. *J. Gresham Machen's the Gospel and the modern world and other short writings*. Phillipsburg, N.J.: P&R Pub., 2005.

McBride, Jennifer M. *The church for the world: a theology of public witness*. New York: Oxford University Press, 2012.

McDermott, Gerald R. *One holy and happy society: the public theology of Jonathan Edwards*. University Park, Pa.: Pennsylvania State University Press, 1992.

Metaxas, Eric. *Bonhoeffer: pastor, martyr, prophet, spy: a Righteous Gentile vs. the Third Reich*. Nashville: Thomas Nelson, 2010.

Miller, Joel, and Kristen Parrish. *The portable patriot: documents, speeches, and sermons that compose the American soul*. Nashville, Tenn.: Thomas Nelson, 2010.

Milton, Michael A. *Cooperation without compromise: faithful gospel witness in a pluralistic setting*. Eugene, Ore.: Wipf and Stock Publishers, 2006.

Naugle, David K. *Worldview: the history of a concept*. Grand Rapids, Mich.: W.B. Eerdmans Pub., 2002.

Neuhaus, Richard John. *The naked public square: religion and democracy in America*. Grand Rapids, Mich.: W.B. Eerdmans Pub. Co., 1984.

Nichols, Stephen J. *Jesus made in America: a cultural history from the Puritans to The Passion of the Christ*. Downers Grove, Ill.: IVP Academic, 2008.

Niebuhr, H. Richard. *Christ and culture*. 1st ed. New York: Harper, 1951.

Peck, Phinehas. *A discourse delivered on the day of general election, at Montpelier, October 9, 1817. ...* Windsor, Vt.: Jesse Cochran, state printer, 1817.

Reagan, Ronald. *Abortion and the conscience of the nation*. Nashville: T. Nelson, 1984.

Sandoz, Ellis. *Political sermons of the American founding era, 1730–1805*. Indianapolis: LibertyPress, 1991.

Schaeffer, Francis A. *Escape from reason: a penetrating analysis of trends in modern thought*. Downers Grove, Ill.: Inter-Varsity Press, 1968.

____. *The God who is there: speaking historic Christianity into the twentieth century*. Chicago: Inter-varsity Press, 1968.

____. *The church at the end of the 20th century*. Downers Grove, Ill.: Inter-Varsity Press, 1970.

____. *Pollution and the death of man: the Christian view of ecology*. Wheaton, Ill.: Tyndale House Publishers, 1970.

____. *He is there and He is not silent*. Wheaton, Ill.: Tyndale House Publishers, 1972.

____. *How should we then live?: the rise and decline of Western thought and culture*. Old Tappan, N.J.: F.H. Revell Co., 1976.

____. *A Christian manifesto*. Westchester, Ill.: Crossway Books, 1981.

____. *The great evangelical disaster*. Westchester, Ill.: Crossway Books, 1984.

____, and C. Everett Koop. *Whatever happened to the human race?*. Old Tappan, N.J.: F.H. Revell Co., 1979.

Shagan, Ethan H. *Popular politics and the English Reformation*. Cambridge: Cambridge University Press, 2003.

Spear, Wayne R. *Faith of our fathers: a commentary on the Westminster Confession of Faith*. Pittsburgh, PA: Crown & Covenant Publications, 2006.

Stott, John R. W. *Our social and sexual revolution: major issues for a new century*. 3rd ed. Grand Rapids, Mich.: Baker Books, 1999.

____. *New issues facing Christians today*. Rev. ed. London: Marshall Pickering, 1999.

____. *The living church: convictions of a lifelong pastor*. Downers Grove, Ill.: IVP Books, 2007.

Torrance, Thomas F., and Richard W. A. McKinney. *Creation, Christ, and culture: studies in honour of T. F. Torrance*. Edinburgh: Clark, 1976.

van Til, L. John. *Liberty of conscience; the history of a Puritan idea*. Nutley, N.J.: Craig Press, 1972.

____. *Liberty, regulation and restraint in the American commonwealth*. Grove City, Pa.: Public Policy Education Fund, 1981.

von Hayek, Friedrich A. *The road to serfdom*. 50th anniversary ed. Chicago: University of Chicago Press, 1994.

Wakelyn, Jon L. *America's founding charters: primary documents of Colonial and Revolutionary era governance*. Westport, Conn.: Greenwood Press, 2006.

Wogaman, J. Philip. *Economics and ethics: a Christian inquiry*. Philadelphia: Fortress Press, 1986.

Woods, Thomas E. *Back on the road to serfdom: the resurgence of statism*. Wilmington, Del.: ISI Books, 2010.

Appendix D

INDEX (SUBJECT)

Appendix E

INDEX (SCRIPTURAL)

CPSIA information can be obtained at www.ICGtesting.com
Printed in the USA
BVOW012130230113

311427BV00007B/9/P